Understanding Digital Literacies

'Finally, a definitive user's guide for the fast changing world of digital media and digital litera-cies.*Understanding Digital Literacies: A Practical Introduction* is lucid, entertaining, spot on, and, while practical indeed, is wholly a theoretically sophisticated and empirically trustworthy guide.'

James Paul Gee, *Mary Lou Fulton Presidential Professor of Literacy Studies, Arizona State University, USA*

Assuming no knowledge of linguistics, *Understanding Digital Literacies* provides an accessible and timely introduction to new media literacies. It supplies readers with the theoretical and analytical tools with which to explore the linguistic and social impact of a host of new digital literacy practices. Each chapter in the volume covers a different topic, presenting an overview of the major concepts, issues, problems and debates surrounding the topic, while also encouraging students to reflect on and critically evaluate their own language and communication practices.

Features of the book include:

*   Coverage of a diverse range of digital media texts, tools and practices including blogging, hypertextual organisation, Facebook, Twitter, YouTube, Wikipedia, websites and games
*   An extensive range of examples and case studies to illustrate each topic, such as how blogs have affected our thinking about communication, how the creation and sharing of digital images and video can bring about shifts in social roles, and how the design of multiplayer online games for children can promote different ideologies
*   A variety of discussion questions and mini-ethnographic research projects involving exploration of various patterns of media production and communication between peers, for example in the context of Wikinomics and peer production, social networking and civic participation, and digital literacies at work
*   End of chapter suggestions for further reading and links to key web and video resources
*   A companion website at **www.routledge.com/cw/jones** providing supplementary material for each chapter, including summaries of key issues, additional web-based exercises, and links to further resources such as useful websites, articles, videos and blogs.

This book will provide a key resource for undergraduate and graduate students studying courses in new media and digital literacies.

Rodney H. Jones is Associate Head and Associate Professor in the Department of English at City University of Hong Kong.

Christoph A. Hafner is Assistant Professor in the Department of English at City University of Hong Kong.

Understanding Digital Literacies
A practical introduction

RODNEY H. JONES
CHRISTOPH A. HAFNER

Routledge
Taylor & Francis Group

LONDON AND NEW YORK

First published 2012
by Routledge
2 Park Square, Milton Park, Abingdon, Oxon OX14 4RN

Simultaneously published in the USA and Canada
by Routledge
711 Third Avenue, New York, NY 10017

Routledge is an imprint of the Taylor & Francis Group, an informa business

British Library Cataloguing in Publication Data
A catalogue record for this book is available from the British Library

Library of Congress Cataloging in Publication Data
Jones, Rodney H.
    Understanding digital literacies : a practical introduction /
    Rodney H. Jones and Christoph A. Hafner.
    p. cm.
    Includes bibliographical references and index.
    1. Media literacy.   2. Mass media—Technological innovations.
    3. Mass media and culture.   4. Educational technology.
    5. Human-computer interaction.   I. Hafner, Christoph A.   II. Title.
    P96.M4.J66 2012
    302.23'1—dc23
    2011041768

ISBN: 978–0–415–67316–7 (hbk)
ISBN: 978–0–415–67315–0 (pbk)

Typeset in Akzidenz-Grotesk
by Swales & Willis Ltd, Exeter, Devon

MIX
Paper from
responsible sources
FSC® C004839
www.fsc.org

Printed and bound in Great Britain by
TJ International Ltd, Padstow, Cornwall

Contents

Illustrations

FIGURES

ACTIVITIES

CASE STUDIES

Acknowledgements

We would like to thank everyone who has shared their 'digital lives' with us and enriched our own understanding of digital literacies. Our students willingly acted as 'guinea pigs', reading the draft chapters of this book and responding with their own stories. Our families and friends also provided us with valuable discussions and insights about digital media in their lives. A special thanks to Janice, Sophie, Thomas, Christopher and Emily for exploring this world with us.

CHAPTER 1

Mediated Me

It's hard to think of anything we do nowadays, from working on projects for work or school to socializing with friends, that is not somehow mediated through digital technologies. It's not just that we're doing 'old things' in 'new ways'. Digital technologies are actually introducing new things for us to do like **blogging, mashing, modding** and **memeing**. Many of the practices that we will be discussing in this book simply didn't exist just a few years ago.

These new practices require from people new abilities and skills, new ways of thinking, and new methods of managing their relationships with others. Some examples of these include:

- The ability to quickly search though and evaluate great masses of information.
- The ability to create coherent reading pathways through complex collections of linked texts.
- The ability to quickly make connections between widely disparate ideas and domains of experience.
- The ability to shoot and edit digital photos and video.
- The ability to create multimodal documents that combine words, graphics, video and audio.
- The ability to create and maintain dynamic online profiles and manage large and complex online social networks.
- The ability to explore and navigate online worlds and to interact in virtual environments.
- The ability to protect one's personal data from being misused by others.

Many people just pick up these abilities along the way by surfing the web, playing online games and posting to **blogs** and **social networking sites**. But people are not always very conscious of how these practices change not just the way they communicate but also 'who they can be' and the kinds of relationships they can have with others.

The purpose of this book is not just to help you become 'better' at mastering these and other 'literacies' associated with digital technology, but also to help you understand how they are affecting the way you make meanings, the way you relate to others, the kinds of social identities you can enact, and even the way you think. We believe that the best way to become more competent users of technologies is to become more critical and reflective about how we use them in our everyday lives, the kinds of things that they allow us to do, and the kinds of things they don't allow us to do.

This book is not just about computers, mobile phones, the internet and other technologies people associate with the 'new **media**' (many of which are not so 'new' anymore). It's about the process of **mediation** itself, the age-old human practice of using tools to take action in the world. In this introductory chapter we will explain the concept of mediation and how it relates to the definition of 'digital literacies', which we will be developing throughout this book. We will also give a brief outline of the structure of the book and the special features we've included for students and teachers.

MEDIATION

A **medium** is something that stands in between two things or people and facilitates interaction between them. Usually when we think of 'mediated interaction' we think of things like 'computer-*mediated* communication' or messages delivered via 'mass *media*' like television, radio or newspapers. But the fact is, all interaction – and indeed all human action – is in some way *mediated*.

This was the insight of the Russian psychologist Lev Vygotsky, who spent his life observing how children learn. All learning, he realized, involves learning how to use some kind of tool that facilitates interaction between the child and the thing or person he or she is interacting with. To learn to eat, you have to learn to use a spoon or a fork or chopsticks, which come between you and the food and facilitate the action of eating. To learn to read, you have to learn to use language and objects like books that come between you and other people and facilitate the action of communication.

These **cultural tools** that mediate our actions are of many types. Some are physical objects like spoons, and books and television sets. Some are more abstract 'codes' or 'systems of meaning' such as languages, counting systems and algorithms. The ability to use such tools, according to Vygotsky, is the hallmark of human consciousness. All higher mental processes, he said, depend upon mediation. You cannot act alone. In order to do anything or mean anything or have any kind of relationship with anyone else, you need to use tools. In a sense, the definition of a person is a human being *plus* the tools that are available for that human being to interact with the world.

These tools that we use to mediate between ourselves and the world can be thought of as *extensions* of ourselves. In fact, the famous Canadian media scholar Marshall McLuhan called media 'the extensions of man'. He didn't just mean things that we traditionally think of as media like television and newspapers, but also things like light bulbs, cars, and human language, in short all **mediational means** which facilitate action. The spoon we use to eat with is an extension of our hand. Microscopes and telescopes are extensions of our eyes. Microphones are extensions of our voices. Cars and trains and busses might be considered extensions of our feet, and computers might be considered extensions of our brains (though, as we will show in the rest of this book, the ways computers and the internet extend our capabilities goes far beyond things like memory and cognition).

The point that both Vygotsky and McLuhan were trying to make was not just that cultural tools allow us to do new things, but that they come to define us in some very basic ways. They usually don't just affect our ability to do a particular task. They also affect the way we relate to others, the way we communicate and the way we think. As McLuhan puts it: 'Any extension, whether of skin, hand, or foot, affects the whole psychic and social complex'. Cars, trains and busses, for example, don't just allow us to move around faster; they fundamentally change the way we experience and think about space and time, fundamentally change the kinds of relationships we can have with people who live far away from us, and fundamentally change the kinds of societies we can build. A light bulb does not just allow us to see at night. It fundamentally changes our experience of circadian rhythms and creates whole new environments for social interaction that did not exist before. A microphone doesn't just make my voice louder. It gives me the ability to communicate to a large number of people at one time, thus changing the kind relationship I can have with those other people and the kinds of messages I can communicate to them.

On one hand, these tools *enable* us to do new things, think in new ways, express new kinds of meanings, establish new kinds of relationships and *be* new kinds of people. On the other hand, they also *prevent* us from doing other things, of thinking in other ways, of having other kinds of relationships and of being other kinds of people. In other words, all tools bring with them different kinds of **affordances** and **constraints**. The way McLuhan puts it, while new technologies *extend* certain parts of us, they *amputate* other parts. For example, while a microphone allows me to talk to a large number of people at one time, it makes it more difficult for me to talk to just one of those people privately. While a train makes it easier for me to quickly go from one place to another, it makes it more difficult for me to stop along the way and chat with the people I pass.

Case study 1: The wristwatch

Before mobile telephones with built-in digital timekeepers became so pervasive, few technologies seemed more like 'extensions' of our bodies than wristwatches. For most people, having a watch on their wrist and referring to it throughout the day was and still is totally natural. In some ways, we even think of watches as part of our minds. Consider the following conversation:

A: "Excuse me, do you know what time it is?"
B: "Sure".
(*looks at his watch*)
"It's 4:15".

In his book *Natural Born Cyborgs*, Andy Clark points to conversations like this as evidence that we consider tools like watches not as separate objects, but as part of ourselves. When B in this conversation says 'sure' in response to the question about whether or not he knows the time, he does so *before* he looks at his watch. In other words, just having the watch on his wrist makes him feel like he 'knows' the time, and looking at the watch to retrieve the time is not very different from retrieving a fact from his mind.

Before the sixteenth century, timepieces were much too large to carry around because they depended on pendulums and other heavy mechanical workings. Even domestic clocks were rare at that time. Most people depended on the church tower and other public clocks in order to know the time.

This all changed with the invention of the *mainspring*, a coiled piece of metal which, after being wound tightly, unwinds, moving the hands of the timepiece. This small invention made it possible for the first time for 'time' to be 'portable'. In the seventeenth century pocket watches became popular among the rich. Most people, though, continued to rely on public clocks, mostly because there was no need for them to be constantly aware of the time.

It wasn't until the beginning of the twentieth century that watches became popular accessories for normal people to wear on their wrists. In the beginning, wristwatches were fashion accessories worn only by women. There are a number of stories about how wristwatches came to be more commonly used. One involves Brazilian aviator Alberto Santos-Dumont, who in 1904 complained that it was difficult to fly his plane while looking at his pocket watch. So his friend, Louis Cartier, developed a watch that he could wear on his wrist, which eventually became the first commercially produced men's wristwatch. According to another account, during World War One (WWI) soldiers strapped their watches to their wrists in order to enable them to coordinate their actions in battle while leaving their hands free to carry their weapons and engage in combat. These early wristwatches were known as 'trench-watches' after the trenches of WWI.

These two examples demonstrate the new affordances introduced by the simple technology of strapping a watch to one's wrist. It allowed soldiers and aviators to do things they were unable to do before, that is, to keep track of time while fighting or flying their planes. Some might even argue that these new affordances contributed to changes in the nature of battle as well as the development of modern aviation.

This ability to 'carry the time around' also introduced new possibilities in the business and commercial worlds. The development of railroads as well as the 'scientific management' of the assembly line factories of the early twentieth century both depended on people's ability to keep close track of the time.

Of course, these developments also changed people's relationships with one another. Human interaction became more and more a matter of scheduled meetings rather than chance encounters. People were expected to be in a certain place at a certain time. The notions of being 'on time' and 'running late' became much more important.

Along with these changes in relationships came changes in the way people thought about time. Time became something abstract, less a function of nature (the rising and setting of the sun) and more a function of what people's watches said. When people wanted to know when to eat, they didn't consult their stomachs, they consulted their wrists. Time became something that could be divided up and parcelled out. Part of managing the self was being able to manage time. Time became like money. Finally, time became something that one was meant to be constantly aware of. One of the worst things that could happen to someone was to 'lose track of time'.

With the development of electronic watches, portable timepieces became accurate to the tenth or even the hundredth of a second. This new accuracy further changed how people thought about how time could be divided up. Before the 1960s, the second was the smallest measurement of time most normal people could even conceive of.

Ever since the development of pocket watches, timepieces have always had a role in communicating social identity and status. After wristwatches became popular, however, this role became even more pronounced. Many people regard watches as symbols of wealth, status, taste or personality. It makes a big difference to us whether or not someone is wearing a Rolex or a Casio. In fact, with the ubiquity of time on computer screens, mobile phones and other devices, the timekeeping function of wristwatches is becoming less important than their function as markers of social identity and status.

Of course, the obvious question is whether it was the development of the wristwatch that brought on all of these social and psychological changes, or the social and psychological changes that brought on the development of the wristwatch. Our answer is: both. Human beings are continually creating and adapting cultural tools to meet the needs of new material or social circumstances or new psychological needs. These tools, in turn, end up changing the material and social circumstances in which they are used as well as the psychological needs of those who use them.

AFFORDANCES AND CONSTRAINTS

As you can see from Case study 1, the cultural tools that we use in our daily lives often involve complicated combinations of affordances and constraints, and understanding how people learn to manage these affordances and constraints is one of the main themes of this book. Throughout we will be examining the ways different kinds of mediational means make different kinds of actions, meanings, social relationships, ways of thinking and social identities either easier or more difficult.

We can divide the different affordances and constraints media introduce into five different kinds: affordances and constraints on what we can *do,* what we can *mean,* how we can *relate* to others, how or what we can *think,* and, finally, who we can *be.*

Doing

Perhaps the most obvious thing we can say about cultural tools is that they allow us to *do* things in the physical world that we would not be able to do without them. Hammers allow us to drive in nails. Telephones allow us to talk to people who are far away. Just as importantly, they allow us to *not* do certain things. Text messages, for example, allow us to get a message across to someone immediately without having to call them (see Chapter 5).

Some of the things that people do with technology are of earth shattering importance, things like landing on the moon or mapping the human genome. However, most of the things these tools allow us to do are pretty mundane like sharing photos with friends, using a search engine to find a place to eat, or acquiring the 'magical power' that we need to reach the next level in an online game. It is these small, everyday actions that we will be most concerned with in this book. These are the actions that are at the heart of everyday literacy practices and ultimately it is these everyday practices that form the foundation for greater achievements like moon landings and genome mappings.

Sometimes when individuals are given new abilities to perform small, everyday actions, this can have an unexpectedly large effect on whole societies and cultures. As we saw above, for example, the ability to keep track of time using a wristwatch was an important factor in the development of other kinds of technologies like airplanes, train schedules, and assembly lines, Similarly, your ability to share random thoughts with your friends on Facebook is having an enormous effect on life beyond your social network in realms like politics and economics.

Meaning

Not only do media allow us to do different kinds of things, they also allow us to make different kinds of meanings that we would not be able to make without them. The classic example is the way television has changed how people are able to communicate about what is happening in the world. Reporting on a news event in print allows the writer to tell us what happened, but reporting on it though a television news broadcast allows the reporter to *show* us what happened and to make us feel like we are there.

The lines of print in a book allow us to make meaning in a linear way based on time – first we say one thing, then we add something else to that. Multimodal web pages and hypertext, on the other hand, allow us to make meaning in a more spatial way, inviting people to explore different parts of the screen and different linked web pages in any order they wish (see Chapters 3 and 4).

Media also affect meaning by changing the vocabulary we use to talk about everyday actions. A few years ago, for example, 'friend' was a noun meaning a person that you are close with. Now, however, 'friend' is also a verb meaning to add someone on a social networking site. In fact, about 25,000 new words are added to the *Oxford English Dictionary* every year, most of them the result of new meanings related to new technologies.

Relating

Different media also allow us to create different kinds of relationships with the people with whom we are interacting. One way is by making possible different kinds of arrangements for participation in the interaction. Does the interaction involve just two people or many people? What roles and rights do different kinds of people have in the interaction? What kinds of channels of communication are made possible: one-to-one, one-to-many, or many-to-many?

A book, for example, usually allows a single author to communicate with many readers, but he or she can usually only communicate to them in relative isolation. In other words, most people read books alone. They may talk with other people who have read or are reading the same book, but usually not *as* they are reading. Also, they normally cannot talk back to the writer as they are reading, though, if the writer is still alive, they might write a letter telling him or her what they thought of the book. The chances of readers actually having a conversation with the author of a book are slim.

A blog, on the other hand, creates very different patterns of participation. First, it allows readers to talk back to writers, to ask for clarification or dispute what the writer has said or contribute their own ideas. Writers can also update what they have said in response to readers' comments. Readers of blogs can also comment on the comments of other readers, that is, readers can talk to one another as they are reading.

The internet, with its chat rooms, forums, social networking sites, social bookmarking sites and other interactive features has introduced all sorts of new ways for people to participate in social life, and people can experience all sorts of new kinds of relationships. They can **'lurk'** in various **online communities** or become active members. They can 'friend' people, 'poke' people, 'spam' people and create many kinds of different 'social gatherings' that did not exist before the development of digital media.

In his famous essay, 'The Relationship Revolution', Michael Schrage (2001) claims that to say the internet 'is about "information" is a bit like saying that "cooking" is about oven temperatures – it's technically accurate but fundamentally untrue'. The real revolution that the internet has brought, he says, is not an 'information revolution' but rather a 'relationship revolution'.

Other than making possible different kinds of social arrangements for participants, media also have an effect on two very important aspects of relationships: power and distance. Technologies can make some people more powerful than others or they can erase power differences between people. For example, if I have a microphone and you don't, then I have greater power to make my voice heard than you do. Similarly, if I have the ability to publish my views and you don't, then I have greater power to get my opinions noticed than you do. One way the internet has changed the power relations among people is to give everyone the power to publish their ideas and disseminate them to millions of people. This is not to say that the internet has made everyone's ideas equal. It's just that more people have the opportunity to get their ideas noticed.

Finally, when our relationships are mediated through technology sometimes they can make us feel closer, and sometimes they can make us feel more distant from each other. When text-based computer chat and email were first developed, lots of people thought that it would be harder for people to develop close relationships through these media since people couldn't see each other's faces. As it turned out, chat rooms and **instant messaging** programs like MSN messenger seemed to facilitate interpersonal communication, self-disclosure and intimacy rather than hinder it. These programs are now used much more for maintaining interpersonal relationships than they are for instrumental purposes (see Chapter 5).

Thinking

Perhaps the most compelling and, for many people, the most worrying thing about technologies is that they have the capacity to change the way we experience and think about reality. If our experience of the world is always mediated through tools, what we experience will also be affected by the affordances and constraints of these tools. Certain things about the world will be amplified or magnified, and other things will be diminished or hidden from us altogether.

One of the first to express this very important insight was the communications scholar Harold Innis (1951/1964). Innis said that each medium has a built-in **bias**, which transforms information and organizes knowledge in a particular way. The two most important ways media affect our experience of reality is the way they organize time and space. Some media make information more portable, making it easier to transport or broadcast over long distances. Some media also make information more durable, that is, they make it easier to preserve information over long stretches of time.

Others have taken this idea even further. The philosopher and literary critic Walter Ong (1982/1996), for example, says that the medium of written language didn't just make it easier for us to preserve our ideas and transport them over long distances to a large number of people, but also changed the way human beings could think. In oral cultures, he argues, because so much had to be committed to memory, human thought tended to focus more on concrete and immediate concerns and to package ideas in rather fixed and formulaic ways. The invention of writing, partly because it freed up people's memories, allowed them to develop more abstract and analytical ways of thinking and, according to Ong, made possible the development of things like history, philosophy and science.

Some people think that digital technologies are having similar dramatic effects on the way we think. The optimists among them see computers and the internet taking over routine mental tasks like calculations and acting as repositories for easily retrievable knowledge, freeing up the brain for more sophisticated tasks like forming creative new connections between different kinds of knowledge. Pessimists, on the other hand, see digital technology taking away our ability to concentrate and to think deeply, weakening our ability to remember things for ourselves and to evaluate knowledge critically (see Chapter 7).

Being

Finally, different technologies have affordances and constraints in terms of the kinds of people that we can be – that is, the kinds of social identities we can adopt – when we are using them. Certain kinds of social identities, of course, require that we have available to us certain kinds of technologies and that we know how to use them. If we want to convince others that we are carpenters, then we'd better have access to tools like hammers, saws, screwdrivers and the like and be able to demonstrate some skill in using them. Similarly, if we want to be doctors, we need to know how to use tools like stethoscopes and medical charts. In fact, some people would argue that nearly all social identities are a matter of having certain tools *available* to us and having *mastered* how to use these tools. We could also put this the other way around, that when we use certain kinds of tools we are implicitly *claiming* certain kinds of identities for ourselves. So when we walk into a lecture theatre and start speaking through the microphone at the podium, we are claiming for ourselves the identity of a professor, and imputing on those listening the identities of students.

Some tools, however, are not necessarily part of such specialized identities. Using a mobile phone, for example, is not something that is reserved for certain professions or social groups. Nevertheless, when you use your mobile phone you are still showing that you are a certain kind of person. For one thing, you are a person who can afford a mobile phone (which not everybody can). *How* you use your mobile phone also communicates something about who you are. A boss, for example, might be able to answer his or her mobile phone during an important meeting, whereas a lower ranking employee might not be able to get away with this. Finally, you might be enacting a certain kind of social identity just by the kind of mobile phone you use. Are you carrying an iPhone or a Blackberry? Is it the latest model or one from two years ago?

Finally, different kinds of technologies can also help you to reveal certain parts of yourself and conceal other parts. The privacy settings on Facebook, for example, allow you to share information with some people in your social network while keeping it a secret from others. The sociologist Erving Goffman uses the metaphor of a play to talk about how we present ourselves to other people. Like actors, he says, we have different kinds of expressive equipment – costumes, props, and various staging technologies – which allow us to create a kind of illusion for our audience. This equipment allows us to reveal certain things to our audience and keep other things hidden. Sometimes we can even reveal some things to some members of the audience while keeping them hidden from others (see Chapter 10).

Activity 1.1: Affordances, constraints and social practices

A. AFFORDANCES AND CONSTRAINTS

Consider the different kinds of technologies listed below and discuss how they have affected:

1. The kinds of physical things people can *do* in particular situations;
2. The kinds of *meanings* people can express in particular situations;
3. The kinds of *relationships* that people can have in particular situations;
4. The kinds of thoughts people can *think* in particular situations;
5. The kinds of *social identities* people can assume in particular situations.

Traffic signals   'Smartcards'   Digital cameras   Cash registers   PowerPoint

B. SOCIAL PRACTICES

Now consider these technologies as parts of wider social practices. What other technologies are they usually used together with and in what kinds of social situations? How do these other technologies and social situations affect what we do with these technologies?

CREATIVITY

As we said above, while new media allow us to do new things, make new kinds of meanings, and think, relate to others and enact our own identities in new ways, they also invariably introduce limitations on what we can do and mean, how we can think and relate, and who we can 'be' when we are using them. Television news, for example, allows for a vivid and dramatic presentation of a story, but may be less suitable than a newspaper or magazine for lengthy and probing analysis. Social networking sites make it easier for us to stay connected to our friends, but make it more difficult to maintain our privacy (especially from advertisers). Caller identification, which is standard on most mobile phones, makes it easier for us to screen our calls, but it also makes it easier for calls that we make to be screened by others. Often the constraints of new technologies are less visible to us than their affordances. We tend to be so focused on the new things we *can* do with a new tool that we don't pay attention to the things we *cannot* do with it.

It would be a mistake, however, to regard affordances as universally good and constraints as universally bad. Sometimes affordances of new technologies can channel us into certain kinds of behaviour or ways of thinking and can blind us to other (sometimes better) possibilities. Constraints, on the other hand, can sometimes spur us to come up with creative solutions when the tools we have at hand do not allow us to do what we want to do. In this way, the constraints of tools can drive creativity and innovation.

Just because different technologies allow us to do some things and constrain us from doing other things does not mean that technologies *determine* what we can do, what we can mean, the kinds of relationships we can have, what we can think, and who we can be. Despite the affordances and constraints built in to the cultural tools that are available to us, human beings always seem to figure out how to do something new with them. We appropriate old tools into new situations, and we creatively alter and adapt them to fit new circumstances and new goals. The psychologist James Wertsch (1993) says that all human actions take place at a site of *tension* between what the cultural tools available to us allow us to do (affordances and constraints) and the ways we are able to *adapt* them to do new things. In fact, managing this 'tension' is an important aspect of the definition of 'literacy' we will develop below and in the rest of this book.

Furthermore, we rarely use media in isolation. We almost always mix them with other mediational means. As we saw with the example of the wristwatch, using one tool (like a watch) often affects how we can use another tool (an airplane). Sometimes the affordances of one medium help us to overcome the constraints of another. More and more, in fact, different media are merging together. Mobile phones, for example, have become devices which we use not just to have phone conversations but also to check email, send text messages, surf the internet, check stock prices and the weather, take snapshots and videos, and play games. Similarly, social networking sites like Facebook are **mashups** of multiple tools, integrating the functions of photo albums, email platforms, instant messaging programs and blogs.

Therefore, instead of thinking about media in a simple, 'one-to-one' way – a single technology with a clear set of affordances and constraints being used to take certain discrete actions – it's better to think of media as parts of systems of actions and activities, meanings and thoughts, social organizations and identities. The applied linguist Jay Lemke (1998a) uses the idea of an 'eco-system' to describe the relationship technologies have to our activities, our relationships, our societies, and to other technologies. We ourselves and the tools that we use are parts of large 'eco-social' systems in which the affordances of one technology might create constraints in other technologies, the meanings that we are able to make in one situation might make possible new meanings in totally different situations, and the actions that we take now might have profound and unexpected effects on relationships and identities we might form in the future.

MEDIATION AND 'MORAL PANICS'

People have always had strong feelings when it comes to new media. This is not surprising since, as we said above, mediation is intimately connected to the ways we go about doing things in our daily lives, the ways we express meaning, relate to others, and even the ways we think. When new ways of doing, meaning, relating, thinking and being start to develop around new media, it is natural for people to feel insecure and to worry that their old ways of doing, meaning, relating, thinking and being that they are used to are being lost or marginalized.

In the past, whenever new technologies arose, people inevitably expressed concerns. When writing was developed, none other than the Greek philosopher Socrates declared it to be a threat to civilization. Under the influence of this 'new media', he insisted, people would lose their ability to remember things and think for themselves. They would start to confuse 'real truth' with its mere representation in symbols. Later, when the printing press was developed, there were those who worried that social order would break down as governments and religious institutions lost control of information. When the cinema came on the scene, some were afraid that people would stop reading books and spend all their time watching movies, and that what they watched would compromise their moral character. And when television became available, many people worried that it would make people stupid or violent, or both.

Similarly a lot of people today – including parents, teachers, and newspaper reporters – are very concerned about the effects of digital media and the new literacies associated with them on society and on individuals. Some of these concerns are justified, and some are based on emotions and insecurity. Interestingly, most of these concerns focus on the five kinds of affordances and constraints that we discussed above. People are worried that digital media are taking away people's ability to *do* some of the things we could do before, or allowing people to do things that they don't think they should do. People are worried that digital media are ruining people's ability to *make meaning* precisely and accurately with language. Some are worried about the effects of digital media on *social relationships*, claiming either that people are becoming isolated from others or that they are meeting up with the 'wrong kind of people'. Some are worried that digital media are changing the way people *think*, causing them to become easily distracted and unable to construct or follow complex arguments. And finally, others are concerned about the kinds of social identities that we are performing using digital media, worrying about how we can tell whether or not these identities are really 'genuine' or about how much of their own identities and their privacy they actually have control over.

We do not mean to belittle any of these concerns. On the contrary, much of this book will focus explicitly on these issues and hopefully facilitate more informed and deliberative debate about them, especially among educators and students. Too many books about digital technologies promote either the extreme view of **technological dystopianism**, that digital technologies are destroying our ability to communicate and interact with one another in meaningful ways, or the equally extreme view of **technological utopianism**, the belief that digital technologies will invariably make us all smarter and the world a better place. We wish to avoid these two extremes. Mediational means like computers and the internet are neither good nor bad – they simply introduce into our social interaction certain affordances and constraints in particular social contexts which we have the ability to respond and adapt to in any number of creative ways, some with positive social consequences and some with negative ones.

Activity 1.2: Digital anxiety

Recall some of the worries that people have about the literacy practices that are developing around digital media that you have heard or read about. See if you can think of concerns that people have in each of the five areas below. In what ways do you think these concerns are justified? In what ways do you think they are not?

1. How digital media are changing what we do and how we do things;
2. How digital media are changing how we express ourselves and use language;
3. How digital media are changing how we relate to other people;
4. How digital media are changing how we think;
5. How digital media are changing the ways we manage our social identities.

WHAT ARE 'DIGITAL LITERACIES'?

Before ending this chapter, it's very important that we explain more about the title of this book and what we mean by it, and especially by the term 'digital literacies'. As we have seen above, using media is a rather complicated affair that influences not just how we do things, but also the kinds of social relationships we can have with other people, the kinds of social identities we can assume, and even the kinds of thoughts we can think. When we talk about being able to use media in this broader sense, not just as the ability to operate a machine or decipher a particular language or code, but as the ability to creatively engage in particular *social practices*, to assume appropriate *social identities*, and to form or maintain various *social relationships*, we use the term 'literacies'.

'Literacy' traditionally means the ability to read and write. Someone who can't read or write is called 'illiterate'. But reading and writing themselves are complicated processes. Reading and writing in different situations requires very different skills. For example, you write an essay for an English class in a different way than you write a lab report for a physics class or a comment on your friend's Facebook wall. The reason for this is that you are not just trying to make different kinds of meanings, but also to establish different kinds of relationships and enact different kinds of social identities. There are also a lot of other activities that go along with reading and writing like looking things up in the dictionary, finding information in the library or on the internet, and figuring out the right way to package information or to 'unpack' it in different kinds of texts. Finally, reading and writing often involve encoding and decoding more than just language. They might also involve using and interpreting pictures, the spatial layout of pages or the organizational structures of texts.

It should be clear from the above that literacy is not just a matter of things that are going on inside people's heads – cognitive processes of encoding and decoding words and sentences – but rather a matter of all sorts of interpersonal and social processes. Literacy is not just a way of making meaning, but also a way of relating to other people and showing who we are, a way of doing things in the world, and a way of developing new ideas about and solutions to the problems that face us.

This view of literacy as a *social* phenomenon rather than a set of cognitive or technical abilities associated with individuals was pioneered by a group of scholars in the 1980s and

1990s who called their approach 'the new literacy studies' (see, for example, Barton, 1994; Gee, 2008; Scollon and Scollon, 1981; Street, 1984). There are also those, however, who study what they call 'new literacies' (see, for example, Lankshear and Knobel, 2006), meaning that they focus on more recently developed literacy practices which are often (but not always) associated with 'new technologies' like computers and the internet.

In this book, what we mean by 'digital literacies' is informed by both of these traditions of research. For us, 'digital literacies' refers to the practices of communicating, relating, thinking and 'being' associated with digital media. Understanding digital literacies means in part understanding how these media themselves may affect the kinds of literacy practices that are possible. At the same time, we do not wish to fall into the trap of **technological determinism**, to suggest that new practices of reading and writing are determined solely by the affordances and constraints of the new digital tools available. An understanding of these affordances and constraints is important, but developing digital literacies means more than mastering the technical aspects of digital tools. It also means using those tools to *do something* in the social world, and these things we do invariably involve managing our social relationships and our social identities in all sorts of different and sometimes unpredictable situations.

To use the terminology we developed above, 'digital literacies' involve not just being able to 'operate' tools like computers and mobile phones, but *also* the ability to adapt the affordances and constraints of these tools to *particular* circumstances. At times this will involve mixing and matching the tools at hand in creative new ways that help us do what we want to do and be who we want to be. In other words, while we may seem at times in this book to focus quite heavily on the 'digital' part of digital literacies, that is, to dwell on the affordances and constraints of these new technologies, what we are really interested in is not the tools themselves, but the process of *mediation*, or, as others have called it, *mediated action* (Scollon, 2001; Wertsch, 1993), the process through which people appropriate these tools to accomplish particular social practices. It is through this focus on *mediation* that we hope to call attention to the *tension* between the affordances and constraints of digital media and the creativity of individuals and groups as they adapt these media to specific social goals and contingencies. As we said above, understanding this tension is central to understanding 'digital literacies'.

How, then, do 'digital' literacies differ from 'analogue' literacies like those involved in print-based reading and writing? Strictly speaking, the process of mediation and the tension between what tools allow us to do and what we want to do with them is fundamentally the same whether you are using pencil and paper or a word processing program. What *is* different, we will argue, are the kinds of affordances and constraints digital tools offer and the opportunities they make available for creative action. In many ways, digital media are breaking down boundaries that have traditionally defined our literacy practices.

One example is the way digital media are breaking down boundaries of time and space. Because of digital technologies we don't have to go to physical places like classrooms, libraries, offices and marketplaces to engage in literacy practices that were previously confined to particular physical places and particular times. Another example is the way digital media are breaking down barriers that traditionally governed the way we thought about language – for example, the distinction between spoken language and written language. One of the most powerful new affordances of digital media is that they make written language more interactive so that writing of all kinds has become more and more like having a conversation. Still another example, which we touched on briefly above, is the way digital media are breaking down the traditional barriers between media producers and media consumers.

Digital media are even breaking down barriers that used to divide literacy practices themselves. Because they facilitate new ways of distributing our attention, they allow us to participate in many practices simultaneously – we can work and study and shop and hold conversations with any number of people all at the same time (see Chapter 6).

Moreover, because digital tools have a different kind of materiality than physical tools like books, they have a greater capacity to be modified (or 'modded'), to be mixed, merged or 'mashed-up' with other tools, and to be adapted to unique circumstances and unique goals. And so mastering many of the literacy practices we will be discussing in this book depends not so much on being able to mimic things that others have done, but rather on being able to mix tools with one another and with environments and people to create *new* meanings and activities and identities, a process which we refer to in Chapter 7 as **hacking**. As Daniel Miller and Don Slater put it in their book *The Internet: An Ethnographic Approach* (2000:14):

> a central aspect of understanding the dynamics of mediation is not to look at a monolithic medium called 'the internet', but rather at a range of practices, software and hardware technologies, modes of representation and interaction . . . What we were observing was not so much people's use of 'the internet', but rather how they assembled various technical possibilities which added up to their internet.

In order to do this, however, we first need to have a good understanding of the fabric of affordances and constraints digital media make available to us to start out with. In the first part of this book we will focus on these new affordances and constraints, looking at things like search algorithms, hypertext, the read-write web, and the ways new technologies facilitate our ability to manipulate visual elements in texts like photographs and videos in ways never before possible. We will also explore how digital media enable and constrain different cognitive and social processes, ways of distributing attention across different tasks and ways of managing our social relationships. At the end of this section we will critically explore the degree to which these affordances and constraints act to promote particular ways of seeing and representing the world, to normalize particular kinds of behaviour, and to advance the agendas of particular kinds of people.

In the second half of the book we will go on to apply this analysis to specific 'literacies' that have grown up around various digital media and within various communities of media producers and consumers. We will examine practices like online gaming, social networking, peer production and collaboration, and practices involving digital media in the workplace.

Each chapter in the book includes a *case study* in which the concepts or principles discussed are illustrated with an example. In addition, each chapter includes *activities* that help you to apply the ideas we have discussed to examining and analysing your own digital literacy practices. At the end of each chapter a list of *useful resources* is provided for those who wish to explore particular topics further, and additional resources, examples and activities can also be found on the companion website for this book. At the end of the book we have included a glossary of terms, and throughout the book, whenever we introduce an important term for the first time, we will highlight it in **bold type** and include a definition in the glossary.

By the time you read this book, many of the 'new literacies' we discuss here will already be 'old' and many of the 'new technologies' may already be obsolete.

Hopefully, however, our framework for understanding media by exploring how they affect what we *do*, how we make *meaning*, how we *relate* to one another, how we *think*, and the kinds of people we can *be* will still be of value. Our real goal is not to teach you about *particular* literacy practices so much as to give you a useful way to reflect on your own literacy practices and how they are changing you.

USEFUL RESOURCES

Print

Clark, Andy (2003). *Natural born cyborgs.* Oxford: Oxford University Press

Gee, J. P., and Hayes, E. R. (2011). *Language and learning in the digital age.* New York: Routledge.

Lankshear, C., and Knobel, M. (2006). *New literacies: Everyday practices and classroom learning* (2nd ed.). Milton Keyes: Open University Press.

McLuhan, Marshall (1964). *Understanding media: The extensions of man*, 1st edition, New York: McGraw Hill; reissued MIT Press, 1994, with introduction by Lewis H. Lapham; reissued by Gingko Press, 2003.

Norris, S., and Jones, R. (eds.) (2005). *Discourse in action: Introducing mediated discourse analysis.* London: Routledge.

Scollon, R., and Scollon, S.W. (2004). *Nexus analysis: Discourse and the emerging internet.* London: Routledge.

Web

Ron Scollon and Rodney Jones, Mediated discourse analysis
http://personal.cityu.edu.hk/~enrodney/mda/index.htm

Pew Internet and American Life Project, Networked creators
http://www.slideshare.net/PewInternet/networked-creators

Alex Couros, Digital literacies and emerging technologies
http://couros.wikispaces.com/emerging+technologies

Video

Michael Wesch, The machine is us/ing us
http://www.youtube.com/watch?v=a-jex5697ec

Howard Rheingold, Digital literacies
http://youtu.be/xMSzgiiSGPQ

Andrea Lundsford, The myths of digital literacy
http://youtu.be/slKu_hZT2BM

Digital Tools

CHAPTER 2

Information Everywhere

Understanding how to cope with and use **information** is one of the most important aspects of digital literacies. Many people nowadays believe that digital technologies have brought about a phenomenon known as **information overload** (Waddington, 1998), a condition characterized by increased levels of stress, confusion and difficulty in making decisions resulting from having 'too much information'.

In this chapter we will argue that the problem of 'information overload' is not so much one of 'too much information', but rather one of defining what we mean by information in the first place, and of understanding how to *create* it by forming strategic relationships between different pieces of data. While digital technologies have dramatically increased people's opportunities to create information, they also provide extremely sophisticated tools for **filtering**, and channelling information. Coping successfully with information involves understanding both the information *creating* and the information *limiting* affordances of digital media.

INFORMATION AND RELATIONSHIPS

Much of the concern about information overload comes from a fundamental misunderstanding of what information is. Think about walking on a busy city street. All around you things are happening. There are thousands of sights and sounds, text everywhere, from shop signs to advertisements on the sides of passing busses, people all around you talking, dressed in different clothes and wearing different expressions on their faces. Most people who find themselves in such situations do not feel they are suffering from 'information overload' because they do not consider everything that is happening around them to be information. They selectively pay attention to and process the **data** which they judge to be important for them. In other words, they *create* information from the data that is available.

And so the first distinction we need to make is between 'information' and 'data'. Data are 'facts' (including sights, sounds, colours, words) which exist in the external world. These 'facts' only become information when we create some kind of relationship with them.

Besides data and information, there is also a third category that we need to consider, and that is **'knowledge'**. Knowledge is what is created when information is integrated into our minds in a way that we are able to adapt it to different circumstances and apply it to analysing and solving problems. Knowledge is created when information is *transformed* in some way – when, for example, it is combined with other information or applied to a particular task in a useful way.

Let's return to the busy city street and consider how the concepts of data, information and knowledge apply. In that environment, when we read the data made available to us on signs and connect it to the data on the map we are carrying, we have created information; when we remember that information and interpret it to the extent that we can not only get from one place to another without having to read the signs, but we can navigate through the city in innovative and creative ways, discovering 'short cuts' and 'scenic routes', then we have created knowledge.

The biggest problem people have in 'managing information' is not that there is too much information but that we have too much data available to us, and we are sometimes not sure how to decide which of it is worth turning into information and knowledge. In other words, we have not adequately worked out how to filter all of the data that is available to us and in a way that results in useful information. The good news is that while digital media add to our confusion by making much more data available to us, they also provide a host of tools for filtering data, and for forming the kinds of relationships that transform data into information and information into knowledge.

And so, to sum up, information is not about 'facts' so much as it is about the *relationships* that we create between ourselves (and other people) and those 'facts', and between different 'facts'. In the first chapter we argued, quoting Michael Schrage (2001), that what is often referred to as 'the information age' is more accurately thought of as the 'relationship age', mostly because people seem to use computers as much to connect with and communicate with other people as they do to search for, store and manipulate information. Now we would like to take that idea even further, arguing that even these practices of searching for, storing and manipulating information are more a matter of *relationships* than they are of data itself. In other words, we would like to argue that information is most usefully seen not as a collection of 'facts', but as a *social practice* based on establishing relationships.

Activity 2.1: Reflecting on your information management habits

A. WHAT'S THERE

Think about all of the data that currently exists in all of your personal storage areas, including the hard drive of your computer, any space on servers or 'virtual disks' that you use, and any webmail or other messaging services (including Facebook) where you store messages and other data as well as physical spaces like bookshelves and desk drawers.

1. How much of this data would you consider 'information' and how much would you consider 'unprocessed data'? Give examples.
2. How much of this 'information' do you think you have successfully turned into 'knowledge'? In other words, how much of it have you been able to integrate with other information in ways that help you to formulate new ideas or solve problems?
3. How much of this data was 'pushed' onto your computer (or other storage area) without you asking for it? Give examples.

4. How much of this data did you actively go out and retrieve from some other place? Give examples.

B. WHAT YOU DO WITH IT

Think about how you manage, organize and use the data in your personal storage areas, including the tools and techniques you use to create information out of data and for limiting the amount of irrelevant data you are exposed to.

1. Do you have a system for organizing your data/information? Is this system useful in helping you find data to create information and find information that you can use to create knowledge?
2. What tools or techniques do you use to access data/information in your own personal storage areas? How effective are these tools and techniques?
3. Do you have a method or methods for identifying and removing irrelevant or unnecessary data from your personal storage areas?
4. Do you have a method or methods for preventing other people from pushing irrelevant or unnecessary data into your personal storage areas?

C. HOW YOU FEEL

1. Do you often feel frustrated when trying to locate relevant data? Explain.
2. Do you often become distracted from what you are doing by the other data available to you or being pushed to you?
3. Do you experience frustration at the amount of electronic data you need to process daily?
4. Do you spend a lot of time organizing and processing data which in the end turns out not to be very useful to you?
5. Do you have the constant feeling that there is data in your personal storage areas that you have failed to process correctly or fully? Do you feel like you have processed the wrong things or have failed to process the right things?

ORGANIZING DATA

The first step in creating information is having data available to us in a way that makes it easy to form useful relationships with it. Throughout history, human beings have come up with various systems of organizing and classifying data. An **organization system** is any system which makes it easy for us to locate the data with which we can form meaningful relationships in order to create information and, eventually, knowledge. Organization systems usually arrange data in relation to other data. They can exist in books or online or even in the arrangement of physical objects (the layout of the streets in a city, for example, can be seen as an organization system).

The most widely used organization system is the **hierarchical taxonomy**. The eighteenth century Swedish botanist Carl Linnaeus is usually considered the father of modern taxonomies. He developed a classification system for plants and animals that is still used by scientists today: a nested hierarchy which classifies all living things first into one of three 'kingdoms', which are then subdivided into classes, orders, genera and species.

Among the best known classification systems of this type are those we find in libraries such as the Dewey Decimal System, developed by American librarian Melvil Dewey in 1873, which consists of 10 main classes of subjects divided into 100 divisions and 1,000 subdivisions, and the Library of Congress System, developed about a quarter of a century later, which allows for more growth of topics and subtopics by using a combination of letters and numbers.

In order to be used effectively, organization systems also usually require technological tools to act as an interface between the system and its users. One of the greatest advances in information technology in the nineteenth century, for example, was the invention of the filing cabinet and its close cousin, the library card catalogue cabinet. You may think that a filing cabinet is not such a big deal, but at the time it was. The idea that you could store documents vertically in different folders for easy classification and access was a tremendous advance. In fact, when the filing cabinet was invented it won a Gold Medal at the 1893 World's Fair.

The development of hierarchical taxonomies and technological tools such as filing cabinets which make searching through them more efficient had a profound effect on the way we interacted with data. It changed what we were able to *do* by making it much easier to locate the data which we needed to create meaningful information. It also affected the nature of the *meaning* behind these relationships since data were arranged in a way that much of their meaning was derived from their relationship with other data. It changed *human relationships* and *identities* by giving to certain people and institutions the power to control knowledge by deciding what belonged in the classification system and where it should be classified. Finally, it changed *the way we thought* about data, first by encouraging us to think of the natural and social worlds as rational and orderly, and second, by making us think of data itself as 'information' (since the classification system itself seems to create a kind of predetermined relationship between pieces of data).

There are, of course, distinct disadvantages to organizing data in this way. Often it is difficult to know exactly where different items should be placed in the series of categories. Classifying books, for example, is often extremely subjective. Whether or not a particular volume is about linguistics or psychology, or about anthropology or sociology, or about history or politics, or even if a work is fiction or non-fiction is often a matter of debate. And so, placing an item in this system always involves judgment, and that judgment is often a reflection of a particular agenda or ideology (see Chapter 7).

The second problem with such a system is that items can occupy only one place in the system at a time. Library books can only have one call number, and no other book can have the same call number. Documents can usually only occupy one folder in a filing cabinet. Of course, it is possible to make multiple copies of a document and store it in multiple places, but after a while this becomes unwieldy, expensive and, in the end, undermines this whole system of classification, which is premised on the idea that there is a place for everything and everything should be in a particular place.

Finally, this system does not really work the way our minds work. We do not usually think in strict categories and hierarchies. Instead, we think associatively, making connections between topics based not just on whether or not they are hierarchically related to each other, but on whether they are related in a whole host of other ways, many of which may not be immediately obvious to others or even to ourselves.

Unfortunately, even up until today, many people have not gone beyond the filing cabinet method of organizing data, despite the fact that digital tools present all sorts of new possibilities. Many 'new technologies' have incorporated the 'old technology' of the hierarchical taxonomy. The file systems on both Windows and Mac OS, as well as many web portals and directories (see below), rely on this system, based on the metaphor that data are like pieces of paper that can be classified and stored in different folders.

NETWORKS AND ORGANIZATION

One of the greatest contributions of digital media when it comes to the way we create and use information has been to make available another way of organizing data which is actually closer to the way the human brain works, a method based on **networked associations**.

What we mean by networked associations is that pieces of data can now be easily linked with other pieces of data based on all sorts of different relationships other than simple hierarchy. This capacity to link different pieces of data together based on a variety of different relationships, in fact, is one of the most important affordances introduced by digital media.

The internet, with its collection of linked web pages, constitutes a kind of natural system of networked associations that has developed organically from the bottom up based on the kinds of relationships people saw between the data they created and encountered on the internet. While this is an extremely powerful way of organizing data, using it requires a very different set of techniques and tools than those we previously used with static classification systems and hierarchal taxonomies.

Besides **linking** (see Chapter 3), another new tool for organizing data which digital technologies make available is the ability to 'tag' data with **metadata** or data which describes a particular piece of data with a set of concepts or references to other data. With **tagging**, rather than putting items into different folders, we put different labels onto the items, and then we can search for them later using single terms or combinations of terms. This allows our information to be organized in many different ways in many different 'places' at once.

The good thing about tagging is that it allows people to organize information in the same way that the brain does, using multiple, overlapping associations rather than rigid categories. For example, in Apple's iPhoto I can tag a picture of my puppy wearing a Santa hat with labels like puppy, cute, and Christmas. Then when I look for that picture I can find it by using any of those key words. More importantly, I can also find other similar photos using combinations of these words and Boolean operators (and/or). For example, I can combine cute and Christmas and find not just my puppy but all sorts of cute things having to do with Christmas like elves and Rudolph the Red-Nosed Reindeer. Or I can combine puppy and Christmas and find all of the pictures that I've taken of my dog on Christmas for the last five years.

Although many software applications support tagging, and you can attach metadata to files in both Microsoft Windows and Mac OS, the place where tagging has become a really central strategy for the organization of data is on the World Wide Web. In the past, whenever we wanted to get data from a public source, like the library, we relied on an expert to organize and classify it for us. The problem was that we were stuck with whatever classification system the expert had settled on, whether we liked it or not. Nowadays, many websites, rather than relying on experts to organize and classify information, rely on users to do this work. On sites like Delicious, Flickr and Amazon, users attach tags to different files or other data that they either upload there or find there, and other people can use these tags to look for things that interest them. Of course, everybody has a different way of tagging based on their own judgments and their own opinions. I might tag a picture of Lady Gaga with words like goddess and sexy, and somebody else might use words like devil and obscene. So, if everybody is adding their own tags to the same piece of information, why doesn't this result in chaos?

The answer is a concept that the philosopher Pierre Lévy (1997) calls **collective intelligence**, a concept that we will discuss in more detail in later chapters, especially Chapter 11. The idea of collective intelligence is that if lots of people make decisions about how something should be classified or organized and you put all of these decisions together, you end up with a system that reflects the collective 'wisdom' of the community.

Many sites that use what has come to be known as **social tagging** present the results in the form of a **tag cloud** so you can visually understand how other people have tagged a particular item or group of items. In tag clouds, the more often a term is used to describe a particular item, the larger the word will appear.

For example, users of the site Library Thing (http://www.librarything.com/) tag books they have read with different key words. So, if you look up the book *Collective Intelligence* by Pierre Lévy, you get the tag cloud shown in Figure 2.1.

One advantage of this practice of displaying tag clouds is that it not only gives you a good way to understand what other people thought the book was about, but it also allows you to search for other books you might be interested in based on key words that are associated with this book.

These systems of classifying data that are invented by the people who actually use the data are called **folksonomies**, as opposed to the rigid, hierarchal *taxonomies* which we discussed above. Taxonomies are 'top-down' – that is, they are invented by experts. Folksonomies are 'bottom-up' classification systems. Some people argue that folksonomies are better than taxonomies because they better reflect the way real people think and classify information in their own minds. Others, however, are more sceptical. The writer Cory Doctorow (2001), for example, points out that collective tagging does not necessarily result in better classification systems for three reasons: 1) people lie (sometimes they just tag things randomly or try to confuse other people); 2) people are lazy (they don't think hard enough when they are doing their tagging); and 3) people are 'stupid' (most people are not very good at thinking up useful tags).

anthropology cognition cognitive science collective intelligence computers cultural anthropology cultural studies cyberculture cyberspace emergence essay essays France globalization hypertext intelligence internet internet studies media media studies media theory new media non-fiction philosophy professional social systems sociology technology web web 2.0

Figure 2.1   Tag cloud
(Retrieved February 12, 2011 from http://www.librarything.com/work/323515, used with permission)

It should be obvious by now that organizing data based on associative networks as opposed to hierarchical taxonomies dramatically changes what we can do with data and the kinds of connections and meaningful relationships that we can form with it. Hyper-linking and social tagging have also had a profound effect on social relationships, to some degree shifting the power to 'create knowledge' away from experts and towards the people who use the data. While this can discourage the ideological control of knowledge by a few powerful people, at the same time, as we will discuss further in the next chapter, it can sometimes make the ideological agendas behind the various associations formed by **hyperlinks** and tags less transparent and easy to detect.

Case Study 2: Search engines

Perhaps the most important and widely used digital tool for turning data into information is the internet search engine. Over the years there have been many different approaches to searching the internet, but nearly all search engines consist of three main components: 1) a *crawler* or *spider*, which is a software program that travels through the World Wide Web and retrieves data to be indexed; 2) the *indexer*, which arranges what has been harvested into a form that can be searched by the user; and 3) the *interface*, which consists mainly of a group of **algorithms** or sets of procedures by which the index is searched and the results of the search are sorted. All three of these components present special kinds of challenges for the designers (and users) of search engines. When they work well, however, search engines provide the enormous affordance of freeing us from hierarchical taxonomies and allowing us to take advantage of the associative networked structure of the internet.

Search engines were not always the preferred way for locating data on the internet. In the early years of the World Wide Web and even into the first years of the twenty-first century, 'directories' or 'web portals' were much more widely used. Portals, like Yahoo and AOL, were originally web pages with lists of links arranged in hierarchical taxonomies according to subject along with, as they developed, more things like news stories, weather reports and horoscopes. In fact, the development of the World Wide Web in the 1990s can in some ways be seen as a competition between the two systems of organization discussed above: the hierarchal taxonomy and the associative network.

The problems with using a **directory** to manage data on the World Wide Web are obvious. First, there is just too much data to fit realistically into a directory, and so the links that are included must always be selected by some central authority. Second, the larger a directory gets, the more time and labour intensive it becomes to search. And finally, as we stated above, directories lock users into rather rigid conceptual categories that may not match with the way they divide up data in their own minds.

Search engines also have problems, mostly having to do with the special technological challenges associated with the three components mentioned above. The first challenge is to develop a *crawler* that can harvest the massive store of data on the web both thoroughly and efficiently. The second is developing a method for indexing the data so that the right kinds of search terms result in the right kinds of results. For example, if you are searching for York, you are probably more interested in York, England than New York, though most of the web pages on the internet containing the word York are about New York. Similarly, if you type in the name George Washington, you are likely more interested in pages *about* George Washington (the person) rather than pages that just mention him or pages about the George Washington Bridge or George Washington University. Lastly, there is the challenge of developing a set of procedures which will return results in a way which can help the user to judge their relevance to what he or she wants to know or do and facilitate the forming of useful relationships with and among these results. This set of procedures is called an 'algorithm'.

Over the years, different developers have gone about solving these problems in different ways. Perhaps the first great advance in search engine design came with the 1995 launch by Digital Equipment Corp. of Alta Vista, a search engine which, for the first time, made the efficient crawling and indexing of the web possible. The problem with Alta Vista and many other search engines of this period was that they lacked an effective algorithm with which to judge the relevance of results and so were open to abuse by 'spammers'.

'Spam' is a term used for unsolicited and usually unwanted data which is pushed onto your computer. The type of spam most familiar to us is email spam, but another important kind of spam is known as 'search engine spam', which refers to web pages which attempt to fool the indexing systems of search engines and 'impose themselves' into the results of unsuspecting searchers. Back in the 90s the most popular method for doing this was 'keyword stuffing' – filling webpages with popular keywords, often hidden (for example white text against a white background) in order to fool crawlers and indexers. For example, a pornography site might secretly embed the names of popular entertainment figures in order to trick search engines into listing them as the results for popular searches.

One of the most important developments in search technology was the invention of the **PageRank algorithm** in the late 1990s by Larry Page and Sergey Brin, two students at Stanford who went on to found Google. PageRank is based on the central idea we used to introduce this chapter: that information is not about 'facts', but about *relationships*. Thus, the 'information value' of any given piece of data comes from the number and strength of the relationships it has with other pieces of data and with other people. PageRank sorts search results in terms of relevance based on the number of other sites which link to them and the quality of these linkages. In other words, the more sites that link to a given site, the more 'important' that site is deemed to be. Not all relationships are equal, of course. If your brother links to your site, that may help you, but not much because not many sites have linked to his site. If, on the other hand, *The New York Times* links to your site, your site will go up in 'information value' since so many other sites have linked to *The New York Times*.

The PageRank algorithm can be expressed mathematically as:

$$PR(A) = (1-d) + d\ (PR(Ti)/C(Ti) + \dots + PR(Tn)/C(Tn))$$

where
PR(A) is the PageRank of page A,
PR(Ti) is the PageRank of pages Ti which link to page A,
C(Ti) is the number of outbound links on page Ti and
d is a damping factor which can be set between 0 and 1.

This algorithm is not the only way that Google ranks search results, but it is the most important and, when it was developed, the most revolutionary method of returning relevant results, resulting in the meteoric success of Google as the search engine of choice for most people at the time this book was written.

Besides the PageRank algorithm, Google also uses other kinds of **data signals** to determine the relevance of particular websites to users' queries. Starting in 2009, it added personalized search features (see below). What this means is that the results you get are not just affected by other people's behaviour in linking pages to one another, but also by your own past search behaviour – the terms you have searched for before and the results you have clicked on. These and other factors go together to help the search engine determine the relevance of particular sites for you (or for the kind of person the search engine thinks you are). If you frequently search for and click on links related to George Washington University, for example, when you search for George Washington, or even just George, chances are that the university homepage will appear high in your results. Personalized search also takes into account your location, and so the term George is more likely to return George Washington University if you are searching from Washington D.C. than if you are searching from Cairo. Google's personalized search also makes use of data that is present in other Google apps such as Gmail and Google Docs. It searches through the emails you have sent and received, for example, and cross references that data with information on what you have searched for in order to get a more accurate idea about what kinds of search results you will find most relevant. Some people are concerned that such practices might violate users' privacy or might make search results too biased towards users' preconceived opinions or ideas about the world (see Chapter 7).

PageRank and personalized search algorithms, however, are not immune from search engine spammers. Search engine spammers have, over the years, attempted various methods to trick the algorithms of search engines, including creating 'link farms' which have no purpose other than to link to other sites and increase their ranking, and installing malicious **cookies** (see below) on people's computers. Consequently, Google and other search companies constantly 'tweak' their algorithms in order to get around such activity, a process which unfortunately sometimes causes legitimate sites from honest purveyors of data to fall in the rankings.

The lesson that can be taken from this brief survey of search is that no matter how good search engines become at delivering to you the data you want and need to create useful information, there will always be limitations. There will always be people who will try to figure out ways to beat the system and to push to you data that you do not want, and sometimes attempts to stop them or to 'personalize' your search can end up making the results too narrow.

Ironically, this situation helps to highlight the affordances of directories, those unwieldy and inefficient systems of organization that search engines promised to save us from. For all of their limitations, at least directories come with a different kind of filter: the judgment of the person who constructed the directory. And so, for certain kinds of data retrieval, especially those in which the reliability of data is very important or which focus on rather narrow disciplinary domains of knowledge, directories can be better choices than search engines. A good example of a useful directory is the Librarians' Internet Index (LII) (http://www.ipl.org/), which promotes itself with the slogan: 'Information you can trust'. The site classifies internet resources by subject, including only those which are deemed by the participating librarians as reliable and relevant to academic or educational pursuits.

One final and very important point about search is that the words people type into search engines themselves become data, especially for people trying to sell things. The words you type into Google's search box as well as the results that you have clicked on, for example, are used to help advertisers to determine which ads might be most appealing to you. Civil libertarians have voiced concern over such practices, citing the invasion of privacy they constitute and wondering about the possibilities of governments using this information to conduct surveillance of citizens.

Aggregated data on search terms is also used by businesses, journalists, anthro-pologists, historians and other scholars to measure trends in what people are interested in or concerned about. John Battelle (2005), former editor of *Wired Magazine*, calls this aggregated data the '**database of intentions**', a record of the thoughts, ideas, desires and fears of human cultures. One important step towards the maintenance of this database is Google's practice since 2001 of publishing yearly aggregated search statistics under the title of 'Google Zeitgeist' (http://www.google.com/intl/en/press/zeitgeist/).

FINDING AND FILTERING

In his book *The Advent of the Algorithm*, mathematician David Berlinski argues that the development of the concept of the *algorithm* at the end of the nineteenth century was the basis for all modern science, especially modern computing. Computers, he says, are physical machines that embody algorithms. Although the mathematical idea of the algorithm is quite complicated, its essence is simply a finite list of precise steps for executing a particular task. A recipe for chocolate chip cookies, for example, can be seen as a simple kind of algorithm.

As we have seen in our case study, algorithms are central to the way search engines work. In fact, they are central to the way all computer programs work. Google's PageRank algorithm, for example, is a series of steps that a computer program executes to determine the number of links to a given webpage matching a particular search term and the value of those links based on the number of links to those linking pages.

The main actions achieved by algorithms are *finding* data that is potentially useful to us based on input we have provided (e.g., search words) and *filtering out* data that is deemed not to be useful to us. Many of the tools that we use to find and filter data are based on very simple algorithms. For example, an **RSS feed** delivers to us blog postings based on a simple formula that selects only postings from blogs we have subscribed to.

Not only is the algorithm an important mathematical concept for digital media, it is also a useful tool for understanding how to manage information. Many of the algorithms involved in delivering data to us are executed by technological tools, mostly computer programs. We can call these **technological algorithms**. One step in making more efficient use of tools like search engines is to understand the algorithms that they use to determine which results to deliver to us.

There are, however, other kinds of algorithms. Some make use of people or groups of people to find useful data and protect from useless data. We can call these **social algorithms** or **social filters.** By participating in social networks (e.g., Facebook, Twitter), for example, which are made up of our friends, colleagues, and other people we respect and trust, we gain access to the data that they consider to be important. In the course of the day, our friends and contacts browse a range of sources on the internet, coming across a lot of uninteresting junk, and a few interesting pieces of data that are worth sharing. The uninteresting junk is 'filtered' out, and the interesting or useful data is passed on by posting a link to a social network site like Facebook, Twitter, or to a social bookmarking site like Delicious or Diigo. When we log on to these networks, we can filter data based on the recommendations of our friends.

Social algorithms are an example of what are known as **agent-based algorithms**, algorithms that involve the interaction between a set of procedures and some kind of agent who can apply the procedures in an intelligent way based on the demands of different circumstances. In many ways, agent-based algorithms are a more accurate means of finding and filtering data than technological algorithms alone. The mental processes that agents use to make decisions about what we may or may not find useful or interesting are often much more sophisticated and complex than those used by computers, taking into account a lot more information and making use of 'fuzzy logic'. This is why your boyfriend is better at choosing a birthday gift for you than a computer (you hope!). And so, social algorithms help us to create information not just by forming relationships with data but also by forming relationships with other people whom we trust.

Personalized algorithms are algorithms that change based on your own choices or behaviour. Perhaps the most basic kind of personalized algorithm is the RSS feed. RSS stands for 'Really Simple Syndication'. It allows owners of a website to send alerts to people who have subscribed to the feed whenever the content of the website changes and to 'push' that new content to subscribers' computers. Subscribers often use RSS aggregators (called 'readers' or 'feeders') to gather together the content of the different websites they have subscribed to.

More sophisticated personalized filters are those that filter data based not on conscious decisions that you have made but on your past *behaviour.* Such filters are essentially prediction engines which examine your past actions on the network (such as what links you have clicked on or what kinds of things you have 'liked' on your social networking site) and try to guess the kind of data (or products) that you are likely to find most interesting and useful in the future. These actions are often recorded and sent back to the server using small programs, which have been installed onto your computer, called 'cookies'. The search personalization features that are part of Google's set of search algorithms that we mentioned in our case study constitute an example of such a personalized filter. Another good example of a site that personalizes search based on users' past behaviour is Amazon.com, which returns results and 'makes recommendations' based on the items you have previously browsed and bought when logged into the site.

While the filtering capacity of algorithms has the enormous advantage of protecting us from unwanted data and making our searches more efficient, there are disadvantages as well. Sometimes filters filter out potentially useful information along with 'spam'. No matter how sophisticated an algorithm is, it can never be absolutely sure about the data you need. Results returned based on criteria such as popularity and relevance are not necessarily the best. Sometimes data that is less popular or falls outside the scope of the things you are usually exposed to is much more useful. It is important, therefore, to be aware of the ways the various algorithms we use filter data and to critically evaluate the criteria they use (see Chapter 7).

Apart from the filtering procedures performed by technological, social and personalized algorithms, there are also the procedures you follow in your own mind when you set about looking for relevant data. All of us bring to the task of information creation certain **mental algorithms**. In other words, whether we are conscious of it our not, we always execute a series of steps when we go about searching for useful data, and just as understanding how Google chooses and filters data for us can help us to use it better, becoming more conscious of the algorithms our own minds execute will make us better at finding useful data and creating useful information. These mental algorithms guide us to perform different procedures based on things like the *purpose* of our search, help us to determine appropriate *search terms*, and assist as we *interact with* and *evaluate* our results.

Recovery or discovery?

One of the most important things to determine before searching for data is what your purpose is for doing so. In some cases, we are attempting to *recover* data which will help us to solve a particular problem. At other times, however, we are not trying to find a specific piece of data, but rather to *discover* what kind of data is out there associated with a certain topic or issue. Some tasks involve both recovery and discovery. Doing research is a good example. Most good research is a process of attempting to discover interesting questions, recovering data that can be used to answer those questions, and then discovering more questions. Most tasks, however, involve primarily recovery or discovery, and if you get lost discovering when all you really need to do is find the answer to the question you have, you end up wasting a lot of time. At the same time, if you are trying to find specific answers before you have sufficiently discovered the best questions to ask, you will also be led astray.

The right word

Searching for data is fundamentally a *linguistic activity*, and for it to go smoothly requires that the words and phrases that you choose as search terms are accurate in terms of meaning, **syntax** and, of course, spelling. Meaning has to do with whether or not the search terms you are using semantically match the kind of data that you want to find. Sometimes you will use words that you believe *describe* the kind of data you are looking for, and sometimes you will simply choose words that you think are in some way *associated* with that data. In choosing search terms, it is important to be flexible and try new terms when the old ones have not delivered satisfying results. Often the search results themselves can help us to refine our searches, suggesting more specific terms or related terms we had not thought of.

Syntax is about the way you combine words together and the order in which you combine them. The syntax that most search engines use is called Boolean logic. Boolean logic does not pay attention to the order of words unless you tell the search engine to. And so, typing 'Lady Gaga' is the same as typing 'Gaga Lady'. If you wish for these words to be found in a particular order as, for example, part of a phrase, you need to surround them with double quotation marks (""). Although some search engines purport to work on the syntax of natural language, most, like Google, do not, and so asking a question like 'Where was Lady Gaga born?' is no more effective than typing a series of words like 'Lady Gaga birthplace'. The most important thing is to be brief, avoiding extra words that might confuse the search engine. Google actually screens out common words like 'the', 'when' and 'where', and so if you want these terms to be included you need to precede them with a '+'. If you want to search for pages that contain either one term or another, you can separate the two terms with 'or'.

The pragmatics of search

Pragmatics is a branch of linguistics which studies 'how we do things with words' and how conversations can be interpreted as a series of *actions* and *reactions*. To approach your search pragmatically means to first realize that, usually, you are not just trying to create information for the sake of information, but that you are trying to *do* something like buy a birthday gift or complete a school assignment. Sometimes people get so wrapped up with collecting data that they forget to ask whether or not the data they are collecting is really going to help them to solve their problem. To avoid this, you can 'think backwards': first determine what you need to accomplish, then determine what kind of information you need, and then think about the kind of data you need to create that information.

Another important aspect of search is that the process of searching for data, whether we are using technical algorithms, social algorithms, personalized algorithms, or relying on our own mental algorithms, is always a kind of *conversation*. When your search engine or social network or whatever tool you are using delivers its results, that is not the end of the conversation, but rather an invitation for you to respond, either by 'interrogating' the results that you have gotten or by further refining your search strategy.

Evaluating data

We will have much more to say about how to 'interrogate' and evaluate data you find on the internet in Chapter 7. For now it will suffice to return to the notion of relationships with which we began this chapter. Usually the best way to judge data you find on the web is to examine the relationships they have to other pieces of data and to different kinds of people who have either produced, used or recommended them. In looking for relationships with people, for example, you might ask who produced the data and what kinds of affiliations they have (e.g., a university, a religious organization, etc.). When it comes to publically available data, it is important to remember that all data has an agenda (see Chapter 7), which is usually to convince you of a certain idea or position or to make you do something (like make a purchase). In looking for relationships between this data and other data, you can consider how the data fits in with the data you already have, the relevance of the data to what you have to do, when it was produced and when you need to use it, and the other sources of data linked to it.

Activity 2.2: Working with algorithms

In this activity you will reflect on and work to refine the various 'algorithms' or sets of procedures for gathering data that help you complete everyday search tasks. Plan a search strategy appropriate for the following scenarios:

1. You want to locate an old friend you went to primary school with.
2. You are writing an essay on whether or not 'collective intelligence' is really a form of intelligence.
3. You want to know how PageRank works.
4. You are going to the beach and you want to know how long before going out in the sun you should apply sunscreen.
5. You want to buy a portable hard disk.
6. You want to find out if a certain professor would be a good supervisor for your planned PhD studies.

For each scenario, write down the procedures that you would go through to locate and retrieve the appropriate data. Provide a list of steps or a 'flow chart', noting when the procedure involves a technological algorithm (such as one provided by a search engine), a social algorithm (such as recommendations from friends in your social network), a personalized algorithm (such as a set of choices you have made in the past), or a mental algorithm (a set of mental procedures you perform yourself such as brainstorming appropriate search terms). As you are doing this, consider the following questions:

1. Does this task primarily require a process of recovering data or discovering data?
2. What kinds of tools (e.g., search engines, social filters) are most appropriate for the job?
3. What do you know about the algorithms that these tools use that can help you to interpret the results that you get?
4. What kinds of questions will you ask about the data you find in order to evaluate its accuracy and relevance to your task?

Most good algorithms have built into them alternative strategies, so make sure to include in your plan alternate routes to take if your initial attempts do not yield the kind of data that allow you to create the information you need.

CONCLUSION

In this chapter we have attempted to address the problem of 'information overload' often associated with digital media by making a distinction between data and information. Data is something that we either find or is 'pushed' to us by other people, and information is something that we *create* by forming useful relationships with this data and among different pieces of data. Forming these relationships always involves using various kinds of tools such as organizational systems and algorithms, and the affordances and constraints of these different tools affects the kind of information we are able to create and what we are able to do with it. In the next chapter we will further explain how we navigate through and create relationships with online data as we consider the new ways of reading and writing that digital media make possible.

USEFUL RESOURCES

Print

Battelle, J. (2005). *The search: How Google and Its rivals rewrote the rules of business and transformed our culture.* Boston: Nicolas Brealey Publishing.

Berlinski, D. (2000). *The advent of the algorithm: The idea that rules the world,* New York: Houghton Mifflin Harcourt.

Davis, C. (2005). *Finding and knowing: Psychology, information and computers.* London: Routledge.

Jones, W. (2007). *Keeping found things found: The study and practice of personal information management.* Waltham, MA: Morgan Kaufmann.

Web

Library thing
http://www.librarything.com/

Google guide
http://www.googleguide.com/

Delicious
http://www.delicious.com/

Librarians' internet index (LII)
http://www.ipl.org/

Google zeitgeist
http://www.google.com/intl/en/press/zeitgeist/index.html

Video

Information overload: The movie
http://www.youtube.com/watch?v=MuwUeVFJF20

Do you suffer from information overload syndrome?
http://www.youtube.com/watch?v=zhoRKxypAwE&feature=related

Google, How Google makes improvements to its search algorithm
http://youtu.be/J5RZOU6vK4Q

CHAPTER 3

Hyperreading and Hyperwriting

With the development of digital media, the activities of reading and writing, which used to be mediated by pen and paper, typewriters and printing presses, are now increasingly mediated by digital tools like web browsers that we access through our computers and other digital devices. This shift from print-based media to digital media has been accompanied by the development of new literacy practices, shaped by the affordances and constraints of digital tools.

Most printed books are designed to be read in a linear way that limits the reading path that we can take. This is not true of all books, of course. Encyclopaedias and dictionaries, for example, are designed to allow us to move from place to place, but we are still restricted by the classification systems of the authors. Printed books also separate us from the people who wrote them and put us in the position of passive recipients of information. In digital media, these design limitations are overcome through three main affordances that are not available in print-based media, namely:

- **Hypertext**;
- **Interactivity**; and
- **Multimedia**.

Let's take multimedia first. Multimedia, by which we mean content that is conveyed as images, audio, video, as well as text, allows us to represent information and make meaning using a wider range of modes (for example visual, aural) than is possible in print. With print technologies it was more difficult to include visual elements in a document and impossible to include aural elements and moving images. Even the relatively straightforward job of inserting a picture on a page posed technical challenges in the early days of print. In contrast, digital technologies have made these operations childishly easy, with the result that we now encounter multimedia everywhere. We consider these changes in detail in the next chapter on **multimodality**.

Another affordance available in digital media is hypertext. In essence, hypertext is electronic text which is 'hyperlinked' to other electronic text. Hypertext is so fundamental to the architecture of the internet that we tend to take it for granted. However, it has had a profound effect on the way writers can structure and organize information, and the way readers can navigate their way through it. Unlike the pages of a book, which unfold in a linear sequence, hypertext can be organized in a variety of different ways.

Finally, digital media provide writers and their readers with the ability to interact with texts in ways that were previously difficult or impossible. For example, if you are reading a book and find an error, then there is no easy way for you to 'write back' to the author and suggest an improvement. In contrast, **web 2.0** technologies allow us to comment on or even annotate the texts that we read online and engage in conversations with the author and other readers about them.

These new affordances of digital media have required people to rethink their understanding of reading and writing, redefine their ideas about what a reader is and what a writer is, and adopt new practices in reading and writing.

HYPERTEXT AND LINKING

Anyone who has ever surfed the internet has experienced hypertext; it is the very fabric that makes up the linked pages of the World Wide Web. As we've defined it above, hypertext is electronic text which is hyperlinked to other electronic text. The term 'hypertext' was coined by American sociologist and philosopher Theodor H. Nelson in the 1960s. In his book, *Literary Machines,* he describes it in this way (1992: 0/2):

> By 'hypertext,' I mean non-sequential writing – text that branches and allows choices to the reader, best read at an interactive screen. As popularly conceived, this is a series of text chunks connected by links which offer the reader different pathways.

A key feature of hypertext, then, is that it allows readers and writers to make use of **hypertext links** in order to organize electronic text in a non-sequential way depending to a large extent on the reader's choice. In essence, the writer of a hypertext document creates a range of choices for the reader, who selects from them in order to create a pathway through the text. A good example of the branching, non-sequential choices in hypertext is the homepage of a website. Often, such a homepage is little more than a series of links, each offering the reader a different possible path to choose from.

Because hypertext allows readers greater flexibility to create their own reading paths, readers play a much more active role in digital media than they do in traditional print-based media. This more active role is reflected in the expressions that we use to describe the activity of online reading. For example, we 'surf' the internet and 'navigate' a website, but we don't usually 'surf' or 'navigate' a book. As a general principle, readers in hypertext are expected to make choices and read in a non-linear, branching fashion. This contrasts with print-based media, where the dominant (though by no means only) expectation is that readers will proceed in a linear way.

Hypertext provides writers with new opportunities as well. Hypertext allows writers to link their texts to other texts on the internet to support and elaborate on their claims. In this way, electronic texts can coherently reference and include prior texts, with writers linking to prior texts in a way that makes them accessible with minimal effort. However, this affordance also creates a new problem. In hypertext it is harder for writers to lead readers through a lengthy argument, because it is easier for readers to navigate away, dipping in and out of a range of online documents.

As a reader and writer of online documents you need to be aware of the affordances of hypertext, and the way that hypertext links ('hyperlinks' or just 'links') can be used to provide order and structure to texts. Links can be used for this purpose in one of two main ways: they can be used to *internally link* different parts of the same text in a logical way, and they can be used to *externally link* the text to other texts on the internet.

Linking internally to structure texts

As suggested, hyperlinks can be used to link different parts of the same online document and organize or structure the text internally. There are three main ways people use hyperlinks to internally organize online texts (illustrated in Figure 3.1). Some hypertexts are organized in a **hierarchical structure**, with the hyperlinks arranged like a menu or a tree-like outline. Similar to the table of contents that you find in a book, this allows readers to see the entire organization of the document at a glance and easily navigate to the part that is most relevant to their needs.

Another popular pattern of organization is the **linear structure** in which parts of the text are organized in a specific sequence which readers have to follow. This kind of organization is common in things like online learning sites or for filling out surveys and forms. For example, the writer of an online learning site might want to break learning material down into a series of fixed steps, perhaps moving from a presentation of information at the beginning of the sequence to a quiz at the end. A linear pattern of organization is also used in blogs (see Case study 3), which tend to organize their content in a linear fashion based on time.

A third pattern might be called the **hypertextual structure** (Baehr 2007). In this case parts of the document are linked to other parts of the document or other documents on the internet (see Figure 3.1) based on relationships of association. For example, some key terms may be highlighted and linked to related pages, definitions or elaborations of terms or concepts.

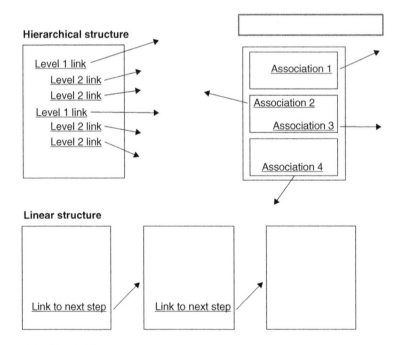

Figure 3.1   Organizational structures in hypertext

Most websites use a combination of these hierarchical, linear and hypertextual organizational patterns. An online shopping site, for example, may have a list of the different kinds of products hierarchically arranged, links that can take you from one product to related products (for example, 'customers who bought this also bought . . .'), and then take you through the check-out process in a linear fashion.

Linking externally to create associations

Hypertext links can also serve to organize an online document externally, by associating the text with other texts on the internet. For example, a website may provide an external links section, which summarizes other resources that readers could be interested in. Or, links to other online documents can be added in the flow of the text to provide more information about concepts relevant to the topic under discussion.

When we use links in this way they create associations, often implicitly suggesting a relationship between linked texts. If you think about it, the same thing happens when you put two sentences next to each other in print (for example, 'He's been behaving very oddly lately. He's in love.' Here the second sentence implicitly stands in a relation of cause and effect with the first). The following is a (non-exhaustive) list of relations that could be implied by a link:

- Cause-effect
- Comparison/contrast
- Example
- Sequence
- Whole-part, or part-whole
- Evaluation

The ability to organize texts externally in this way provides a new affordance for writers, allowing them to easily juxtapose different texts. This affordance can be exploited in creative and playful ways, for example where links create unexpected associations to humorous effect. On the other hand, links can also be used to contrast different texts and viewpoints in critical, thought-provoking ways.

It is important to remember that when authors link to an external source, they often neglect to tell us what relation they see between the two texts. As a result, the relation has to be inferred by the reader. Also, links can have the effect of subtly changing the way that a text is read, by providing clues to the underlying assumptions of the writer (see Chapter 7). For example, our reading would probably change if a website about terrorism linked to another website about a particular political or charitable organization. In this example, we would probably infer that the author sees the organization as similar to, or even as an example of a terrorist organization and we would have to evaluate this association. A careful and critical reading of links can provide useful additional information about a writer's underlying assumptions and attitude.

As we noted above, readers in hypertext are expected to play a more active role than readers in print-based media. Nevertheless, writers still exert a lot of influence over the construction of the text. When we read a hypertext document, although we are able to create our own reading path by selecting the links to follow, we don't have any choice about which links have been made and which links have not been made. These choices, which can determine the limits of our reading trajectory, are made by the writer. Thus, educational theorist Nicholas Burbules (1998) reminds us that it is important to adopt a critical stance when interpreting links in hypertext. In particular, we should pay attention to the following questions:

- What associations does the writer make?
- What associations does the writer **not** make?
- What assumptions do these (non-)associations reveal?

READING CRITICALLY IN HYPERTEXT

The following example may serve to illustrate how the choices that writers make when they use hyperlinks can affect our reading of an online document. The text comes from the technology news blog *TechCrunch* and describes the adoption of a new policy to ban gambling in the virtual world *Second Life* (London Lab, 2003).

> ### *Second Life* Bans Gambling Following FBI Investigation
> Duncan Riley, July 25, 2007
>
> An on-going investigation by the FBI into gambling in *Second Life* is believed to be directly related to Linden Lab's sudden decision to ban all forms of gambling on *Second Life*.
>
> The FBI investigation commenced in April and was considering the legality of online gambling within the virtual world. The US Government prohibits most forms of online gambling.
>
> (Retrieved June 7, 2011 from http://techcrunch.com/2007/07/25/second-life-bans-gambling-following-fbi-investigation/)

The post goes on to consider possible actions (arrests, prosecutions) open to the FBI and comments on the likely loss of revenue that *Second Life* will face when casino owners are forced to pull out. The post is written in a neutral, objective style similar to a news report. It contains three hyperlinks, which are underlined in the text. The first link ('*Second Life*') is an internal link to a webpage providing information about Linden Lab, the company that runs *Second Life*. The second link ('sudden decision') is an external link to a post on the *Second Life* blog, 'Wagering in *Second Life*: New Policy', introducing the new policy on gambling. Both of these links serve to elaborate on information provided in the article but are otherwise unremarkable.

The third link ('in April') is another internal link, this time to an existing blog post by a different TechCrunch writer (April 4, 2007). This post, 'G-Men Visit *Second Life* Casinos, Stay for the Brothels', serves both to elaborate on and to evaluate the FBI investigation. The linked post conveys a strong anti-government bias and pokes fun at the FBI investigation. In particular, the writer suggests that the FBI agents ('G-men' or 'government men') are in fact more interested in cybersex than they are in investigating online gambling in *Second Life*.

In this example then, the writer links to online texts authored by *TechCrunch* and Linden Lab, but chooses not to link to any government sources. This choice of links reveals an underlying assumption that the linked sources are more valuable and trustworthy than information provided by the government. The choice of links also introduces a very subtle bias into the article, because the government's position is not as fully represented as other viewpoints.

If readers follow the 'in April' link, this is also likely to change the way they read the original post. On the one hand, the original post appears to provide a neutral account, avoiding any clear stance on the part of the writer. Yet, read in conjunction with the linked post, the original post adopts more of an anti-government stance.

IS HYPERTEXT MAKING YOU STUPID?

Walter Ong (1996), whose work we mentioned in Chapter 1, claimed that the transition from orality to literacy did not just change the way we communicate, but also the way we think. Print literacy, he said, restructured human consciousness, making us less dependent on formulaic ways of thinking as aids to memory and more able to engage in abstract reasoning. More recent research in the field of reading confirms that learning how to read results in physiological changes in the brains of children, and even learning how to read different languages results in different kinds of changes (see, for example, Wolf 2007).

If the transition from orality to print literacy engendered changes in the way we think, it's not unreasonable to suppose that the shift to reading hypertext might also be resulting in cognitive changes. Some recent research supports this supposition. A study conducted by Rowlands and his colleagues (2008) on how young people use electronic resources in their studies, for example, found that early exposure to hypertext likely helped their participants develop good parallel processing skills needed to move efficiently from one document to another. The researchers worry, however, that the sequential processing skills necessary to follow the logical progression in longer narrative works were not being as strongly developed.

This worry is shared by a number of other writers on digital literacies, most notably Nicolas Carr (2011), author of *The Shallows: How the Internet Is Changing the Way We Think, Read, and Remember,* who argues that reading hypertext may be compromising our ability to read conventional texts and follow complex arguments. The constant stimulus of moving from document to document, he claims, 'short-circuits both conscious and unconscious thought, preventing our minds from thinking either deeply or creatively. Our brains turn into simple signal-processing units, quickly shepherding information into consciousness and then back out again'.

There are, of course, those who disagree with Carr. One is the famous cognitive scientist and linguist Steven Pinker. Pinker (2010) points out that distractions to information processing have always existed, and people have always developed strategies to deal with them. The ability to reason and follow logical arguments does not come from the media that we use, he says, but from effort and education. Although different media may have the power to affect the way we deal with information, we are not passive victims being 'reprogrammed' by media.

Another flaw in this argument is that it assumes that 'deep', linear reading is an inherent quality of all print literacy practices, and that this kind of reading is inherently better than other forms of reading for grasping complex arguments. Research in reading, however, has shown that the reading of print documents – especially by the most advanced readers – is not always linear. Rather, good readers develop strategies to interact with documents in extremely creative and flexible ways, as Andrew Dillon and his colleagues (1989) found in their study of how academics read print-based journal articles.

Case study 3: The blog

Rebecca Blood (2002) considers the **blog**, or 'weblog' as it was originally called, to be the first 'native genre' of the internet. Unlike other early text forms on the internet (email, for example), the blog has no obvious predecessor in print-based media. One of the reasons for this is that blogs draw on the communicative affordances of digital media in a way that has created something unique. Blogs can therefore teach us a lot about the new practices of reading and writing in hypertext.

So, what is a blog? The term 'weblog' was coined in 1997 by Joan Barger, author of one of the earliest blogs, Robot Wisdom (www.robotwisdom.com). He defined it as 'a web page where a web logger "logs" all of the other web pages she finds interesting'. Early examples of weblogs basically consisted of frequently updated lists of links with minimal commentary. These weblogs served to draw the attention of their readers to sources of news which might not be covered in the mainstream media.

Many blogs today still perform this function of drawing attention to and providing critical comments on particular events of interest. In addition though, some blogs perform the function of an online journal, where authors simply describe and reflect on the events of their lives.

Early blogs were maintained by web enthusiasts who had some basic knowledge of html, the hypertext mark-up language used to create web pages. Some technical knowledge (though not a lot) was needed to participate. This all changed in 1999, when a number of platforms were developed to facilitate the process of blogging, among them LiveJournal and Blogger. The blogging platforms that we are familiar with now developed out of these. Today, blogs are characterized by their ease of use: the technical barriers have been removed and it has become possible for anyone to maintain a blog.

Today's blogging platforms share a number of technical features that make blogs what they are. As suggested, they have an easy-to-use rich text editor to create and update posts. Once created, posts are displayed on the home page of the blog in reverse chronological order with the most recent post at the top of the page. As time goes by, posts are moved off the homepage and into an archive, but they can still be accessed through their **'perma-link'**, the permanent, unique URL of the post. Finally, each post provides a form for **commenting**, so that readers can 'write back' to the author of the blog.

As well as these technical features, there is an interesting social convention that is also unique to blogs: the **blogroll**. A blogroll is a list of links to other blogs which the blog author reads and recommends, and it is usually displayed on a side-bar. Bloggers can use this blogroll to establish a kind of blogging community, similar to the lists of friends that you see in profiles on social networking sites.

So, what does all of this mean for the practice of reading and writing on the internet? Blogs illustrate the way digital media affects how we read and write in several ways.

First, because of the possibility of hyperlinking, information can be organized differently than in analogue media, and so different kinds of meanings can be made. When you write a blog post, you typically link to other sources of information and make comments. This can be creatively exploited, for example by linking to contrasting perspectives on the same issue, and drawing attention to different underlying assumptions. You could even link to old posts written by yourself, and revise and develop your ideas. In this way, blogs illustrate the way that reading and referencing prior texts has become a very important part of writing on the internet.

Second, the practice of commenting illustrates the changing relationship between reader and writer in the digital age. Readers of blogs are empowered to 'write back' to writers and influence their ideas, in a way that would previously have required great effort. Reading and writing in blogs is much more like having a conversation than like reading or writing a book. These reader–writer relationships are also illustrated by the social convention of the blogroll, which we described above. Blogs illustrate the way that online contexts lend themselves to the development of communities of readers and writers who collaborate in the on-going process of knowledge creation.

Third, because anyone can set up a blog and become a media producer, blogs illustrate changes in the power relationships associated with media. The power to publish and reach an audience is now available to all, and authors can now bypass the process of selection that was necessary for publishing in print-based media like newspapers with their editorial boards. As the barriers to publication have been removed, systems of quality control that were associated with publishing in the past have also been removed. As a result, writing in digital media has lost some of the authority that writing in print-based media used to have.

Finally, blogs illustrate how digital media has changed the ways that people think about the practices of reading and writing. Because of the kinds of interactions described above, bloggers tend to see the activities of reading and writing as interlinked, each one feeding into the other. Publishing a post is not regarded as the end of the process, but rather as part of an on-going contribution to 'the conversation'. In this sense, writing in digital media like blogs is always evolving and always unfinished.

INTERACTIVITY, COMMENTING AND PARTICIPATING

One of the most important developments in recent years has been the move from 'web 1.0' to 'web 2.0', from the 'read-only web' to the 'read-write web'. In the early days of the internet, the World Wide Web was dominated by the few players who had the technical knowledge necessary to publish their work. For most people, the World Wide Web was a 'read-only' experience: they were able to browse the internet but not publish to it. However, subsequent developments in technology reduced these technical barriers, so that ordinary people were able to publish online. Today's online platforms (like blogs, **wikis**, social networking sites, etc.) allow us to not only read, but also to write: hence the term, the 'read-write web'.

One affordance of the read-write web is the interaction made possible by the comment function in blogs, the discussion page in wikis, and so on. As the case study of the blog shows, it is now possible for readers and writers to easily interact about an article online. As a result there has been a shift in the relationship between reader and writer, with readers now empowered to 'write back' and contribute their own point of view.

Of course, this kind of interaction between reader and writer is not unique to online contexts. Think of the 'letters to the editor' in print-based newspapers, where writers and readers exchange their views, referring back to previous letters and making 'comments'. With the ease with which readers can engage with writers in digital media, interactivity and **participation** have become features of nearly all online writing. Most people would probably agree that blog posts and other kinds of online writing are more interesting to read if you also take a look at the comments and feedback that they receive.

The blog example also illustrates how this kind of interaction between readers and writers can lead to the establishment of specialized online writing communities. As noted above, with blogs, such communities can be established by following the convention of the blogroll and linking to other blogs that discuss similar topics. In such communities, readers and writers enter into a collaborative relationship, providing feedback on each other's work (see Chapter 11). Rebecca Black's research (see, for example, 2005, 2006) into fan fiction writers in FanFiction.net provides interesting glimpses into this kind of writing community.

Black describes fan fiction as 'writing in which fans use media narratives and pop cultural icons as inspiration for creating their own texts' (2006: 172). She notes that printed fan fiction has been around for many years, but that with the read-write web, fans now have 'the opportunity to "meet" in online spaces where they can collaboratively write, exchange, critique and discuss one another's fictions' (172).

In her 2006 case study, Black describes the experiences of Tanaka Nanoko, an English language learner and successful writer of Japanese *anime*-based fan fiction. She shows how Nanoko communicates with her readers through the 'author notes' that accompany her writing, and how she uses these notes to present herself to her readers, provide them with additional background, encourage particular kinds of feedback, and express her gratitude to readers and reviewers. In the author notes, Nanoko explicitly identifies herself as an English language learner and this appears to have an effect on the kind of feedback that she receives from readers. Readers' feedback is supportive of her writing development: some readers gently suggest improvements to aspects of her writing, while others admire her skill as a multilingual and multicultural writer.

Communities like FanFiction.net underscore the kinds of relationships between readers and writers facilitated by digital media. Writing is often now seen more as a collaborative, social activity, where the participative process of writing together is as important as the actual writing itself. In view of this, part of learning how to be a good reader increasingly involves developing practices of commenting and participating in particular communities of writers.

Activity 3.1: Online reading and writing

Read the blog post by Will Richardson below, posted to his blog *Weblogg-ed* on June 18, 2009 (http://weblogg-ed.com/2009/writing-on-the-internet/). What does this post tell us about online reading and writing? Consider especially:

1. How does the author use quotations?
2. How does the author use links? What kind of relations do they establish?
3. How does the author try to manage interaction and commenting?
4. According to the author, how has online reading and writing changed?
5. Do you agree or disagree with the author's views? Why?

Writing on the Internet

Just a couple of quotes that I've run across of late to add to the reading and writing conversation. I love this one by Donal Leu:

> *Another difference from earlier models of print comprehension is the inclusion of communication within online reading comprehension. Online reading and writing are so closely connected that it is not possible to separate them; we read online as authors and we write online as readers [Emphasis mine.]*

And this from Deborah Brandt at the University of Wisconsin Madison in a great article from the Chronicle titled 'Studies Explore Whether the Internet Makes Students Better Writers':

> *Some of the resistance to a more writing-centered curriculum, she says, is based on the view that writing without reading can be dangrous because students will be untethered to previous thought, and reading levels will decline. But that view, she says, is 'being challenged by the literacy of young people, which is being developed primarily by their writing. They're going to be reading, but they're going to be reading to write, and not to be shaped by what they read.' [Emphasis mine]*
>
> *(See also Kathleen Blake Yancey's wonderful essay 'Writing in the 21st Century' if you haven't already.)*

I know as a long-time high school expository writing teacher (who really misses that classroom), my curriculum would be decidedly different today than five years ago. There would have been a lot more situated practice in reading as a writer and developing the skills necessary to track and participate in the distributed conversation that hopefully occurs. I find it fascinating to consider the ways in which social technologies afford all sorts of potentially global, immediate connections around what we write. And I still think that a basic shift here is that we can no longer look at publishing as the final step in the process but see it instead as somewhere in the middle. Maybe even see it as the start of something.

Interested to hear from teachers who have begun to rethink or rewrite curriculum in light of the potentials of the technologies.

MASHUPS AND REMIXING

As we've seen, hypertext and interactivity provide readers and writers with new ways of organizing and associating text, as well as relating to each other. In addition, electronic text can be easily shared through the internet and copies made by others. As a result, writers now have the ability to create new kinds of digital texts or artifacts that incorporate and appropriate the works of others: for example, the 'mashup' or the '**remix**'. The well-known internet scholar Lev Manovich (2007) suggests that we now live in a '**remix culture**' and goes so far as to claim that the 'World Wide Web [has] redefined an electronic document as a mix of other documents'.

A mashup, in music, is the creative combination of two or more songs, which when combined create something new and distinct from the original. The term is also used to describe the combination of two or more websites, for example when a web designer combines Google Maps with the photo-sharing website Flickr and creates a new website that allows users to view photos of particular locations on a map. Similar to a mashup, the term remix was originally used with specific reference to music. It referred to an alternative version of a song that was technically edited and modified to create something new.

Both terms, mashup and remix, have expanded beyond their original contexts of use and can now be used in a more general sense to refer to new and original texts or cultural artifacts that have been created out of existing works. Although the difference between a mashup and a remix is not always clear, most consider remixing a process of altering or re-engineering aspects of an existing work and 'mashing' as combining two or more (sometimes seemingly incommensurate) works together. This practice of borrowing and building on existing work has become very common in digital media. Because of the way that mashups and remixes build on the work of others, they pose some interesting questions, of both a philosophical and practical nature. They challenge us to rethink beliefs about originality, intellectual property and ethics.

At the philosophical level, we need to begin by observing that the practices of digitally mashing and remixing texts has obvious predecessors in print media. The most obvious of these is the practice of quoting, where the author explicitly incorporates the words of another person in their text. Most people would accept that a text that uses quotations appropriately can still be considered an original text. This is in spite of the fact that it builds on previous texts.

In fact, we can take this further by pointing out that, if you think about it, all original texts build on previous texts in some way. The famous Russian literary critic Mikhail Bakhtin (1986: 89) said that texts are 'filled with others' words, varying degrees of otherness or varying degrees of our-own-ness', and the French philosopher Roland Barthes said a text is just a 'tissue of quotations' (1977: 146).

Nevertheless, some people are concerned that the remix culture is fostering plagiarism in educational institutions like universities. They point to cases where students have submitted work that reads like a patchwork of online articles cut and pasted into their assignments without any proper form of attribution. Such cases clearly pose a serious problem, but they are often relatively easy to resolve because they are so obviously unoriginal.

Others are concerned about broader issues related to the ownership of texts, intellectual property and copyright, especially in relation to commercial, pop culture texts like movie-clips and songs. Owners of this kind of commercial content are understandably upset about the ease with which perfect digital copies of their work can be circulated, remixed and 'mashed' into the work of others. They see remixing as a kind of stealing, which deprives them of their ability to profit from their own work.

Lawrence Lessig, an American legal scholar who specializes in intellectual property and cyber law, considers the effect of current intellectual property law on the production of cultural artifacts such as mashups and remixes. He argues that the law acts to constrain creativity and the development of culture, by unnecessarily limiting the extent to which people are free to build upon the creative work of others. In his 2004 book, *Free Culture*, he suggests that when it comes to the creation of cultural texts we have moved from a 'free culture' to a 'permission culture', providing a number of examples to support this idea, including that of Walt Disney and Mickey Mouse. Lessig notes that one of the first Mickey Mouse cartoons, *Steamboat Willie* (distributed in 1928) was based on a silent film by Buster Keaton called *Steamboat Bill, Jr.*, which appeared in the same year. According to Lessig (2004: 22–23), 'Steamboat Willie is a direct cartoon parody of Steamboat Bill'.

Such creative borrowing was commonplace at the time, but, given the current legal framework, people today have less freedom to borrow and build upon the creative works of the Disney Corporation in the way its founder borrowed and built upon the creative works of others. Nevertheless, despite these legal constraints and because of the affordances of digital media (which make texts both more reproducible and more mutable) remixing and mashing have become common forms of creative production on the internet. Remixes and mashups are much more than simply a matter of copying: they require a creative re-working of the source material so that when it is placed in the new context and mixed up with texts from other sources, it takes on a new meaning or significance.

Lessig points out that a major change in the way that culture is produced now as compared to Walt Disney's day is that prior to the internet, culture was produced by a small elite group who had access to the media. In the age of digital media, however, the barriers to publishing have been removed, opening the way for thousands upon thousands of 'amateur' publishers to contribute to the creation of cultural texts. By 'amateur' Lessig means that these people are involved in cultural production for the love of it, rather than for monetary reward. Often they are very talented and create cultural texts of great interest. Such people want to share their creations.

But this is where the law of copyright gets in the way. Copyright law automatically protects creative works (for example, books, songs, films, software) and prohibits others from making copies without the consent of the copyright holder. Under US law, these protections last for the author's entire life, plus seventy-five years (or ninety-five years altogether for a corporation). If an author does nothing, the protections will apply whether or not they want them, and whether or not they want to share their creative works with others so that they can sample and remix them.

Realizing the law put severe constraints on the creation of cultural texts within the remix culture, Lessig proposed a system, called 'Creative Commons Licensing', to make it easier for people to create and remix cultural texts. The system works by making available carefully drafted but easy-to-understand licenses, that clearly describe what intellectual property rights the creator wants to reserve. Using a creative commons license, you can specify that your creative work is available for others to use, subject to a range of possible conditions. For example, you could specify that future remixes of the work must attribute the creator of the original, must not be for commercial purposes, and/or must also be issued under a creative commons license (see http://creativecommons.org for the full range of licenses).

Even though copyright law lags behind technological developments of digital media, a remix culture has developed in which the new texts that people are creating explicitly mix and build upon the prior texts of others. At the same time, this practice of remixing must be governed by an appropriate ethical framework. The creative commons licenses identify the most important elements of this framework in the choices that they offer creators: attribution (do you want credit for your work?); commercial use (do you want others to profit from your work?); and future participation (do you want others to share their work too?).

Activity 3.2: Remix culture

Consider the two quotations about remixing from Lev Manovich (2007) below:

A   *The other older term commonly used across media is 'quoting' but I see it as describing a very different logic than remixing. If remixing implies systematically rearranging the whole text, quoting refers [to] inserting some fragments from old text(s) into the new one. Thus I think we should not see quoting as a historical precedent for remixing. Rather, we can think of it as a precedent for another new practice of authorship [. . .] that, like remixing, was made possible by electronic and digital technology – sampling.*

B   *[W]e are left with an interesting paradox: while in the realm of commercial music remixing is officially accepted, in other cultural areas it is seen as violating the copyright and therefore as stealing. So while filmmakers, visual artists, photographers, architects and web designers routinely remix already existing works, this is not openly admitted, and no proper terms equivalent to remixing in music exist to describe these practices.*

Discuss the following questions:

1.   How are the practices of quoting, sampling, mashing and remixing similar or different?
2.   In your view, how original and creative is remixing?
3.   Do you think the practice of remixing should be accepted?
4.   If you do, what ethical guidelines do you think remixers and mashers should follow?

CONCLUSION

New technological tools and affordances of digital media have had a demonstrable effect on the ways that we can 'do' reading and writing. First, hypertext and the associated practice of linking allow us to make new kinds of meanings, organizing text in non-sequential ways and linking to other texts to create sometimes subtle associations. Second, hypertext and the interactivity of the read-write web have changed the way that readers and writers relate, with readers moving from the position of passive recipients of information to active collaborators in the process of knowledge creation. Third, the ability to easily copy digital texts has led to the development of a 'remix culture' in which writers explicitly create new cultural texts by building upon existing prior texts.

All of these changes contribute to an evolution in the way that we think about reading and writing. Hypertext has blurred the boundaries of reading and writing and many people now see the two activities as essentially interconnected. The read-write web has facilitated the development of online communities of readers and writers and as a result reading and writing are now perceived as more collaborative, social activities than they were before. Finally, now that anyone can participate in the creation of cultural texts and publish their work online, published writing has lost much of the perceived authority that it had in the days of print media. Of course, an equally striking development is the way that digital texts now incorporate multiple modes, with print, image, audio and video all working together to create meaning. We examine this shift from page to screen and the associated shift from print to image in the next chapter on multimodality.

USEFUL RESOURCES

Print

Black, R. W. (2006). Language, culture, and identity in online fanfiction. *E-Learning and Digital Media, 3* (2): 170–184.

Blood, R. (2002). *The weblog handbook: Practical advice on creating and maintaining your blog.* Cambridge, MA: Perseus Publishing.

Landow, G. P. (2006). *Hypertext 3.0: Critical theory and new media in an era of globalization.* Baltimore: John Hopkins University Press.

Lessig, L. (2004). *Free culture: How big media uses technology and the law to lock down culture and control creativity.* New York: Penguin Press.

Snyder, I. (1996). *Hypertext: The electronic labyrinth.* Carlton South, Vic: Melbourne University Press.

Snyder, I. (ed.) (1998). *Page to screen: Taking literacy into the electronic era.* London: Routledge.

Web

Rebecca Blood, Weblogs: A history and perspective
http://www.rebeccablood.net/essays/weblog_history.html.

Dave Winer, What makes a weblog a weblog?
http://blogs.law.harvard.edu/whatmakesaweblogaweblog.html.

George Landow, Cyberspace, hypertext, and critical theory
http://www.cyberartsweb.org/cpace/

Earth Album
http://www.earthalbum.com/

Programmable Web
http://www.programmableweb.com/

Creative Commons
http://creativecommons.org/

Video

Lee Lefever, Blogs in Plain English
http://www.youtube.com/watch?v=NN2I1pWXjXI

Thru You: Kutiman mixes YouTube
http://thru-you.com/

TED, Lawrence Lessig, Re-examining the remix
http://www.ted.com/talks/lessig_nyed.html

CHAPTER 4

Multimodality

It should be obvious that making meaning has always involved more than just words. In speech aural elements such as the pace, rhythm and the tone of your voice, as well as visual elements such as your gestures, facial expressions and body language all contribute to the message that you send. Similarly, in writing the use of visual elements such as font, colour, spacing and accompanying images can have an effect on the meaning you make. Spoken and written texts have always drawn on multiple **modes**: aural and visual, as well as verbal and textual.

In this chapter, we will focus on the way the affordance of multimedia mentioned in the last chapter makes it easier for users of digital media to combine multiple **semiotic modes** based on different systems for meaning making. This practice of combining multiple modes is known as 'multimodality', and texts that are made up of a combination of modes in this way are called **multimodal** texts.

One effect of technological developments in digital media has been to greatly increase the multimodal content that we normally encounter in texts. This is most obvious in the texts that we encounter on screens, because these digital texts can incorporate audio and video in a way that print-based texts cannot. As a result, a range of new literacies are needed to cope with the proliferation of images, graphics, video, animation and sound in digital texts. These new practices follow a shift in the dominant organizing principle of texts from the primarily textual mode of the page to the primarily visual mode of the screen.

This shift towards images is also visible in printed texts, which now tend to incorporate more visual elements than before. One example of this is the way that newspapers have become increasingly visual: the quantity of images has increased, and their quality has improved (from black-and-white to colour). The same can be said of scientific texts (Lemke, 1998b). A similar trend is, of course, also observable in the pages of the World Wide Web, which have become increasingly multimodal as digital technologies have improved. You can see this shift towards the visual mode if you compare the two webpages from our institution, City University of Hong Kong, shown in Figures 4.1A and 4.1B. The first page, from 1997, shows the text-only mode, an option which was necessary at the time because slower internet connections made the rendering of graphics more cumbersome; the second page shows the CityU homepage at the time of writing.

When you are writing for the screen, it is now much easier to make use of visual resources like images, layout, font and formatting. In this chapter we will focus on the implications of this for practices of 'reading' and 'writing' (or perhaps more aptly, 'designing'). It is increasingly important for readers and writers to understand the logic of visual communication.

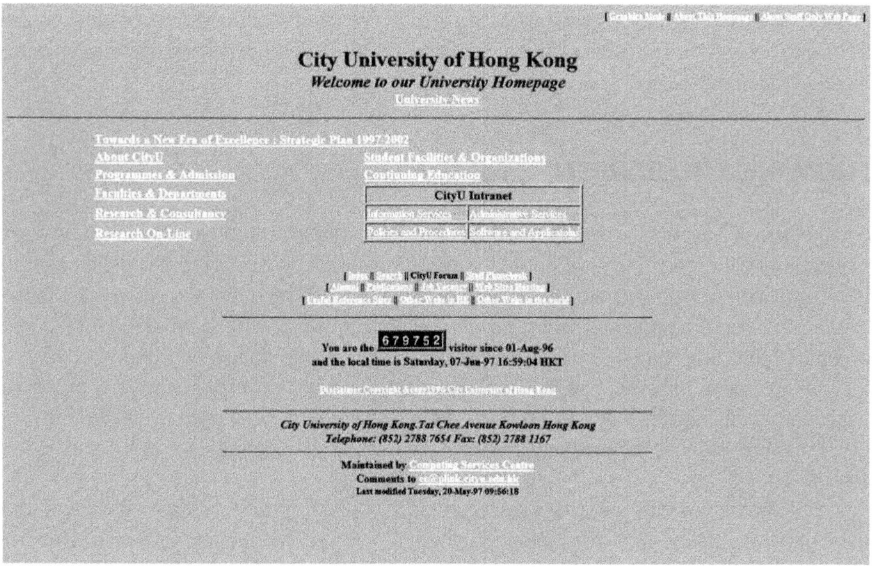

City University of Hong Kong
Welcome to our University Homepage
University News

Towards a New Era of Excellence : Strategic Plan 1997/2002
About CityU
Programmes & Admission   Student Facilities & Organizations
Faculties & Departments   Continuing Education
Research & Consultancy
Research On-Line

CityU Intranet

Information Services   Administrative Services
Policies and Procedures   Software and Applications

[Info][Search][**CityU Forum**][Staff Phonebook]
[Courses][Publications][Job Vacancies][Web Sites Directory]
[Useful Reference Sites][Other Webs in HK][Other Webs in the world]

You are the **679752** visitor since 01-Aug-96
and the local time is Saturday, 07-Jun-97 16:59:04 HKT

Disclaimer Copyright © 1996 City University of Hong Kong

City University of Hong Kong. Tat Chee Avenue Kowloon Hong Kong
Telephone: (852) 2788 7654 Fax: (852) 2788 1167

Maintained by Computing Services Centre
Comments to cc@plink.cityu.edu.hk
Last modified Tuesday, 20-May-97 09:56:18

Figure 4.1A   City University of Hong Kong home page (1997)
(Text mode, retrieved June 7, 1997 from http://www.cityu.edu.hk, used with permission)

Figure 4.1B   City University of Hong Kong home page (2011)
(Retrieved January 29, 2011 from http://www.cityu.edu.hk, used with permission)

In particular, they need to be aware of 1) the affordances and constraints of text and images, 2) how to design for the visual space of the screen, and 3) how image and text can be combined to make meaning.

FROM PAGE TO SCREEN

Gunther Kress, a pioneering scholar in the field of multimodality and visual design, describes the evolution in media from the printed page (for example in books) to the digital screen (for example in webpages). According to Kress, the underlying principles with which these media organize information is different, with books 'organized and dominated by the logic of writing' and the screen 'organized and dominated by the image and its logic' (Kress, 2003: 19). Kress believes that the technological affordances of digital media, as we've described them above, will inevitably shape the future of writing as well. Writing will become more visual as it increasingly adopts the logic of the image that is promoted by the screen.

So, what is the difference between the logic of writing that dominates the page and the logic of the image that dominates the screen? Writing, like speech, follows a temporal and sequential logic. For example, when you tell a story in speech, the story unfolds in time and as a result you are forced to organize your story into a kind of sequence. Similarly, in writing, the logic is sequential. Even though writing is fixed in space (as words on a page) rather than unfolding over time, readers are still, for the most part, expected to process it in a linear and sequential way.

By comparison, the logic of the image is spatial/simultaneous: all of the information in an image is displayed simultaneously, with different elements of the image related to one another in space. Because of this spatial logic, images tend to have a more direct effect, often provoking an immediate emotional reaction from viewers. In addition, images tend to be more 'polysemous'; that is, they are capable of sending numerous messages at the same time. This can create a challenge for communication as viewers of images are sometimes presented with a range of competing messages to choose from or to integrate.

Because of these different affordances and constraints, the mode that you use makes a difference to the kind of meanings that you can make. Meanings in images are more 'topological', that is, images are capable of representing continuous phenomena, like the changing slope of a hill, or the various shades of colour in an object. In contrast, meanings in text are more 'typological'. Language describes things in terms of categorical choices: for example, we say the hill is 'steep', or the colour is 'blue'.

Different modes have different underlying assumptions and require you to make different kinds of choices. When you write a sentence in English you typically follow the syntax: subject–verb–object, and as a result you have to explicitly describe who is doing what to whom (and in what order), or who is related to whom (and how). In contrast, when you draw a picture, you have to be explicit about the spatial relationships between the entities.

For example, if you describe in writing a traffic accident that you witnessed, you might say 'The truck hit the car' and commit to a particular relationship of agency (with the truck, in this case, doing the 'hitting'). On the other hand, if you draw a diagram to represent the accident, then you might depict the truck and car in collision on the road and commit to a particular spatial relationship, i.e. where exactly on the road the collision occurred and from what angle. Your diagram would also explicitly show whether other vehicles were present at the time, and where exactly on the road they were. The picture, however, may not contain the same information about agency that your sentence did.

As we move from the page to the screen, we are witnessing a change in the amount and quality of information that is communicated through images. The increased role of visual aspects of communication necessarily has an effect on the way that we 'read' and 'write'. With respect to writing, an understanding of the different affordances and constraints of different modes can help you to select appropriate modes in your writing and combine modes more effectively. We will consider these issues in more detail below.

With respect to reading, different strategies also have to be developed. In traditional texts like books, where writing is the dominant mode, a preferred reading path is usually evident. In English texts you begin at the top left of the page and proceed in a linear way to the bottom right. But when writing is no longer the dominant mode, as with many digital texts like webpages, we need to develop different kinds of reading paths. In order to negotiate reading paths through such multimodal texts, Kress (2003: 159) suggests we first scan the page to identify the modes it draws on, and then decide which mode (if any) is dominant. We can then read the text as an image by interpreting the spatial relationships between entities on the page, or as written text by following the linear/sequential logic of writing.

Activity 4.1: Sign language?

Consider the poster in Figure 4.2 and discuss the following questions:

- What visual elements has the designer of this text used?
- What message is conveyed by these visual elements?
- What message is conveyed by the textual elements, i.e. the words on the page?
- How do the textual elements interact with the visual elements?
- What effect does this interaction create?
- Give examples of other texts that combine textual and visual elements (including images) for effect. How do the textual and visual elements interact?

VISUAL DESIGN: LAYING OUT THE SCREEN

In reading a webpage, the very first visual cue that you are confronted with is its layout. The designer has made choices about the composition: where different elements are placed on the page, how big these elements are, and so on. From your experience of reading webpages, you probably have some idea about where you usually find different elements: for example, navigation menus, main stories, and advertisements. However, you might not realize how such choices about composition can affect your reading of the text. In this section, we consider how visual elements are arranged in various ways and how we go about 'reading' them.

In their book, *Reading Images: The Grammar of Visual Design* (1996/2006), Gunther Kress and Theo van Leeuwen take up this question. They analyse visual layout in much the same way that linguists analyse the structure of sentences, examining the different functional elements and how they are combined to make meaning. They acknowledge that their analysis is limited to images in western cultural contexts, and so the details of their theory

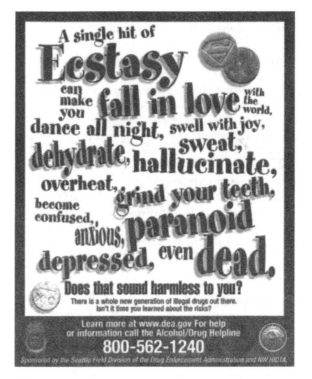

Figure 4.2   Drug Enforcement Administration poster

may not apply as well in other cultures. In spite of this limitation, the analysis provides valuable insights into the way designers arrange elements in multimodal texts.

Kress and van Leeuwen point out that visual layout can be divided into different regions: the left and the right, the top and the bottom, and the centre and the margin. In some cases, there are very clear divisions between these different regions: for example, in a two-page magazine spread, where the page margin creates a natural division between left and right.

Let's first consider the relationship between left and right. In western cultures, the traditional page is read from left to right, moving from given to new information (Halliday, 1994). In this context, **given information** is presented as that which we already know or agree on, often assumed cultural knowledge. **New information** is the new message yet to be agreed upon that the reader is intended to take from the text, and may therefore be presented as problematic. Multimodal texts organized using the spatial logic of the image often follow a similar given–new structure, with the given information on the left and the new information on the right.

As an example, consider the Twitter login screen shown in Figure 4.3. There is a clear left-right division on this screen, created by the blank space between the left and right sides above the yellow line. On the left of the screen, we see (from top to bottom): the Twitter logo; and the slogan 'Follow your interests: Instant updates from your friends, industry experts, favourite celebrities and what's happening around the world'. This message about global connection is subtly reinforced by the background image, which shows a map of the world. On

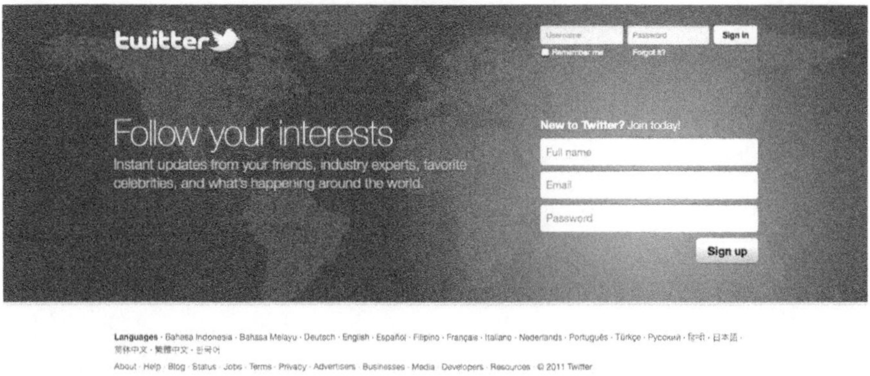

Figure 4.3   Twitter login screen
(Retrieved September 23, 2011 from http://www.twitter.com)

the right of the screen we see the login form, and below that a signup form. On this screen Twitter and what it does are presented as 'given': the page assumes that we have some cultural knowledge about this social networking site. The login or signup forms are presented as 'new', and we are invited to notice them and take action. For those who are not already members, the signup form is truly 'new'; for those who are already members, the login form acts as a gateway to the rest of the website and all of the 'news' from people in their social network.

The homepages of most websites follow a similar 'given–new' textual pattern. The navigation bar typically appears on the left of the page with the main, newly updated content to the right of it. In such cases, the navigation bar is presented as 'given' or taken-for-granted, and we are asked to notice the new message towards the middle and right of the page.

Another possible visual relationship is between the top and bottom of the page. According to Kress and van Leeuwen, the bottom represents the **real**, i.e. concrete reality and factual information, while the top represents the **ideal**, i.e. the aspired to promise, hope, or ideologically foregrounded information. It is not surprising, therefore, that the login form on the Twitter page appears on the top with the signup form below it, a subtle encouragement to non-members to aspire to the 'ideal' condition of membership.

The Chanel website, whose layout is illustrated in Figure 4.4, also demonstrates the way in which designers can use horizontal division. At the top and taking up most of the page is a video of a fashion show with models wearing this season's garments. This is the ideal to aspire to. At the bottom of the page are a number of links to more detailed information about the fashion lines: these allow viewers to browse more videos, access online catalogues, locate Chanel stores, contact the company or subscribe to their newsletter. It is also the place where the legal information related to the website is presented. The lower part of the page contains the 'real': concrete information about the products that customers need in order to achieve the 'ideal'.

Kress and van Leeuwen also describe the relationship between centre and margin. Sometimes multimodal texts are organized around a dominant element in the centre that gives meaning to the other elements that surround it. As Kress and van Leeuwen (2006: 196) note: 'For something to be presented as Centre means that it is presented as the nucleus of the information on which all the other elements are in some sense subservient'.

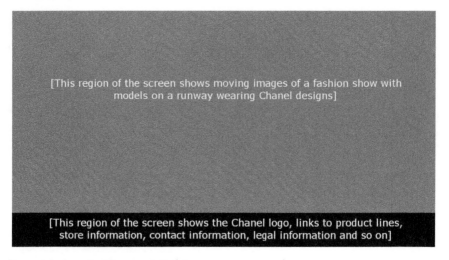

[This region of the screen shows moving images of a fashion show with models on a runway wearing Chanel designs]

[This region of the screen shows the Chanel logo, links to product lines, store information, contact information, legal information and so on]

Figure 4.4   Layout of Chanel website (http://www.chanel.com/)
(Based on http://www.chanel.com/fashion/8#8)

One example of such a centre-margin composition is the Google homepage (see Figure 4.5). On this screen, with the possible exception of the Google logo, every element is subservient to the single search bar in the middle of the screen. In the upper left and upper right margins, there are links to Google services, including the option to sign in and customize settings. In the banner we observe a similar left-right organization to the Twitter page, with the various company services presented as given information on the left, while user options are presented as new information on the right. The central block around the search bar also follows a bottom–top organization with the company logo in the position of ideal, and information about the company, advertising and privacy in the position of real.

Figure 4.5   Google homepage (Retrieved January 31, 2011 from http://www.google.com.hk)

This last example illustrates how the organization of elements in multimodal texts can combine patterns. The different regions, as well as their associated meaning potential, are summarized in Figure 4.6. The figure also illustrates the way in which these different information structures might overlap on a given page or screen. Keeping these visual information structures in mind should help you to make choices about visual design, especially the layout of the screen in digital media, in a more informed way.

In designing the layout of webpages, it is also helpful to take into account the way that people read them. Some eye-tracking research (Nielsen, 2006) indicates that people approach the reading of a webpage in a number of horizontal and vertical movements which approximate an 'F-shaped' pattern. This research suggests that people begin with a horizontal movement along the top of the page, continue with another horizontal movement along the middle of the page and end with a vertical movement down the left side of the page. It follows that the text in these regions (top, middle, left) is more likely to be noticed by readers of webpages. Many web designers seem to understand this and often use the top and left of the screen to locate the information that they consider most important.

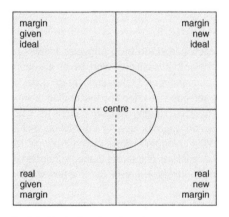

Figure 4.6   Meaning potential of textual regions in an image
(adapted from Kress and van Leeuwen, 2006)

Case study 4: Digital images and digital video

Digital cameras have made taking, processing and sharing pictures and video much easier and much cheaper than it was in the days of film. The images captured are stored as digital files on small memory devices. These digital images provide a number of affordances:

1.   Digital images are cheap to store: you can take as many as you like;
2.   Digital images are immediate: you can view them instantly on a screen;
3.   Digital images can be cropped, manipulated, and deleted from memory;
4.   Digital images can be shared through the internet.

Because taking pictures and making movies has become so easy, many people now find themselves engaged in new multimodal literacy practices as producers of digital images and digital video.

One example of such a new literacy practice is digital film-making, sometimes referred to as '**digital storytelling**'. A **digital story** is a short film which combines digital images, video and audio in order to create a personally meaningful narrative. The practice allows people to adopt the role of film-maker, using multimodal forms of representation in order to create and share their stories with a potentially wide audience. The practice is popular in educational contexts (see, for example, Hafner and Miller, 2011), but has also been adopted in the mainstream media, with a number of large projects encouraging members of the public to create and share digital stories. One example of such a project is the BBC's 'Telling Lives', completed in 2005, which collected digital stories from ordinary people and shared them through the BBC's website grouped in categories such as: stories of ancestry; talking teenagers; World War Two memories; and other categories based on place of origin (http://www.bbc.co.uk/tellinglives/).

Another new literacy practice is **video blogging**, also known as **vlogging**. A **video blog** can take a form similar to a traditional blog, i.e. as a website with regular posts that readers can leave comments on. However, instead of posting text for the audience to read, the **vlogger** posts a video for the audience to watch. This video is usually also uploaded to video sharing websites, such as YouTube or Blip.tv, and these websites also provide opportunities for interaction, including text comments and 'video responses'. Video blogging allows ordinary people to assume the role of news reporter, investigating issues of interest to them, shooting relevant footage, and editing together a video report, often very similar to a newscast.

Practices like digital storytelling and video blogging require us to understand and exploit the multimodal resources (both aural and visual) available in video. In terms of multimodal content, digital stories and video blogs can vary from very simple creations to semi-professional movie-like productions. An example of a more complex digital story is 'As Real as Your Life', a short film created by game designer Michael Highland (2006) (http://youtu.be/fxVsWY9wsHk). In this story, Highland documents his video game addiction, using a range of visual effects that reinforce the message that 'the boundary in my brain that divides real from fantasy has finally begun to crumble'. These visual effects include:

- Close-up shots of the narrator's face in the flickering light of a video game;
- Shots of the narrator sitting inside a TV set, playing a video game;
- Shots of 'real' and game worlds juxtaposed in sequence or side-by-side;
- Washed out shots of the 'real world' overlaid with game-like animations.

These and other visual effects contribute to the sense of a blurring of the 'real' and virtual worlds that are the subject of the film.

This example illustrates the kind of literacy practices involved in creating an effective digital film. Composing for video requires you to not only script a narrative but also create a **storyboard** that maps the narrative onto a sequence of images, i.e. the scenes in your story. To do this effectively, it is important to have an understanding of the 'grammar of visual design', that is how images can be used to create particular meanings.

Posting and sharing images and video (through online platforms like Facebook, YouTube and Flickr) is itself a multimodal practice, because of the need to combine the image or video with surrounding text. When you post your image, you often have the option to provide a textual title, caption or tag. The text that you provide can interact with the image in different ways, depending on how consistent the textual and visual messages are. Sharing images and video in such websites also opens up the possibility for interaction in an on-going conversation, benefitting from the affordances of interactivity and practices of commenting that we described in the last chapter. This conversation can itself incorporate a multimodal element, as when different people annotate a picture in Flickr or respond to a video by posting another video on YouTube.

One example of this kind of multimodal online sharing and exchange was provided by Carey Jewitt in 2010 at a conference in Sydney, Australia. She described an art exhibition by Olafur Eliasson called 'The Weather Project' which was held at the Tate Modern art gallery in London in 2003–04. The exhibition featured a large-scale installation in the so-called 'turbine hall' of the gallery, a 3,400-square-metre, five-storey space. The space was mostly empty, except for a large disc of light at one end, which took on the appearance of the sun. A fine mist-like spray was pumped into the space and the ceiling of the room was covered with mirrors. What's interesting about all of this is the way that people responded to it. Visitors lay on the floor, bathed in the artificial sunlight, and stared up at the mirrored ceiling, waving and making shapes with their bodies. And they used their digital cameras to record themselves and each other. In a sense the people became a part of the installation.

Many of the digital images and videos created were subsequently uploaded and shared on the internet. As a result, the exhibition was effectively moved into online spaces, where people could continue to discuss and reflect on the experience that they had in the museum. This online exchange was beyond the control of the museum curators and therefore allowed the public to take a more proactive role in disseminating the artwork than is traditionally possible for such events.

This case study illustrates how cheap and easy access to tools for capturing, manipulating and sharing digital images and video has led to the development of new literacy practices. First, the practice of creating digital images and video draws on multiple modes: the visual and aural as well as the textual. As a result, 'readers' and 'writers' of digital media now need to understand the meaning-making affordances and constraints of these multimodal resources. In addition, placing a greater reliance on modes other than text forces us to rethink what it means to read and write in new media. Second, the creation and sharing of digital images and video can bring about shifts in roles that affect the ways that we relate to one another. A medium that was previously only available to a small, technically knowledgeable elite has now become available to anyone with access to a digital camera and an internet connection. This has paved the way for ordinary people to act as film-makers and television news reporters, with the potential to reach and influence a wide online audience.

THE WORLD IN PICTURES: DESIGNING MULTIMODAL TEXTS

As the case study shows, we are beginning to communicate with more visual resources: images and video. Images now bear an increasing load in the communication of meaning, especially on the internet. We therefore need to consider how we can draw on these visual resources when we create texts. Here we will explore 1) how image and text interact on the page or screen, 2) how images represent reality and create interactions, 3) how images appeal to the emotions, 4) how images are combined to create visual sequences in videos.

Image text interaction

If you are composing a multimodal text, you will have to consider which modes are best suited to conveying your meaning. As noted earlier, the written and visual modes offer different affordances and constraints, with writing following a more linear/sequential logic, and image a more spatial/simultaneous one. As a result, speech and writing are generally considered to be better suited to the representation of sequential relations and categorical distinctions (for example of difference and relationship). On the other hand, as Lemke (1998b: 87) points out, image is more suited to the representation of 'degree, quantity, gradation, continuous change, continuous co-variation . . . varying proportionality, complex topological relations of relative nearness or connectedness'. It is common for steps in food recipes to be described sequentially in writing, for example, and to be accompanied by pictures of stages of the completed dish, which allow the reader of the recipe to see fine gradations of texture, colour, shape and proportion that they can compare with their own creations.

As in the example of the recipe, writing and image are often combined in such a way that the two modes interact. You can see a simple example of this kind of interaction when pictures are given captions, for example in newspaper articles or photo essays. Another example from new media is when photos are posted on social networking sites like Facebook or Twitter, with an accompanying (often humorous) message. In these cases, the image and text serve to **frame** (create the context for) each other, providing additional contextual information to help us interpret them. Similar kinds of framing relationships can be observed in longer newspaper texts that are accompanied by images: both the text and the image have a potential framing effect on each other.

Where such relationships between text and the image are created, we may also observe a concurrence, complementarity, or divergence in the message of the text and the message of the image. If the textual and visual information is in concurrence that means that the essential messages are the same and reinforce each other. The information can also be complementary, with text or image presenting slightly different information, which 'colours in' the details of the message in the other mode. Len Unsworth (2004; 2008: 390), in his examination of school science explanations on CD-ROM and the World Wide Web, notes that the images complement text in three main ways: 1) by explaining the 'how' or 'why' of an event in the main text (enhancement), 2) by providing additional information to that in the main text (extension), and 3) by restating or specifying what is in the main text (elaboration).

Finally, the visual and textual information sometimes diverge in meaning, carrying messages that are incompatible with each other. In particular, this might be observed where the 'tone' of an image, the attitudes and emotions that it conveys, differ from those in the accompanying text. For example, a newspaper article about a rogue banker whose irresponsible actions have ruined the lives of many ordinary people would be difficult to reconcile with a head and shoulders portrait of that individual smiling in a sympathetic way. Such conflicting meanings are often used to create irony or humour (as in Figure 4.7).

Interaction and involvement

As noted earlier, the simultaneous logic of images means that they are able to evoke an immediate emotional reaction in a way that writing cannot. As such, they can powerfully influence our attitude towards a particular subject or event. Many historians explain the strong opposition to the Vietnam war among the US public in the 1960s as a result of the rise of both television news and photojournalism, both of which brought images of dead and dying soldiers and civilians into people's living rooms.

The emotional impact of images has a lot to do with the way they create interpersonal relationships with viewers (see Chapter 7). Kress and van Leeuwen (2006) note that such interactions in images can be between different kinds of participants: represented participants (i.e. those in the picture) and interactive participants (i.e. the producer and the viewer). The producer of an image can draw on a range of techniques in order to engage and involve their audience, express power relations, and express modality (how truthful something is). The kinds of resources that can be drawn on include:

- For involvement: Gaze, distance of shot, camera angle (frontal/oblique).
- For power relations: Camera angle (low/eye-level/high).
- For modality: colour saturation, colour differentiation, colour modulation, contextualization, representation, depth, illumination, brightness.

Audience involvement can be achieved by drawing on resources of gaze, distance, and camera angle. Images of people or animals looking directly out of the image at the viewer 'demand' some kind of response from the audience, for example to identify with the subject, to take action and so on. The kind of response demanded is usually conveyed through the use of a facial expression. In contrast, pictures of people or animals that do not look directly at the viewer in this way simply 'offer' the subject for reflection or contemplation. These two kinds of images are referred to as **offer images** and **demand images**.

The distance of the shot, whether close-up, medium shot, or long shot, also has an effect on audience involvement. As you might expect, close-up shots (head and shoulders) correspond to close personal distance, whereas long shots and extreme long shots correspond to far social distance. News presenters are typically shot from the waist up (a medium-close shot), which corresponds to far personal distance: they are still 'in our personal space', but not too close.

Camera angle can also influence the degree to which we identify with figures in a picture: we identify more if the shot was taken from a frontal angle (looking directly at the subject from the front), than an oblique angle (looking across the subject from the side). As suggested above, camera angle can also be used in order to convey power relations: a low angle, looking up at the figure conveys a sense that the figure has power over the viewer, while the reverse is true for a high angle looking down.

Finally, there is the question of what Kress and van Leeuwen call 'modality': how 'truthful' the representation is portrayed to be. Various effects can be applied to images using software like Photoshop, and these may have an effect on how real or lifelike the picture looks. For example, the popular sepia tone is achieved by applying a simple tint which has the effect of reducing the colour differentiation in the picture to a single brown-gold spectrum. This gives the picture a warmer tone, and evokes photographs taken in the early days of photography. Although the colour in such pictures is less true to life, the effect can nevertheless serve to make an image seem more realistic by giving it an aura of authenticity. Other effects such as colour saturation (too high or too low), or blurring or emphasizing outlines can be used in order to give pictures a dream-like, surreal quality.

Appeals to emotion and visual arguments

Because images appeal to our emotions in a way that text does not, we need to be aware of the ways images often present 'visual arguments'. The ad in Figure 4.7 provides an interesting example of a visual argument, with an appeal to emotion. The ad pictures a calf, and the words 'Fashion victim'. The shot is about medium distance and it is a 'demand' with the calf looking directly at the camera: we are invited to identify with and feel sorry for the calf.

Figure 4.7   PETA advertisement
(used with permission)

Like all visual arguments, this one is less direct than a verbal argument. The argument itself relies on us to make connections and formulate the proposition ourselves. In order to understand the argument that this ad makes, we need to formulate the proposition 'cows are victims of the fashion industry' and the argument 'it is wrong to wear leather because if you do you are supporting this victimization'. The risk, of course, in giving the reader so much responsibility is that he or she might misinterpret the message.

Another reason why this ad is effective is because of the way that it combines the words with the picture (an example of text image interaction, as described above). The words evoke the fashion industry with a clever play on the phrase 'fashion victim'. This phrase, which is usually used to refer to a person who decides what to wear only based on what is trendy, is used ironically here to refer to the calf. At the same time, the picture arouses our emotions in a way which is not possible with written text. Critics of visual communication consider such ads to be dangerous precisely because they appeal to emotions, and not to reason.

Visual sequences in video

The design principles that we have discussed so far in relation to images can also be applied to the design of video. In essence, a video presents the viewer with a sequence of images, each of which can be designed to interact with surrounding text, create interactions with viewers, and appeal to emotions. Videos differ from images because they are in fact a sequence of images, and so they mix the affordances of image with the affordances of writing. On the one hand, videos present visual information organized according to the spatial/simultaneous logic of the screen. On the other, they also present textual information, the scripted narrative, voiceover and dialogue that unfolds over time, and this is organized according to the linear/sequential logic of speech and writing.

Any serious attempt to work with video requires that you take both this visual and verbal logic into account. In particular, it is necessary to plan the sequence of images that the viewer will see, the transitions between them, and any accompanying voiceover, scripted dialogue, sound effects or soundtrack. One tool that can be used to portray this combination of modes is the storyboard: a visual representation of the story that displays a series of sketches showing different scenes in the story with accompanying script and notes about the soundtrack for each visual frame (see Figure 4.8, which shows a blank template for a storyboard). In creating a storyboard you can consider visual elements such as composition, camera angle and distance, as well as how these visual elements interact with surrounding written or spoken text and soundtrack.

Another important issue in video design is pace: how quickly or slowly the images and film unfold in time. If the visual information is presented too quickly then the video may seem overwhelming, but if it is presented too slowly the video may seem dull. Finally, in video, sound effects and music play a very important role. A video without a soundtrack, or with a poorly chosen one, is much less likely to be effective than one which uses sound in an appropriate way to complement the visual and verbal messages.

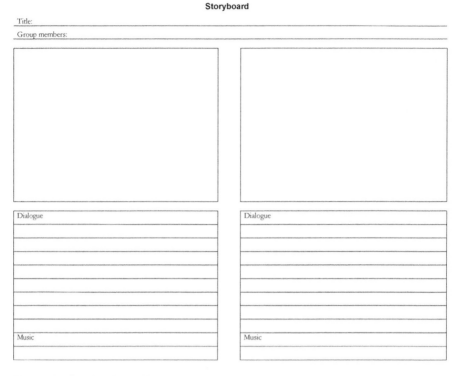

Figure 4.8   Storyboard template

Activity 4.2: Storyboarding

Imagine that you are going to create a video about a significant moment in your life. In this activity, your task is to create the storyboard or visual representation for that video. You will need to:

1. Recall a moment in your life that was significant to you (for example, your first day at university, your first date);
2. Make notes about the people, events, and objects in your story;
3. Create a storyboard, with at least 5 shots, that tells your story visually;
4. Remember to include in each scene a visual representation of the action, an accompanying script, and a note about the kind of soundtrack to play;
5. Remember to draw on some of these techniques:

    a. Involvement: Gaze, distance of shot, camera angle (frontal/oblique);
    b. Power relations: Camera angle (low/eye-level/high);
    c. Modality: Any special effects (colour differentiation, etc.).

CONCLUSION

In this chapter we have considered the ways that texts in the digital age have become increasingly multimodal, combining text with image, audio and video. In particular, we have discussed the affordances and constraints of writing and image and we have seen that written and visual modes follow a different logic: the written mode being linear/sequential and the visual mode spatial/simultaneous. As a result of these different logics, the current trend towards visual communication challenges us to rethink the way we represent the world. As Kress (2003) suggests, we are moving from 'the world told' to 'the world designed'.

We have also discussed some principles of visual design as they apply to webpages where text is easily combined with digital images and digital video. Webpages draw heavily on visual elements and so need to be read and designed in a different way than most written texts, according to principles of composition and layout that have been observed in images. As a result of the ease with which digital images and video can be inserted into digital text, writers now need an understanding of how images and video can engage an audience, how they can be combined with text and sound, and how they can appeal to emotions and be used to construct visual arguments. As we will see in the next chapter, however, despite the new prominence of visual communication in digital media, many contexts continue to rely almost entirely on text in ways that are making us rethink the affordances and constraints of written language.

USEFUL RESOURCES

Print

Jewitt, C. (2005). Multimodality, 'reading', and 'writing' for the 21st century. *Discourse: Studies in the Cultural Politics of Education 26* (3): 315–331.

Kress, G. (2003). *Literacy in the new media age.* London: Routledge.

Kress, G. R., and van Leeuwen, T. (2006). *Reading images: The grammar of visual design*, 2nd edition. London: Routledge.

Lemke, J. L. (1998b). Multiplying meaning: Visual and verbal semiotics in scientific text. In J. R. Martin and R. Veel (eds.) *Reading science: Critical and functional perspectives on discourses of science.* London: Routledge, 87–113.

Unsworth, L. (2008). Multiliteracies and metalanguage: Describing image/text relations as a resource for negotiating multimodal texts. In J. Coiro, M. Knobel, C. Lankshear, and D. J. Leu (eds.) *Handbook of research on new literacies.* New York: Lawrence Erlbaum, 377–405.

Web

BBC, Telling lives
http://www.bbc.co.uk/tellinglives/

Centre for Digital Storytelling
http://www.storycenter.org/

Tate Modern, Olafur Eliasson, The weather project
http://tate.org.uk/modern/exhibitions/eliasson/about.htm

Video

Mary Kalantzis and Bill Cope, New learning: Transformational designs for pedagogy and assessment: Videos
http://newlearningonline.com/multiliteracies/videos/

Edutopia, Digital media empower youth
http://www.edutopia.org/digital-generation-youth-network-video

Michael Highland, As real as your life
http://www.youtube.com/watch?v=fxVsWY9wsHk

CHAPTER 5

Online Language and Social Interaction

In the last chapter we discussed how images, video and other modes function in digital communication. Despite the importance of such modes, however, written language still remains our primary tool for communication in online environments. At the same time, language use, especially when it comes to things like spelling, grammar, and the use of abbreviations and other non-standard forms, is one of the most controversial aspects of digital literacies. Teachers and parents frequently complain about the language young people use when instant messaging, mobile texting and posting to social networking sites, and journalists frequently portray online language as substandard and impoverished (see Thurlow, 2006; 2011 for examples).

What these journalists, teachers and parents are reacting to, of course, is not all language found on the internet, but rather the language often used with interactive media like chat, instant messaging, mobile text messaging and micro blogging, language which in studies across numerous contexts has been found to contain a number of specific linguistic features, including:

- Frequent use of acronyms (e.g., 'btw', 'lol')
- Shortened forms (e.g., 'k' for 'okay')
- Less attention to standard spelling, capitalization and punctuation
- Letter homophones (e.g., 'u' for 'you', 'oic' for 'oh, I see')
- Creative use of punctuation (e.g., multiple punctuation such as '!!!!' or ellipsis marks '. . . . .')
- Spelling based on sound, sometimes to mark a regional accent or special style of speech (e.g., 'kewl' or 'cooooool')
- Lexicalization of vocal sounds (like 'umm', 'uh huh', 'haha')
- **Emoticons** and other keyboard generated graphics (e.g., '=.=')
- Creative use of typographical space and layout
- Formulaic openings and closings (e.g., 'sup'; 'bb')

The linguist David Crystal argues that digital media are giving rise to a new 'variety' of language which he calls 'netspeak' – a type of language 'displaying features that are unique to the internet . . . arising out of its character as a medium' (Crystal, 2001: 18). He further divides 'netspeak' into various sub-varieties associated with specific digital media such as the 'language of emails' and the 'language of chat groups' (Crystal, 2001: 148, 165).

Despite worries that this so-called new variety of language is threatening people's ability to produce more standard varieties and compromising their ability to communicate effectively, there is little evidence that this is the case. In fact, some evidence shows the opposite. Alf Massey and his colleagues (2005), for example, have found that students who spend more time instant messaging and texting tend to write more complex sentences, use a wider vocabulary and have more accurate spelling and capitalization in their English examinations. Similarly, multiple studies done by Bev Plester and her colleagues have shown that students who use SMS ('txt') language more frequently actually perform better in standardized measures of English proficiency (Plester, Wood and Bell, 2008; Plester, Wood and Joshi, 2009). Another important finding of research on online language is that it is not as non-standard as many people think. In her 2004 study of the instant messaging language of US university students, Naomi Baron (2004) found that only 0.3 per cent of the words or symbols they used were abbreviations (e.g., 'hrs', 'cuz'), less than 0.8 per cent were acronyms (e.g., 'lol', 'brb'), and only 0.4 per cent were emoticons.

In this chapter we will consider how digital media affect the way we use language to conduct interactions online. First we will briefly review how linguists and communication scholars have approached online language, discussing how traditional approaches tend to regard text-based digital communication as an 'imperfect replica' of either face-to-face conversation or more traditional written communication rather than as a unique form of communication with its own special uses and characteristics. We will then go on to consider how the affordances of text-based communication have actually made new forms of interaction possible and given rise to unique and creative ways of making meaning and enacting social identities.

MEDIA EFFECTS AND USER EFFECTS

There are a number of different ways that scholars have gone about trying to account for the linguistic features of text-based digital communication. On the whole, however, these explanations can be divided into two main types: those which focus on the *media* and how they constrain 'normal' language use, and those that focus on the *users* of media, their social identities and their relationships with the people with whom they are communicating.

Approaches which focus on media effects see the unique linguistic features of text-based digital communication as the result of the affordances and constraints inherent in digital media. The most conspicuous affordance of digital media is interactivity (see also Chapter 3). Unlike most written communication, text-based digital communication involves all kinds of opportunities for interaction between the people writing messages and the people receiving them, whether it is the more or less 'real time' (**synchronous**) interaction of chat and instant messaging or the 'delayed' (**asynchronous**) interaction of email and blogs.

At the same time, however, digital media also place significant constraints on interaction. One set of constraints, particularly in more synchronous types of digitally-mediated interaction, has to do with time. Not only does typing, for most people, require more time than speaking, but there is an inevitable delay between the time a message is typed and the time it is received by one's interlocutor. Even the most advanced chat system using the fastest data connection cannot imitate the synchronicity of face-to-face conversation.

Another set of constraints has to do with space. Some digital media limit the number of characters allowed in one 'turn' (for example 160 characters for most SMS text messages and 140 characters on Twitter).

The proliferation of acronyms and abbreviations in digital text are, from this perspective, seen as attempts to compensate for these constraints. They help to facilitate rapid responses in chat and instant messaging environments in which those who produce messages faster are often more successful at maintaining conversations (see, for example, Jones, 2005b), and they allow users to pack more meaning into a shorter space, thus compensating for limitations on the maximum number of characters per turn. Such an explanation, however, does not entirely account for why such features also frequently appear in contexts which do not involve these constraints, for example blogs and emails.

Another kind of constraint of text-based digital communication that is often seen to affect language use involves what communication scholars refer to as **media richness**. Although chat, instant messaging and 'texting' are in many ways like face-to-face conversation, they lack the 'rich cues' (like tone of voice, facial expressions and gestures) that are available in face-to-face interaction. Just as abbreviations and other forms of shorthand are seen as a way of compensating for constraints of time and space, emoticons, and nonstandard typography and spelling are often seen as a way of compensating for the relative lack of 'richness' of text by giving users ways to communicate their emotions and attitudes that imitate face-to-face conversation.

In face-to-face communication we use facial expressions, gestures and vocal quality to supplement our verbal messages with what linguists call **contextualization cues** – signals that create a 'context' within which our words should be interpreted. Such cues convey information on what we are 'doing' when we are communicating (for example, joking, complaining, or arguing) and how the verbal part of our message is meant to be taken. When we shift from a serious 'frame' to a joking one, for example, we might change the expression on our face, adjust our posture, make certain kinds of gestures or change the pitch, volume or intonation of our voice.

Of course none of this is possible in text-based communication. Users of text, however, have developed their own ways of issuing such signals. In fact, many of the unique features of digitally-mediated text mentioned above actually function as contextualization cues that communicators use to strategically frame and reframe their messages.

The following excerpt from an instant messaging conversation illustrates how things like punctuation and emoticons can be used as contextualization cues in text-based communication.

> Barnett: u're. . . .~?!
> Tina: tina ar . . . .
> a beautiful girl . . . .
> haha . . .
> ^_^
> Barnett: ai~
> i think i'd better leave right now . . . .^o^!

(from Jones 2012a)

In this example, Tina signals that her characterization of herself as 'a beautiful girl' is playful and facetious by adding 'haha . . .' and the emoticon ^_^. Similarly, Barnett also signals that he is not entirely serious about leaving by adding a *tilde* (~) to his interjection 'ai' (signalling a lengthening of the vowel sound) and ending his contribution with the playful emoticon ^o^ (a clown's face). Without these cues to signal participants' attitudes towards what they are saying, it would be difficult to interpret the utterances as they were meant to be.

There is, however, a danger in regarding the unique features of text-based digital communication simply as substitutes for the kinds of cues we use in face-to-face conversations. Such a position rests on the assumption that there is a more or less one-to-one correspondence between emoticons and facial expressions, or between certain forms of non-standard spelling and actual speech, a correspondence that does not always exist in practice. A smiling emoticon in an instant message may not mean the same thing or serve the same function as a smile in a face-to-face conversation, and just because somebody writes things in a certain way does not mean that they would pronounce them in that way in voice-based interactions. While the systems of emoticons and typography used in text-based communication might draw upon the semiotic systems of facial expressions and phonology, they are not simply replications of these systems in writing. They are systems in their own right, with their own conventions and their own sets of affordances and constraints. This was brought home to us recently when Christoph's daughter asked him, 'Dad, how do you say ":p" in real life?'

One good example of how emoticons in text-based communication can be used in ways that do not have clear correspondences in face-to-face conversation is the posture emoticon 'orz', common in the texting and instant messaging of Japanese, Chinese and Korean speakers. The symbol is meant to convey someone bowing or 'kowtowing', and has many possible meanings depending on the context in which it is used. It might be used to express frustration, despair, sarcasm, or grudging respect. This and other posture emoticons (as well as abbreviations like 'ROFL' –'rolling on the floor with laughter') demonstrate ways users of text-based communication can animate their verbal messages that would be either impossible or inappropriate in face-to-face communication: it is unlikely that those who use this symbol would ever actually 'kowtow' to an interlocutor in a face-to-face conversation.

The biggest problem with approaches that focus on media effects is that they start from the assumption that text-based digital communication is an 'imperfect replica' of some other mode of communication against which it should be judged. When judged against less interactive forms of written language like newspapers and books, the language of text-based digital communication is found to lack precision, clarity and 'correctness'. When measured against face-to-face conversation, text-based digital communication is found to lack 'richness'. Either way, this approach constitutes a 'deficit model', one which explains the features of digitally-mediated text as 'compensation' for not being enough like spoken language or enough like written language, rather than as responses to the media's unique set of communicative affordances. Not only do people *do* very different things with text-based digital communication than they do with written texts or with verbal conversations, but text-based digital communication has itself introduced into social life a whole array of new kinds of interactions which are not possible using traditional writing or voice-based conversation (see below).

An even more obvious problem with approaches that focus solely on media effects is that they fail to account for the great variety of language use within particular media. Many tweets and instant messages, for example, contain no abbreviations at all, text messages can sometimes be written in rather formal and standard language, and the linguistic register you would use to post a comment on the wall of the official Facebook page of your company would likely be different from that you would use to post a comment on your best friend's wall.

The way scholars have come to account for this variation has been to focus on the *users* of text-based communication: who they are, their relationships with and attitudes towards the people with whom they are communicating, and what they are communicating about.

Below are two Facebook status updates, one from President Barak Obama (a), and the other from a fifteen-year-old student named Kayla Dakota (b).

(a) Barack Obama

High-speed wireless service is how we'll spark new innovation, new investment, and new jobs – and connect every corner of America to the digital age.

(b) Kayla Dakota

truth is, I don't like our health class at all. . . . UGHHH ahahaha *holds up two fingers* . . . and I miss film club. we should like . . . make our own film club: (

It's easy to see how the language that President Obama uses is very different from that Kayla uses. Whereas President Obama's contribution is written in rather formal style with standard spelling and grammar, much like a conventional written text, Kayla's uses frequent ellipses (. . .), sound words ('UGHHH ahahaha'), an emoticon '(:' (a left facing smiley), the intensifier 'like', and a parenthetical description of a gesture (*holds up 2 fingers*), a practice known as **emoting**.

It is also not hard to imagine *why* these two Facebook users deploy such different linguistic resources. One reason has to do with the people they are communicating with. Kayla is communicating with her friends, and the informality and playfulness of her language helps her to maintain a close relationship with them. The President, on the other hand, is addressing his constituents. Although the people who receive this message in their news feeds are all Facebook 'friends' of Barack Obama, chances are they are not as close with the President as Kayla's Facebook friends are with her.

Another reason has to do with who they are. President Obama and Kayla are from different generations, of different genders, and hold different social positions. Although both President Obama and Kayla have many different styles of communicating available to them for different situations, in general we can say that US Presidents and teenage girls tend to use language rather differently. We would probably think it odd if the President were to write something like 'it would be sooooo kewl if we had faster wifi *holds up 2 fingers* then we could like . . . hook the whole country up to the internet!'

Linguists have found different patterns of emoticon use, spelling, slang, code mixing and even turn taking among people of different ages, different genders and from different regions. They have found, for example, that teenagers are more likely to use emoticons than adults, and women are more likely to use them than men (Huffaker and Calvert, 2005; Witmer and Katzman, 1997). They have also found that speakers of vernacular varieties of language like 'Singlish' (Singaporean English), colloquial Arabic and Swiss-German sometimes use features from these dialects in their digital interactions in ways they do not in more conventional forms of writing.

The linguist James Paul Gee (2008) calls the different styles of speaking and writing associated with different kinds of people and different social groups **social languages.** Scholars of computer-mediated communication have found that particular communities of users or occupants of particular **affinity spaces** (see Chapter 8), such as contributors to a particular blog, players of a particular online game, or friends in an online social network, tend to employ unique 'social languages' which mark them as members of the group. The more competent and creative they are at using these languages, the more accepted or respected they are in the group. David Crystal (quoted in Kleinman, 2010) says that language is 'like any badge of ability. If you go to a local skate park you see kids whose expertise is making a skateboard do wonderful things. Online you show how brilliant you are by manipulating the language of the internet'. Sometimes people also use these social languages to exclude people who are not in their social group from their interactions. Crystal (2008) gives the example of young people using abbreviations like 'prw ttyl' ('parents watching, talk to you later') in their text messages.

Activity 5.1: Analyzing online language

A. ANALYZING INTERACTIONS IN DIFFERENT MEDIA

Collect samples of different kinds of text-based digital interactions (emails, IM conversations, Facebook wall posts, IM chats, SMS conversations) and answer the following questions:

1. Which kinds of interactions have the most emoticons, non-standard spellings, abbreviations and short forms? Which kinds of interactions have the least?
2. To what extent can you explain these features based on the constraints of the medium used, particularly constraints on time, space and media richness?

B. ANALYZING LINGUISTIC FEATURES

Save the history of a text-based chat, instant messaging session or SMS interaction and circle all of the uses of emoticons, abbreviations or non-standard spelling or punctuation.

1. How would the interaction be different if the emoticons were removed and the non-standard features were standardized? Would this affect how the utterances might be interpreted?
2. Which features (emoticons, abbreviations, unconventional spellings or punctuation) function as contextualization cues? How do communicators use them to frame and reframe their messages?

Although an approach to text-based digital communication that takes users' identities and relationships as its starting point helps to explain why different people use language differently online, it still fails to fully capture the unique affordances of this form of communication. In the rest of this chapter we will shift our focus away from how media affect our language use and how different people use language differently, and turn to the process of *mediation* itself, the process through which people creatively engage with the affordances and constraints of media to perform unique social actions. A focus on mediation begins with the questions: what are people *doing* with text-based digital communication that they cannot do with other forms of communication, and how do they use the kinds of linguistic features we have discussed above as resources to perform these actions?

WHAT ARE WE DOING WHEN WE INTERACT ONLINE?

After the web entrepreneur Evan William's initial success in developing Blogger, a simple tool which allowed anyone to design and manage their own blog, he turned his attention to a new project: audio blogging. The idea was that bloggers could make their blog posts more expressive by embedding recordings of their own voices. This attempt to enhance the text-based communication of blogging with the 'richer' mode of voice-based communication, however, didn't take off. So Williams tried a different strategy. Rather than trying to make blogging richer, he developed a platform that placed even *more constraints* on users, not just limiting them to text, but also confining them to posts of only 140 characters long. He called this new platform Twitter.

One lesson we can take from the success of Twitter is that the richness of a communication channel does not necessarily correspond to how useful people actually find it. A similar lesson can be taken from the fact that, although nearly all personal computers sold nowadays come equipped with webcams and most IM clients and many social networking sites facilitate video chats, very few people actually engage in this form of interaction. A 2010 survey by the Pew Research Centre found that most of those surveyed hadn't even tried to use such tools, and that on a typical day only about 4 per cent of US internet users participate in video calls, chats, or teleconferences. Most people seem to prefer the more 'impoverished' medium of instant messaging.

The reason for this has to do with what economists call **transaction costs**.

Imagine you are in a used record shop and find a vintage vinyl disk from a band you listened to in high school called the Iridescent Pineapples. You really want to tell your friend, Fred, also a Pineapple fan, about it, but there are many things that keep you from calling him: it's the middle of the day and you don't want to interrupt him at work; you owe him ten dollars and are afraid he might ask you about it; you just don't want to go to all the trouble of going through the pleasantries of starting a phone conversation, asking how his girlfriend is, listening to him complain about his boss, or face the difficulties inherent in ending a phone conversation. In other words, because the effort and trouble – the transaction costs – of giving this piece of information to Fred are too high in relation to the importance of the information, you resolve to wait and tell Fred about your find at some later date, but you end up forgetting and miss the chance to share this information with him.

Text-based media substantially lower the transaction costs of communication. And so, instead of calling, you might use your mobile phone to text Fred, saving yourself the trouble of engaging in a full-scale conversation and avoiding the risk of inconveniencing him with a phone call. Or you might 'tweet' the news to your social network, alerting not just Fred but all of your other Pineapple-loving friends.

In general, the 'richer' a medium of communication is, the higher the transaction costs are for using it, simply because users have to attend to more modes. The transaction costs of traditional forms of verbal interaction include not just the necessity of engaging in all sorts of conversational rituals like opening, closing and making small talk, but also the necessity of constantly attending to one's tone of voice, facial expressions and gestures as well as those of one's interlocutors, of constantly showing that one is listening, and of responding in a timely manner to the utterances of others. Text-based communication, on the other hand, saves people the trouble of having to pay attention to other modes like facial expressions and vocal quality. In face-to-face conversation, you could not get away with using no facial expressions at all, but you can with text. From this perspective, the interesting thing about emoticons is *not* that they are necessary to compensate for the lack of facial expressions in text-based digital communication, but that they are *not* a necessary feature of such communication. Their optional status allows people to be more creative about when and how to use them.

In addition, text-based digital communication usually gives people more time to compose and respond to utterances, especially if the interaction is asynchronous. It sometimes even gives people the option not to respond at all. If Fred or others in your social network do not respond to your tweet about the Iridescent Pineapples, you probably won't hold it against them.

Finally, because text-based communication does not require users to devote so much attention to how they look and what they are doing when they are interacting, it allows them to do other things at the same time, including having other interactions with other people (see Chapter 6). This is especially important when one wants to maintain a separation between these different interactions. One study by Jones (2008), for example, found that one reason teenagers like instant messaging is that they can talk with their friends without their parents overhearing, and another study by Ling (2004) showed that teenagers use mobile phone texting not just to stay in contact with their friends but also to stay out of reach of their parents.

In the last chapter we discussed how digital media introduce new affordances through increasing our opportunities for multi modal communication, but the opposite is also true. It also introduces new affordances through increasing opportunities for monomodal communication using only text, which make the kind of low-stakes interactions people engage in using tools like Twitter and SMS possible. Before digitally-mediated, text-based communication, many of the kinds of interactions that are a regular part of many people's daily practices were either not possible or not particularly practical. People did not regularly phone up friends or drop by just to say 'hi' or to tell them what they had for dinner, for to do so would have taken too much time and effort.

Some of these new kinds of interactions have more to do with maintaining our relationships with others than actually conveying information. One particular practice that text especially facilitates, for example, is the practice of 'sharing'. Because of its low transaction costs, text makes it easy for people to share their thoughts, ideas, experiences and feelings with others. It also makes it easier for people to reciprocate, or to ignore such messages if they so choose.

What people are mostly doing when they 'share' is not so much transacting information as maintaining a sense of connection with their friends. Below is an example of an instant messaging conversation between two teenagers that takes place over the course of several hours on one evening:

> (6:40 pm) Cheesecake: hihi
> (7:08 pm) SnowBread: wowo
> (9:33 pm) Cheesecake: kaka~~~
> (11:05 pm) SnowBread: ~^.^~

It is quite clear from the content of these messages as well as the length of the intervals between them that Cheesecake and Snowbread are not engaged in anything like what we would normally call a 'conversation'. Rather, they are simply working to maintain a virtual connection with each other.

In a famous study of the way teenagers use mobile phone text messaging, Sara Berg, Alex Taylor and Richard Harper (2005) compare the exchange of text messages to the practice of gift giving. What many teenagers are doing when they send text messages to each other, they argue, is not exchanging information, but exchanging tokens of friendship. Earlier studies on internet relay chat (see, for example, Bays, 1999) made the same observation.

Of course we are not arguing that the practice of gift giving was not possible or practical before the invention of the mobile phone. What was not possible or practical, however, was the kind of constant exchange of virtual gifts that many young people engage in as part of their friendship rituals. And so, in a very real sense, text-based digital communication has changed the way many people 'do' friendship.

At the same time, text also facilitates completely instrumental interactions: a boy informing his girlfriend that he's going to be late, a wife asking her husband to pick up a carton of milk, or an employee informing her boss that she has completed a report. Again, it is not that these interactions did not take place before text-based digital communication, but rather that they took much more time and energy. Calling his girlfriend to say he's going to be late increases the likelihood that the boy is going to have to explain why. By walking down the corridor to tell her boss that she has finished a report, the employee wastes both the boss's time and hers. Text helps to make such purely instrumental transactions more efficient.

These new forms of interaction that text-based digital communication facilities remind us of the fact that communication is more than one thing: lots of different kinds of activities go under the name of communication, and different modes and media tend to encourage different kinds of communication and different relationships between the people communicating (see Chapters 7 and 8). In a study of how families use video chat, for example, Ames and his colleagues (2010) point out that video communication – with its particularly high transaction costs – is not generally used by families for casual exchanges, but rather it is used on those occasions when family members wish to highlight the 'specialness' of the communication and to reinforce their identity as a family.

Case study 5: 'Why do guys text instead of call?'

This is a question asked by one of the posters on an online advice site called Girls ask Guys.com. The poster writes:

> Recently I have been seeing this guy for about 4 months. We really hit it off and enjoy each other alot! I just don't get it, our lines of communication are mostly thru emails and text. I don't understand, as text and emails can be very confusing. So, any advice?
>
> (http://www.girlsaskguys.com/Dating-Questions/39234-why-do-guys-
> text-instead-of-call.html)

As it turns out, this is a rather common 'problem': A Google search for 'Why do guys text instead of call' reveals that this question has been asked by different people on a whole range of advice websites including Guys Speak.com, Yahoo Answers, and Topix.com. To avoid being sexist, we should note that this behaviour is not restricted to 'guys'. One can also find people asking: 'Why do girls always want to text instead of talk?'

The other users of Girls ask Guys.com reply to this poster with a number of possible explanations: the girl's boyfriend might be shy, he might be a 'computer/tech fanatic', or it might be that he's just not that into her. In light of what we said above about the affordances of text-based communication, however, it is likely that there are some much better reasons why this guy, along with many other people, sometimes prefer text-based communication to voice-based communication, even when it comes to intimate relationships.

Here are some of the advantages of texting somebody you are in a romantic relationship with.

It provides an 'emotional buffer' and facilitates the discussion of intimate topics

Because text-based communication avoids the necessity of having to manage bodily aspects of communication like facial expressions, it decreases the discomfort or fear some people feel when talking to people they have strong feelings for. Text-based communication also makes it much easier to manage the impressions that we present to others, lowering the risk that unintended information might be 'given off' or 'leaked' (Goffman, 1959) through our facial expressions or tone of voice. In the early days of text-based digital communication, many scholars thought that, because of its lack of 'richness', it was not particularly suited for communicating emotions. This assumption has turned out to be completely false. In fact, most people who use text-based communication frequently have experienced that it can facilitate what the communications scholar Joseph Walther (1996) calls **hyperpersonal communication**.

It's discreet

By texting, a person can avoid having their conversation overheard by friends, family members or other people in the vicinity. This is especially important when one is discussing particularly intimate topics. This discrete or 'secret' nature of text-based communication can also have the effect of heightening the sense of intimacy between users.

It allows for more considered communication

The asynchronous nature of text-based communication gives users the opportunity to craft more thoughtful, considered and creative messages that better communicate how much they care for each other.

It facilitates 'flirting'

A lot of the communication that goes on in intimate relationships involves teasing, flirting and *double entendre*, forms of communication that depend as much on what is *not* communicated as what is. Text-based communication facilities the linguistic ambiguity that makes flirting possible. It also leaves more space for interpretation. The cultural critic Allucquére Stone (1995: 92) points out that 'low bandwidth' communication can sometimes have the effect of increasing 'erotic tension' between communicators, allowing them to generate 'complex fantasies . . . from a small set of cues'.

It gives partners a way to test their feelings for each other

In most romantic relationships, especially in the early stages, people often feel the need to check to see if their feelings are reciprocated by the other person. This is usually done through conversational rituals ('I love you . . .', 'I love you, too'). The exchange of text messages, like the gift-giving rituals among friends we discussed above, give people a way to test and to strengthen the sense of reciprocity in the relationship, which helps to create the basis for future intimacy.

It makes other forms of communication more 'special'

As we said above, the choice of different kinds of media communicates different intentions and different levels of commitment to an interaction. By using text messages for most day-to-day communication, romantic partners can reserve 'richer' forms of communication like phone calls and video chats for times when they want their interaction to seem more special. In new relationships, moving from periodic texting to periodic phone calls can sometimes function as a signal that the relationship is moving to a 'more serious' stage.

It's persistent

What we mean by persistent is that one is able to save text messages. The obvious advantage of **persistence** is that it allows communicators to look back and check what was said at earlier times in the interaction. For romantic partners, persistence has the added advantage of allowing them to preserve their conversations as 'keepsakes' much in the way people in the past saved love letters.

MEANING AND CREATIVITY

It should be clear from the discussion above that making more modes of communication available in an interaction does not always result in 'more meaning' being conveyed, in the same way that, as we noted in Chapter 2, more data does not always result in more information. In fact, linguists have been pointing out for some time that quite a lot of communication occurs indirectly and that meaning is conveyed both in what is *not* said as well as in what is said. Depending on the context and the relationship between communicators, a text message containing a single smiley can express just as much as an elaborate verbal utterance.

Sometimes the constraints of text-based communication themselves have the effect of encouraging people to come up with new and creative ways to express things, just as the constraints of strict poetic forms like the sonnet encourage creativity in literature. When, as in Twitter, you have only 140 characters to express a rather dense set of meanings, for example, you must learn to choose your words wisely and employ them inventively.

In 2011, The University of Iowa Tipple School of Business, tired of receiving dull and formulaic admissions essays, invited applicants to submit their admissions essays as 'tweets' and offered a scholarship to the most creative effort. The purpose of this, according to the director of admissions, was to gauge how imaginative applicants could be when asked to express themselves concisely, a key demand of business writing. The winning applicant chose to write his tweet in the form of a haiku, an ancient Japanese poetic form, creatively combining one of the newest forms of communication with one of the oldest forms (Snee, 2011).

Text-based digital communication does not just encourage creativity through its limitations, but also through its flexibility, especially the way it makes it easy for users to mix different kinds of linguistic resources. Of course, such mixing is not entirely confined to text-based digital communication. In fact, people have been mixing linguistic resources in their verbal communication for a long time. People who speak more than one language or variety of a language, for example, regularly mix languages, especially when they are speaking to other multilinguals. What is special about text-based digital communication is that it can be *multi-scriptural* as well as multilingual, allowing users to add into the mix features like abbreviations that are only possible in writing.

This multi-scriptural capacity of text is particularly evident in the communication of those whose language is not traditionally written with the Roman alphabet. One variety of multi-scriptural language that has developed on Russian and Ukrainian blogs, for example, is called 'padronkavskiy zhargon' – a mixture of Russian and Ukrainian rendered phonetically and often full of puns and profanity. Another example is what has come to be known in China as 'Martian Language' (火星文), a combination of Chinese characters, Romanized Chinese words, English words, symbols, abbreviations and emoticons.

Playing around with language in this way opens up all sorts of new possibilities for meaning making that are not normally available in voice-based conversation or traditional written communication. Carmen Lee (2007), for instance, discusses how teenagers in Hong Kong creatively mix different forms of English and Chinese writing in their instant messaging language, sometimes rendering Chinese using characters, as in traditional writing, sometimes writing it as Romanized words, and sometimes using English transliterations. She gives the example of an instant message in which a user describes a part-time teacher at his university by rendering the Chinese expression '厄飯吃' (which is used to describe someone who only works for money) using the English words 'cheat rice eat'. This strategy allows the user to maintain the cultural meaning of the idiom without having to change input methods. The new coinage, which is neither English nor Chinese, also carries a kind of ironic playfulness.

Another example of how the mixing of linguistic resources increases users' capacity to make meaning can be seen in the frequent insertion of Romanized final particles (for example: 'ar', 'a', 'r~' and 'lor') at the end of English messages by Chinese speaking IM and SMS users. In all dialects of spoken Chinese these particles are very important because they carry information about the attitude one has towards what one is saying or the person one is talking to. In Standard Written Chinese, however, most of these particles are absent, and they, of course, do not exist in English. When Chinese speakers use them in their instant messaging and SMS language, they gain the advantage of being able to express their feelings and attitudes more clearly and create a sense of closeness with the people with whom they are communicating. In other words, they increase the meaning potential of both written Chinese and written English.

TEXTUAL SELVES

One final affordance of text-based digital communication we would like to mention is the way it facilitates the creation of new kinds of identities. Since the early days of the internet, commentators have noted how text-based digital communication allows people to assume different persona. Sherry Turkle (1995: 14), in fact, argues that one of the main affordances of text-based communication is that it gives to users 'the ability to assume a role as close to or as far from one's "real self" as one chooses'. Men can pretend to be women, adults can pretend to be children, and novices can pretend to be experts. One of the most iconic jokes about the internet is a 1993 *New Yorker* cartoon of two dogs sitting in front of a monitor, one saying to the other, 'On the internet nobody knows you're a dog'.

There are, of course, lots of potential problems with text-based identity play. It can, for example, be used as a tool for antisocial behaviour such as online deception or harassment. At the same time, there are also many positive aspects of 'identity play'. Turkle (1995) has pointed out that text-based communication gives to teenagers the unprecedented opportunity to explore their potential by 'trying on' different kinds of identities in the safety of their own home.

Often when people engage in text-based identity play, they are not so much 'pretend-ing' to be someone else as exploring different aspects of their 'real life' identities. A good example of this can be seen on the Twitter feed of Erica's Fish (@ericasfish), part of which is reproduced in Figure 5.1).

ericasfish Erica's Fish
The human's sick today. I'm unable to make her tea, but I AM able to swim back and forth in an entertaining manner.
18 Dec 09

ericasfish Erica's Fish
Some days, I wish I were a tuna. The human would come home and faint from fear! Sadly, she's more likely to get a fork and a bib.
17 Dec 09

ericasfish Erica's Fish
Pardon my absence. The human briefly rescinded my Internet privileges after I started playing dead when visitors came by.
15 Dec 09

ericasfish Erica's Fish
Feeling flamboyant today, people! Who wants a martini?
5 Dec 09

ericasfish Erica's Fish
The human secured a seat for me at the Thanksgiving table. I am still misty-eyed over this. I rode home in the cup blowing kisses at her.
29 Nov 09

Figure 5.1   Excerpt from Erica's Fish's Twitter feed (used with permission)

The important thing to note here is that, by pretending to be her fish, Erica is not trying to 'fool' anybody. Rather, she is communicating about herself, what happens to her and how she feels about it *through* her fish. In other words, rather than separating herself from her 'real self', Erica uses text-based identity play to view and comment on her life from a different perspective, a process which not only helps her to share different aspects of herself with her followers but also helps her to reflect upon her day-to-day activities in a new and creative way.

Most discussions of text-based identity play emphasize the 'mask-like' function of text (Danet 1998), its ability to facilitate impersonation. A much more important aspect of text, however, is the way it helps people to create different aspects of their 'real' identities online through cultivating different kinds of writing styles and inventing things like screen names and message signatures, and through aligning themselves to various groups and communities by using different social languages.

Activity 5.2: Text-based communication and creativity

A. THE AFFORDANCES OF TEXT

Make a list of the things you can do with text-based communication that you cannot or would not do in face-to-face communication. Why does text make these things easier to do?

B. WRITING A 'TWEET'

Try to summarize as many advantages of text-based communication as you can in the form of a 'tweet', limiting yourself to 140 characters.

C. IDENTITY PLAY

Try to impersonate another person, animal or inanimate object in an instant messaging interaction and see if your interlocutor can guess who or what you are impersonating. How do you use language and non-linguistic features of text-based communication to construct your false identity?

CONCLUSION

In this chapter we have discussed some of the reasons why the language of text-based digital communication is so different from other kinds of written and spoken language. We have also considered why text-based communication continues to be the most pervasive mode of digital interaction, even when other more multimodal alternatives are readily available. One reason we discussed was the low transaction costs of text, a factor which encourages people to engage in many kinds of interactions which would involve too much time or effort using other modes. Another reason we mentioned was the unprecedented amount of control text-based communication gives people over managing the meanings they make and the identities they create. Finally, we discussed how sometimes the very constraints that seem to make communication more difficult can actually foster more creative forms of self-expression.

One aspect of digital interaction we touched upon briefly in this chapter was the fact that text-based communication, along with other forms of digitally-mediated interaction, sometimes make it possible for people to simultaneously engage in multiple activities and multiple interactions. This is a phenomenon which we will take up more fully in the next chapter when we discuss how digital media make available affordances for distributing our attention across different activities at the same time, and how being able to both efficiently distribute attention and attract the attention of others have become important skills in the digital age.

USEFUL RESOURCES

Print

Baron, N. (2010). *Always on: Language in an online and mobile world.* New York: Oxford University Press.

Crystal, D. (2001). *The language of the internet.* Oxford: Oxford University Press.

Crystal, D. (2011). *Internet linguistics: A student's guide.* London: Routledge.

Harper, R. H. R. (2011). *Texture: Human expression in the age of communications overload.* Cambridge, MA: MIT Press.

Thurlow, C., and Mroczek, K. (eds.) (2011). *Digital discourse: Language in the new media.* Oxford: Oxford University Press.

Web

Internet world users by language 2010
http://www.internetworldstats.com/stats7.htm

NetLingo: The internet dictionary
http://www.netlingo.com/

BBC, Zoe Kleinman, How the internet is changing language
http://www.bbc.co.uk/news/technology-10971949

Video

David Crystal: How is the internet changing language today?
http://www.youtube.com/watch?v=P2XVdDSJHqY

TED, Rives: A story of mixed emoticons
http://www.ted.com/talks/rives_tells_a_story_of_mixed_emoticons.html

Cingular commercial: 'bff Jill'
http://youtu.be/4nlUcRJX9-o

CHAPTER 6

Attention Structures

With digital media, the number of communication tools available to us at any given time has increased dramatically. Email, instant messaging, social networking and the World Wide Web all compete for our attention. At the same time, digital tools also provide us with new ways to structure our attention and allow us to distribute attention across different activities and interactions. In this chapter we will consider the ways digital media are affecting how we structure, manage and even think about attention.

The practice of distributing attention in order to perform multiple tasks simultaneously is known as **multitasking**. Research into multitasking has focused on two different processes: task switching, where people switch their attention from one activity to another (for example, between their email, instant messenger and the report they are writing); and dual tasking, where people are engaged in two or more activities at the same time (for example, listening to music while writing their report). In addition, technology consultant Linda Stone (n.d.) describes another aspect of multitasking: what she calls the state of **continuous partial attention**. This, she says, is a stressful state where people are constantly, but only partially, attending to the information from their communication devices, motivated by the fear of 'missing something'.

For some, such practices are a cause for concern. They worry that they interfere with people's ability to pay attention to a single task in a sustained, in-depth way. Nicholas Carr, whose work we described in Chapter 3, describes his worries in the following way (2011: 1):

> I used to find it easy to immerse myself in a book or lengthy article. My mind would get caught up in the twists of the narrative or the turns of the argument, and I'd spend hours strolling through long stretches of prose. That's rarely the case anymore. Now my concentration starts to drift after a page or two. I get fidgety, lose the thread, begin looking for something else to do.

Others, however, like Steven Appelbaum and his colleagues (Appelbaum, Marchionni and Fernandez, 2008) point to an apparent paradox in the research on multitasking. They note that, according to this research, multitasking is detrimental to task completion. Yet, at the same time, as multitasking in the workplace has been on the rise, workers' average productivity has increased, not decreased. If multitasking hinders task completion, this does not appear to be reflected in the overall value of contributions made by workers to the companies that they work for. Perhaps the practice of rapidly switching between different projects at work is adding some other kind of value, allowing workers to provide immediate responses to the demands of their clients, for example.

The ability to manage and distribute attention across a range of competing activities is increasingly important in the digital age. Knowledge workers (see Chapter 12) are expected to be able to manage numerous different projects at the same time, dividing attention between them. At both work and at home people are engaging with much richer media environments than they used to. Environments like this require us to make decisions about what to attend to at any given moment. As the rhetorician Richard Lanham (1994: n.p.) puts it, 'If one is looking for a glimpse of what literacy will look like in the future, the fighter cockpit is a good place to look'.

One important though sometimes neglected aspect of digital literacies is this ability to use digital tools to manage, distribute and focus attention. In this chapter we will examine the demands digital media make on our attention as well as the affordances and constraints of media that help us to structure our attention. We will then go on to discuss the effects of digital media on the way that we think about attention, the value that we place on it, and the strategies we use to attract it.

DIGITAL MEDIA AND POLYFOCALITY

Digital media create two main challenges for the way that we manage and distribute our attention. First, with the shift from page to screen, designers are able to draw on the affordances of hypertext, interactivity and multimedia (see Chapters 3 and 4) to present many different kinds of information to us at the same time, all competing for our attention. Second, digital media make it possible for us to engage in numerous different activities and interactions at the same time, strategically shifting our attention between them.

Digital video games provide an excellent example of the way that the design of a screen can require us to distribute attention efficiently. As an example, consider the first person shooter game *Counter-Strike* (Valve, 2000), where players take on the roles of terrorists or counter-terrorists and work in competitive teams in order to achieve their objectives. As is often the case in such video games, the screen is divided into a visual display of the virtual world which the player is moving through, with other texts and tools for acting on that world arranged around the edges of the display (see Chapter 9). Among the peripheral texts and tools that are available to the player are: a radar map of the terrain, text-based chat for communication with other players, a timer, and a money and ammunition counter.

Coping with the environment of *Counter-Strike* requires players to shift attention across a range of multimodal signs, including the visual, the aural and the textual. Players have to attend to the 'physical' features of the virtual world that they are moving through, while at the same time keeping track of communications (on the left side of the screen) and their stock of ammunition (on the right side). In addition, bodies and objects in the game communicate their position through the sounds that they make, so players must become accustomed to attending to and analyzing sounds in the virtual world: gun shots ricocheting off walls, footsteps as they become louder or softer, the squeak of doors and the crunch of gravel. Furthermore, just as with other computing activities, the virtual spaces created by *Counter-Strike* often spill into and interact with the physical spaces in which the game is played. In Hong Kong, for example, some people like to play such games together with their friends in busy commercial gaming centers where the sights and sounds occurring around them compete for their attention with what is happening on the screen in front of them.

The example of *Counter-Strike* demonstrates the **polyfocality** of texts and practices involving digital media. Rather than directing their attention at a single focal point, players distribute their attention among *multiple foci*. Furthermore, the example shows that attention is often distributed not only *within* the virtual world of the game, but also *between* the virtual world and the physical locations where players are situated. Therefore, to understand how attention is distributed in computer-mediated communication, we have to look not only at virtual environments, but also at physical settings.

This kind of polyfocality is common in computer-mediated activities. Studies of secondary school students (see, for example, Jones, 2010) show that students using computers frequently switch among a range of simultaneous activities and interactions. For example, while doing their homework they might also be watching TV out of the corner of their eyes, checking their friends' Facebook status, surfing the web, and chatting with several different people on MSN about their homework. In such contexts, attention can shift among at least three different kinds of space: 1) physical spaces (where the participants are located); 2) virtual spaces (for example, chat rooms, web pages, virtual worlds); and 3) screen space (windows, toolbars, writing spaces).

In the last chapter we talked about how the affordances and constraints of text-based digital communication, such as low transaction costs and an inability to monitor the physical activities of other people, help to facilitate multitasking. In fact, one of the most common questions people ask one another in such interactions is: 'What are you doing?' This question belies the fact that participants expect their interlocutors to be engaged in other activities besides the chat. In this sense, text-based communication is very different from face-to-face interaction, where you are often expected to give your conversational partner your undivided attention. To illustrate this difference, consider an online chat which Rodney observed (Jones, 2009: 18), in which one participant described how her uncle was dying of cancer and how unhappy this was making her. At the same time as consoling her friend, the other participant in this interaction was engaged in a number of other activities, including surfing entertainment websites and downloading music. This polyfocality was unproblematically accepted as a normal part of the interaction. By contrast, it is almost impossible to imagine a face-to-face encounter where someone would engage in other, unrelated tasks during a conversation about such a serious topic.

Polyfocailty, however, is not a new phenomenon introduced by digital media. In fact, almost all interaction involves participants doing more than one thing at a time. Scollon and his colleagues (1999), for example, in studying the literacy practices of Hong Kong university students in the early 1990s, before digital technologies became widely available, noted that even then the students rarely focused on one thing at one time. Instead '[w]hen they watch television, they also listen to music and read or carry on conversations; traveling on the bus or Mass Transit Railway they read and listen to music – most commonly they "read" while chatting, watching television and listening to music on CD' (p. 35).

It might even be argued that our ability to multitask is a major part of what makes us human. One type of cognitive behavior that plays a big role in multitasking is called 'branching', which involves keeping a goal in mind over time while at the same time being able to allocate attentional resources to other tasks. Research suggests that this process takes place in the anterior prefrontal cortex, a region of the brain especially well developed in humans as compared to other mammals (Koechlin *et al.*, 1999). It's quite likely that this evolutionary advantage was key to the survival of our species, especially in those early years when we depended on hunting for our food. Without the strength, speed or equipment (claws, fangs, tusks) of other animals, prehistoric humans had to rely on their superior ability to attend to many different things at once, scanning complex landscapes in search of their prey, while at the same time keeping track of their fellow hunters and staying alert to possible danger, in much the same way as people playing complex multiplayer shooter games like *Counter-Strike*.

With computer-mediated communication this kind of polyfocality has become more efficient. The way that digital tools are designed helps us to distribute attention among a variety of different **attentional tracks** (Goffman, 1974). For example, in chat clients like MSN, messages from different people appear in separate windows which helps users to manage, prioritize and keep track of multiple, simultaneous conversations in a way that is not possible in, for example, a physical interaction with a group of friends in which many people are trying to talk at one time. Furthermore, the conversations themselves are 'persistent' in the sense that a history of previous messages is recorded, making it easy to scroll back to check what was said before or suspend the interaction and resume it at a later time. People we chat with are also organized into contact lists, which can be categorized and linked to personal information. Finally, the degree to which we make ourselves available to others can be modulated through adjusting our online 'status' (for example 'online', 'away', 'do not disturb', 'invisible' and so on).

The kinds of tools described above help us to manage both the cognitive and social aspects of paying attention. Although attention is usually thought of as a purely cognitive phenomenon, attending to conversational interactions involves a social dimension as well. Paying attention means more than just focusing your mental energy on a particular exchange, remembering who you are talking to and what you are talking about. It also involves sending appropriate signals or feedback to other participants in order to *show* them that you are paying attention. The kind of feedback that you need to send will depend on who you are talking to and what the goals of your interaction are.

As we've suggested, digital media make it easier to manage the cognitive load of multiple simultaneous interactions, by allowing us to easily monitor multiple attentional tracks. Ironically, the relative lack of 'richness' of computer-mediated communication, often considered a constraint of the medium, is also what makes it easier to manage the social element of paying attention. It is easier for us to give the appearance of attention (i.e. timely feedback, even when it involves sending one-word messages or emoticons) to multiple conversation partners in text-based chat and instant messaging than it would be in face-to-face conversation (see Chapter 5).

Activity 6.1: Multitasking and distributing attention

Read the vignette below and answer the questions:

> Ming is a 19-year-old student studying in a university in Hong Kong. Every evening after dinner she switches on her IBM laptop, which is connected to the high-speed wireless LAN in her residence hall, and works on her school assignments. While she is working she intermittently answers email and instant messages (IM) from her classmates as well as her friends and family members.

Sometimes she chats with three or four people at a time using a chat and IM software popular with her friends. She also has her mobile phone next to her computer just in case somebody wants to call her. Occasionally it lights up with an SMS (short message service) from a classmate. She is an avid fan of all kinds of music from indie to hip-hop, and she almost always listens to mp3 files through her earphones when she's working on the computer and swaps songs with other fans using a 'peer-to-peer' file sharing application. Ming's roommate, Mei Lin, sits on the other side of their small room, typing into her own laptop and watching her small portable Sony television. Mei Lin likes to spend time browsing a bulletin board system (BBS) from China where young people express their ideas about culture and politics, and she likes to talk with Ming about some of the news and opinions she finds on it, and sometimes these comments develop into heated exchanges of opinion between the two roommates. These debates, however, rarely significantly interrupt the ongoing tempo of messaging, chatting, emailing, surfing the web, downloading music files, watching TV, and working on homework assignments.

(Jones, 2009: 13–14)

1. Do you multitask in the way described above? How? Why/Why not?
2. How can digital tools/interfaces help you to manage and distribute your attention?

    a. How can they help you make yourself 'available'/'unavailable'?
    b. How can they help you to juggle multiple communicative activities and interactions?

3. Are some digital tools/interfaces better for multitasking than others? Consider the interface of the operating system on computers (for example Windows, Mac OS, Linux) and on smartphones or tablets (for example iOS, Android, Windows Phone).

ATTENTION STRUCTURES

It should be clear from the descriptions of polyfocality above that computers are having a significant effect on the way that we organize and distribute our attention. As we have pointed out, attention is distributed not only across screen space (application windows) and virtual space (different websites, chats and virtual worlds), but also across physical spaces (classrooms, living rooms, internet cafés). We also noted that, because attention is socially constructed, interpersonal relationships (either with online chatmates or with others in the same physical location) can have an effect on the way that attention is distributed. In this section, we describe a framework that you can apply in order to understand the way attention is distributed in interaction.

A key concept in the framework that we propose is that of the **attention struc-ture**, introduced by the rhetorician Richard Lanham in his 2006 book, *The Economics of*

Attention. In Lanham's work, attention structures are the technological means used by people to make sense of the overabundance of information that they face in the digital age.

Here we will use the term 'attention structure' to refer to the patterns of orientation to time and space which individuals use to attend to elements of an interaction (Jones, 2005a, c). In interactions, we structure our attention according to these patterns, attending to certain elements and not attending to others. In other words, an attention structure is a way for us to distribute our attention in a particular communicative situation.

This view of attention structures is influenced by the work of the linguist Ron Scollon, who pointed out that every human action takes place at the intersection of three elements: 1) a person with all of his or her memories and experiences (what Scollon calls the **historical body**); 2) the social relationships we have with other people (what he calls the **interaction order**); and 3) the kinds of communication tools that we have to help us organize our attention (what he calls the **discourses in place**).

Distributing attention can be seen as a kind of social action, which involves these three main factors, as illustrated in Figure 6.1.

What this model highlights is the fact that attention is neither solely inside your head nor solely outside of it. It is distributed among mental structures, social relationships and communication tools. When these three components work together in sync, we have the feeling that our attention is flowing right, that we're attending to what we need to attend to, we're doing our jobs efficiently. To see how this framework works, let's return to the example of the video game, which we considered earlier.

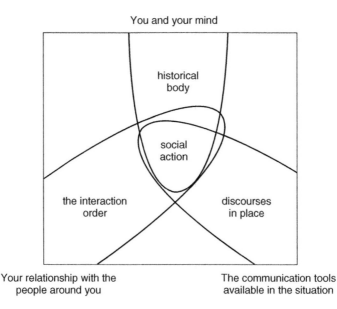

You and your mind

historical body

social action

the interaction order

discourses in place

Your relationship with the people around you

The communication tools available in the situation

Figure 6.1   Factors affecting the distribution of attention (adapted from Scollon and Scollon 2004)

The attention structure adopted in the game depends first on the 'discourses in place', that is the kind of texts and tools that you encounter in the game. These include the visual display of the game world, and stats like ammunition counters. These texts and tools serve to draw your attention in different ways, and you have to attend to them selectively according to the needs of the moment. In addition to the texts and tools on the screen, your attention is also drawn to texts and tools in the physical environment where you are playing the game. Depending on the situation these may be more or less relevant to the game, for example, if you are playing at home alone or in a group in a gaming center or internet café.

Second, different players bring different attention structures to the game, depending on (among other things) their prior experience of playing the game. As you develop the skills of playing the game, particular attention structures are established and maintained within your 'historical body'.

Finally, the attention structures adopted depend on the 'interaction order', the social relationships between players. For example, if you know the people you are playing with well, then you will probably pay them a different kind of attention than if you do not. You will also pay a different kind of attention to your teammates than you do to your opponents.

Digital media are having an effect on the kinds of attention structures that people adopt in a whole range of different situations. One setting where conflicts in attention structures can sometimes be observed is in schools. If you observe young people using computers out of school, you notice them adopting the kind of polyfocal attention structures that we described earlier. However, studies of the use of computers in schools (see, for example, Jones, 2010) show that these polyfocal attention structures sometimes come into conflict with what is expected of students when they are using computers in the classroom.

In Hong Kong, English classes are sometimes conducted in computer rooms known as Multimedia Learning Centres (MMLC). What is striking about these lessons is the way that these computer rooms have been infiltrated by practices from the traditional classroom. For example, although these rooms were introduced in order to encourage a new kind of interactive and experiential learning, the texts and tools (the 'discourses in place') that are used in these contexts and the ways they are arranged sometimes discourage this. Computers, for example, are arranged in rows following a 'panoptican' model (Foucault, 1977), with the screens facing the back of the room. The space reproduces the interaction order of the traditional classroom, where the physical setting channels attention towards the teacher, and the teacher, standing in front, can observe all of the students. Ironically, at the same time the setting limits the teacher's ability to monitor students' activities, and so the teacher has to wander up and down the aisle to see what students are doing or else attend to her own computer screen in the front of the room to monitor their computer use.

The computer activities that students do in these rooms are sometimes extremely limited. For example, in one class we observed students read a text from their textbook and recorded their recital using the computer (Jones, 2010). The textbook, not the computer screen, was the text that students were expected to focus their attention on. The text displayed on the computer screen, which would normally be considered the most important in such settings, here was almost totally inconsequential. Students' screens showed simply an interface based on the controls of a tape recorder.

Figure 6.2 and 6.3   A Multimedia Learning Centre in Hong Kong

Into these interaction orders and discourses in place, teachers and students bring 'historical bodies' which are habituated to different kinds of situations, both traditional classrooms and out-of-school computer use. However, the lesson in the computer room doesn't fit with experiences of either of these situations. Just as teachers find themselves in classrooms in which the traditional ways of monitoring students doesn't work, students find themselves in front of computer screens but unable to make use of the attention structures that they are used to drawing on outside the classroom (see Figures 6.2 and 6.3).

It should come as no great surprise that the computer room is unpopular with teachers and students alike. The problem is the way the discourses in place, the interaction orders and the historical bodies don't fit together. Attention structures from traditional classrooms and traditional literacy practices in many ways contradict the orientations towards time and space that are characteristic of computer use for these students. In other words, the activities that students are meant to do in the computer room are 'out of sync' with the technology they are supposed to use and with the attention structures that have developed in their historical bodies through years of computer use at home. A similar point is made by Michael Wesch in his video 'A Vision of Students Today' (see Useful resources), in which he explores the difficulties twenty-first-century students have when they enter 'nineteenth-century-style' lecture halls.

The point of this discussion is that whether or not multitasking is good or bad depends very much on the circumstances in which people engage in it. The attention structures appropriate for playing *Counter-Strike* are not the same as those appropriate for reading a novel, and those that a stock trader needs to cultivate are different from those needed by a diamond cutter. Many of the cognitive and social problems we encounter around the issue of attention, especially as it relates to digital media, arise because the attention structures being used don't fit the circumstances of the task at hand, or because the attention structures people bring to the situation, those made possible by the media available, and those associated with the social relationships and circumstances of the situation are somehow 'out of sync'.

THE ATTENTION ECONOMY AND DIGITAL LITERACIES

Just as technological advances have led to greater demands on our attention, requiring us to manage and distribute it in a more polyfocal way, these technological advances have also been accompanied by profound cultural and economic changes. There has been a shift in many places from an industrialized economy based on the exchange of physical goods to a knowledge-based economy based on the exchange of information (see Chapter 12). However, some economists have pointed out that in such an economy, the most valuable commodity is not information, but attention. The scholar Herbert Simon puts it like this:

> in an information-rich world, the wealth of information means a dearth of something else: a scarcity of whatever it is that information consumes. What information consumes is rather obvious: it consumes the attention of its recipients. Hence a wealth of information creates a poverty of attention and a need to allocate that attention efficiently among the overabundance of information sources that might consume it.
>
> (Simon 1971: 40–41)

This observation has led others like Michael Goldhaber (1997) to propose that we are not so much living in an information economy, as in an **attention economy**, where value is created from the exchange of attention and '[w]hat matters is seeking, obtaining and paying attention'. Digital media and the internet facilitate participation in this economy, by creating new channels for distributing attention. Ordinary people are now empowered to reach a wide audience by publishing their own content and commenting on the content of others (for example in blogs and social networking sites, see Activity 6.2). As you might expect, this new economy brings traditional values into question, requiring us to rethink our assumptions. In particular, it requires us to rethink the importance of attention.

Goldhaber maintains that in order to *get* attention, you have to *give* attention, otherwise your audience will lose interest and take their attention elsewhere. This is an important point for advertisers, especially those launching social media campaigns (for example, in Facebook). Brands that want to get the attention of customers are increasingly viewing the process as a two-way exchange rather than the one-way communication that characterizes traditional advertising. The emphasis is on developing new kinds of relationships with customers, and, in many cases, moving towards 'engaging customers in the design of products for themselves' (MacLeod, 2000, cited in Lankshear and Knobel, 2002: 29).

Goldhaber notes that some people (he calls them 'stars') are better at attracting attention than others (he calls them 'fans'). Stars are able to command more attention partly because they pay **illusory attention** to fans, that is, they give the illusion of personal attention even though they are addressing a large audience. Goldhaber illustrates this concept with the example of a presenter at a conference, who, while talking to a large crowd, makes eye contact with individuals in that crowd. In digital media, social media tools like Twitter and Facebook provide opportunities to pay illusory attention (see Case study 6).

Another point that Goldhaber makes about attention is that it is something which can be passed on by someone who has it. In the conference presentation, it is normally the presenter who holds the attention of the audience, but he or she can pass this attention to others, as when a member of the audience asks a question. At this point the presenter (along with everyone else) focuses their attention on the questioner. A good example from digital media is the way that hypertext links from a well-known website with a sizeable audience can draw the attention of readers to other, lesser-known websites. As we noted in Chapter 2, the PageRank algorithm which Google uses in order to rank search results is based on similar principles of giving and getting attention.

If you accept the idea of an attention economy with attention as the valued commodity, then you have to adjust your ways of thinking about certain concepts. For example, our traditional way of thinking of privacy as freedom from the public gaze is not especially appropriate for people participating in an attention economy. People have to be 'out there' in order to attract attention. In addition, intellectual property laws that forbid people from copying and distributing a creator's work also seem out of place. This kind of copying and distributing draws attention to the creator, thus increasing their 'wealth' in the attention economy. In other words, wealth comes not from the exchange of 'intellectual property', but from the exchange of attention.

A number of important digital literacy practices associated with the attention economy are emerging. They include practices of managing and distributing attention by filtering information in the manner described in Chapter 2. They also include activities which involve us in getting and giving attention, as when we post, share and comment on content on the internet. Education experts Colin Lankshear and Michele Knobel (2002) review a number of practices associated with getting and giving attention such as 'contact displaying' (wearing eye-catching messages), 'memeing' (spreading ideas), 'scenariating' (describing possible futures), 'attention transacting' (sharing information), 'culture jamming' (spoofing), 'transferring' (linking to popular personalities), and 'framing and encapsulating' (developing attractive conceptual 'angles'). Central to these practices is a need to be original in order to secure the attention of others. As Goldhaber (1997) notes, 'this new economy is based on endless originality, or at least attempts at originality'.

Let's take the practice of 'memeing' as an example. The idea is to attract attention by participating in the creation or distribution of a powerful, original idea, known as a meme. The British biologist Richard Dawkins describes memes like this:

> Examples of memes are tunes, ideas, catch-phrases, clothes fashions, ways of making pots or of building arches. Just as genes propagate themselves in the gene pool by leaping from body to body via sperms or eggs, so memes propagate themselves in the meme pool by leaping from brain to brain via a process which, in the broad sense, can be called imitation. If a scientist hears, or reads about, a good idea, he passes it on to his colleagues and students. He mentions it in his articles and his lectures. If the idea catches on, it can be said to propagate itself, spreading from brain to brain. When you plant a fertile meme in my mind you literally parasitize my brain, turning it into a vehicle for the meme's propagation in just the way that a virus may parasitize the genetic mechanism of a host cell.
>
> (Dawkins 2006: 192)

What Dawkins is saying is that ideas are like genetic characteristics in species and evolve or die out in the same way. Just as biological organisms evolve based on the natural selection of genes, cultures evolve based on the natural selection of memes. So, when we talk about a YouTube video 'going viral', this is what we mean. Ideas become popular, and then become more popular based on the fact that they are popular in the first place, just like search results on Google. Originating a meme, or playing a significant role in its distribution, is one way of attracting attention.

In order to attract attention effectively, one also needs to gain some understanding of how social filters (see Chapter 2) function in focusing and amplifying information and in distributing and drawing people's attention to content. Anthropologist Michael Wesch (2008) describes how a video that he created and uploaded to YouTube 'went viral'. Two days after uploading the video it had 253 views, and the number of views grew exponentially from there. The video appeared in social filtering websites like Digg (http://www.digg.com) and Delicious (http://www.delicious.com). It spread through the blogosphere where its progress was tracked by Technorati, a blog search engine which ranks content. Through this user-generated filtering and user-generated commentary in blogs, the video was exposed to new audiences far beyond the YouTube website where it was originally uploaded. Ultimately, the video became so popular that it was featured on the television news, translated into 12 different languages within a matter of months, and as Wesch says, 'it went all over the world from there'. The video in question is 'Web 2.0 . . . The Machine Is Us/ing Us' (Wesch, 2007) and at the time of writing has over 11 million views.

While digital media have undoubtedly given people the tools with which to attract attention, some are concerned that this is leading people to do 'anything' as long as it gets attention. In the documentary film 'Peep Culture', writer Hal Niedzviecki sets out to understand some of the attention-seeking practices he observes in popular culture (see http://www.thepeepdiaries.com). He becomes a life caster, recording every moment of his life with web cameras set up in fixed locations around his home and broadcasting the video stream to the internet. He goes on a boot camp for reality television hopefuls where he is taught to turn himself into a 'brand', tell his 'story', and 'market' himself for mass-consumption. In light of his experiences, he notes: 'point a camera at us, and we change. The question is, what are we changing into, what are we becoming?'

Case Study 6: Social media

Social media refers to participatory forms of digital media such as blogs, wikis, podcasts, social networking sites, and social bookmarking sites. What these digital tools and technologies have in common is that the content is user-generated and shared in a social environment. Because social media platforms allow individuals to easily create and share content through the internet, they provide us with opportunities to get and give attention. In other words, they provide us with the means to participate in the attention economy. Not just individuals, but commercial brands as well are eagerly adopting social media in an effort to get people's attention. However, for these marketing campaigns to succeed, a new approach has to be adopted, one that treats promotions in social media as different from traditional media advertisements.

Here we will examine the social media platform Twitter (http://twitter.com) and identify literacy practices that involve getting and giving attention. Twitter is a micro-blogging service which was launched in 2006 (see Chapter 5). It allows you to share information in the form of short posts (called 'tweets') up to 140 characters in length. The original interface asked users to answer the question 'What are you doing?' though at the time of writing this has been replaced with the question 'What's happening?'

When you post a tweet, it is usually (depending on privacy settings) published to the internet, as well as being broadcast to your 'followers', i.e. the users in your network who have subscribed to your tweets.

People tend to tweet about whatever has their attention at the time: from everyday occurrences ('coffee!') to brief observations about issues of interest. This practice of tweeting has been criticized by those who feel that such brief, superficial communications erode people's attention spans, discouraging meaningful engagement with a topic. However, tweets are often linked to other, richer media like blog posts, YouTube videos, or news items.

The frequent exchange of short status updates in tweets allows people to be in **perpetual contact** (Joinson, 2008), continuously aware of what their friends and contacts are doing. Whether this kind of perpetual, always-on contact is desirable is again a matter for debate. As pointed out at the beginning of this chapter, participating in social media can lead to a need to pay 'continuous partial attention' in an effort not to miss anything (Stone, n.d.). This can in turn contribute to an artificial sense of constant crisis.

No doubt this sense of constant crisis is only heightened by the huge volume of data generated in social media sites like Twitter. The Twitter blog reported that in March 2011, there were on average 1 billion tweets sent per week, and the number of tweets sent in a single day on March 11, 2011 was 177 million (@twitter 2011). Obviously, the sheer number of tweets generated by all of your contacts can create a drain on limited resources of attention, very similar to the problem of information overload discussed in Chapter 2. As a result, we have to learn new strategies for distributing our attention, and adopt appropriate attention structures.

One strategy is to pay selective attention to just a portion of the data generated. Some people find it helpful to think of Twitter as a stream of data to occasionally dip into, rather than as a series of communications that must be read and processed. Technological tools can also be used to focus attention where it is most needed. For instance, a Twitter client like TweetDeck allows you to visually sort tweets into columns based on (for example) social group or topic, and this in turn reduces the effort needed to scan the feed (see also Chapter 2 on filtering information).

One social practice that has developed in order to facilitate this kind of selective attention is the practice of tagging tweets with '**hashtags**' which use the '#' key and a descriptive tag. For example, an educator could add the text '#edchat' to indicate that the tweet is relevant to education issues (similar to the process of social tagging, described in Chapter 2). Other educators can, if they want, pay selective attention by filtering tweets based on a search for the hashtag. The practice also benefits the sender of the tweet by drawing the attention of a particular community (in our example, the community of educators who use the #edchat tag). In other words, hashtags can be used to strategically get and give attention.

As we've explained, the form of one-to-many communication in Twitter allows users to broadcast to a potentially very large audience. If you are skillful, you can use your tweets to create the illusion of individual attention to members of this group, what Michael Goldhaber calls giving 'illusory attention'. The challenge here is to write the tweets in such a way that your followers feel personally touched, even though they realize that the tweets are being broadcast to large numbers of others. Twitter is sometimes used in this way by well-known individuals like celebrities, sports stars, and politicians. With relatively little effort these individuals can now maintain a new channel of communication with their fans and supporters, using their tweets to create the illusion of proximity and attention.

However, using Twitter solely as a broadcast channel in this way tends to be frowned upon by the user community. As well as broadcasting your tweets, you are expected to interact with others in ways that give them genuine individual attention. One way to give individual attention is by 'following' individuals. If you decide to 'follow' an individual, you subscribe to their tweets. That individual will be notified that you are following them and can decide to reciprocate your attention, by following you back. Sometimes, people follow others in order to gain more followers, in the hope that by giving attention to others they can attract more attention for themselves.

Another practice that has emerged as a way of giving individual attention is the practice of '@replies'. In essence, this is a tweet that replies to another tweet. To send a reply, you use the '@' symbol and username of the originator of the tweet (e.g., '@cahafner'). This kind of tweet appears in your public timeline visible to all, so it can serve to draw attention to your addressee. In addition, other users can get an idea of how often you broadcast, how often you reply, and might use that information when they decide whether or not to follow you. Another, more private channel for giving individual attention in Twitter is 'direct messaging'. A direct message ('dm') does not appear in your public timeline the way a reply does, and can only be read by the receiver of the message.

As well as giving attention in the various ways described above, Twitter provides those who participate with an opportunity to get attention. The amount of attention that you are getting can most easily be measured in the number of followers that you have. For example, at the time of writing, Lady Gaga has 8,856,896 followers and is following 144,274 users. Obviously, her real-world popularity carries over into the 'twittersphere'. For ordinary people, attracting a similar amount of attention would be difficult: it is a question of somehow standing out from the crowd. Thus, Goldhaber (1997) suggests that in an attention economy, the need to attract attention translates into a need to be original.

This case study shows how the literacy practices that have evolved in Twitter can be interpreted in terms of the attention that people give and get. Twitter provides a powerful means for us to participate in the attention economy and seek attention for ourselves. However, to succeed in promoting ourselves with a social media tool like Twitter, we have to develop new ways of thinking about promotion. Where in the past, broadcasting might have been an appropriate strategy, we now need to think about how to engage others in an exchange that involves both getting and giving attention.

Activity 6.2: Getting and giving attention with digital media

A. ATTENTION ONLINE

As we said above, apart from placing demands on how we manage and distribute our attention, digital media and the internet also provide tools for us to get and give attention. For example, web 2.0 platforms like blogs and social media tools like Twitter allow us to get attention by posting information about our own activities, and give attention by commenting on the activities of others. But with the vast amounts of information out there, what can we do to make sure people pay attention to the information that we post ourselves? The following list summarizes some possible suggestions, taken from various sources on the internet:

- Do something cool and/or stupid;
- Be controversial;
- Interview cool people;
- Post pictures and video;
- Give your work a great title;
- Write a guest post for a large blog;
- Leave comments on relevant blogs or social media channels;
- Create a poll.

Search the internet for examples of the above strategies. How effective do you think they are? Which strategies would be most likely to get your attention? Which would you be most likely to use? Can you find examples of other kinds of strategies?

B. ATTENTION IN ONLINE DATING

One place where people are especially concerned with getting attention is on online dating sites, where they often try to compose their profiles in such a way as to attract a potential romantic partner. Go to an online dating site like OKCupid or Match.com and look at some of the profiles people have left there. What strategies do they use to make their profiles unique and attract the attention of other users? Do you think people use different strategies to attract different kinds of people?

Useful links:
- http://www.okcupid.com/match?fromWhoOnline=1anddiscard_prefs=1anduse_prefs=1
- http://www.match.com/search/index.aspx?lid=2

C. ATTENTION IN SOCIAL MEDIA

Choose a social media site that you have used before (such as YouTube, Digg, Facebook, Twitter or Google +). What tools does the site make available to people to efficiently distribute their attention by filtering data? What tools does the site make available for helping people attract the attention of others?

CONCLUSION

In this chapter we have approached the concept of attention from two distinct vantage points. First, we considered the way in which computer-mediated activities, such as video games and online chat, foster polyfocal attention structures. These attention structures can be understood as distributed among historical bodies (you and your mind), discourses in place (texts and tools) and interaction orders (your relationships). Second, we pointed out that the deluge of information which we are experiencing in the digital age leads to a scarcity of the human resource of attention. We described the emergent attention economy and how this economy promotes different ways of thinking. In this new economy, originality and other literacy practices of strategically managing, getting and giving attention take on great importance. Of course, getting and giving attention is never an ideologically neutral activity: behind the content that consumes our attention are people or organizations whose motives we must evaluate in a critical manner. The need to develop a critical stance towards digital tools and the content of the messages we receive through them is the topic of the next chapter.

USEFUL RESOURCES

Print

Appelbaum, S. H., Marchionni, A., and Fernandez, A. (2008). The multitasking paradox: Perceptions, problems and strategies. *Management Decision, 46* (9): 1313–1325.

DeCastell, S., and Jenson, J. (2004). Paying attention to attention: New economies for learning. *Educational Theory 54* (4): 381–397.

Jones, R. H. (2010). Cyberspace and physical space: Attention structures in computer-mediated communication. In A. Jaworski and C. Thurlow (eds.) *Semiotic landscapes: Text, image, space.* London: Continuum, 151–167.

Lanham, R. A. (2006). *The economics of attention: Style and substance in the age of information.* Chicago: University of Chicago Press.

Lankshear, C., and Knobel, M. (2002). Do we have your attention? New literacies, digital technologies, and the education of adolescents. In D. Alvermann (ed.) *Adolescents and literacies in a digital world.* New York: Peter Lang, 19–39.

Web

Goldhaber, Michael H., The attention economy and the net.
http://firstmonday.org/article/view/519/440

The Globe and Mail, Hal Niedzviecki gets deep into the peep culture
http://www.theglobeandmail.com/news/arts/television/hal-niedzviecki-gets-into-the-peep-culture/article1906669/

Linda Stone, Continuous partial attention.
http://lindastone.net/qa/continuous-partial-attention/

Video

Michael Wesch, A vision of students today
http://youtu.be/dGCJ46vyR9o

Frontline, digital nation: Life on the virtual frontier
http://www.pbs.org/wgbh/pages/frontline/digitalnation/view/

Peepculture
http://youtu.be/yf59ckL5FZI

CHAPTER 7

Critical Literacy

So far we have focused on various affordances and constraints of digital media and explored how these affect the ways people do things, make meanings, manage their relationships with others, construct their identities and think. In this chapter we will take a more critical stance towards digital technologies, attempting to discover how these affordances and constraints embed particular **ideologies** and the agendas of particular people or groups. The word 'critical' as we are using it here doesn't mean that you need to find fault with digital media or the practices people engage in with it. What we really mean by a critical stance is a *conscious* stance – a stance that puts you in the position to 'interrogate' the ideologies and agendas promoted in the texts that you encounter via digital media and by digital media themselves.

TECHNOLOGY AND IDEOLOGY

Ideologies are systems of ideas, practices and social relationships that govern what is considered right or wrong, good or bad, and normal or abnormal. These systems are extremely powerful. They can determine which people in a society are included and which are marginalized, who has power and who doesn't, and how wealth and other resources are distributed. The problem with ideologies is not that they are necessarily bad, but that most people are unconscious of them, taking the particular ideology they subscribe to as the 'truth' rather than simply as one of many possible 'versions of reality'. As a result, it is difficult for them to question the assumptions of their own ideology.

One place where we can see ideology at work is in the way people talk about digital media. As we mentioned at the beginning of this book, many people are upset about digital technologies and the new kinds of literacy practices associated with them. They are afraid these technologies are affecting our minds and our relationships in negative ways and point as evidence to things like cyber-bullying, internet 'addiction', the erosion of personal privacy, the supposed deterioration of our language (see Chapter 5), and the apparent shortening of our attention spans (see Chapter 6).

As we said in the first chapter, the introduction of new media has always made people uncomfortable, but their worries often turn out to be unfounded. At the same time, it is important not to dismiss concerns about the effects of technology out of hand. Many of them are based on legitimate concerns that are supported by scientific evidence. The trick is to separate the reasonable arguments from those based on emotion and exaggeration.

It is also important to remember that sceptics of digital technologies are not the only ones that trade in emotion and exaggeration. Those who uncritically extol the supposedly positive effects of digital media are equally guilty.

The writer Evgeny Morozov, author of *The Net Delusion* (2011), for example, talks about the way the Western media portrayed the 'dramatic' role of Twitter and other social networking sites (see Chapter 10) in the Iranian protests of June 2009. The problem with this portrayal, claims Morozov, is that it was probably wildly exaggerated. Most of the 'tweets' about the protests, he points out, came from outside of the country rather than inside of it and there is no strong evidence that digital social networking (as opposed to old-fashioned word of mouth) played a significant role in the organization of the protests. Finally, he reminds us that, whether or not digital media played a role, the revolution was *not* successful – the government of President Mahmoud Ahmadinejad not only retained power, but itself harnessed the power of the internet and social networking sites to round up critics and encourage citizens to inform on dissidents.

The main problem with both digital sceptics and digital utopians is that they often focus on the technology itself without paying enough attention to the social contexts in which it is used and the intentions of those who use it. This position is known as techno-logical determinism, a belief that technology controls people's thoughts and behaviour. The opposite of this position is one which argues that technology is ideologically neutral and that people can do whatever they want with it. This position is equally problematic. The position we have been taking in this book is that the truth lies somewhere between these two extremes, and the first step to taking a critical stance towards digital media is to understand *both* the potential for technology to control us and our potential to exercise control over technology.

MEDIATION

In the first chapter we introduced the concept of *mediation* as the foundation of our approach to digital literacies. All human actions, we pointed out, are *mediated* through tools, either technological tools, like telephones and computers, or symbolic tools like languages and other semiotic systems. The crux of the concept of *mediation* is that we cannot interact with the world without doing it though some kind of *medium*, and the media that we use play an important role in determining how we perceive the world and the actions we can take. And so part of *mediation* has to do with how we are to some degree 'controlled' by the tools that are available to us to take action.

There are at least four ways that media can exert control over us. The first is through what we have been calling *affordances* and *constraints*. Different tools make some actions more possible and other actions less possible. They reveal certain aspects of reality and conceal others. They amplify participation in certain kinds of social practices and social groups, and constrain participation in others. In the last five chapters we have given examples of the affordances and constraints of various tools from hypertext to digital video. In the chapters in this section we have sometimes emphasized the affordances over the constraints. This is a natural reaction to any new technology – people tend to be more focused on the new things it enables them to do rather than the limitations it might impose. Taking a critical stance towards media means being just as conscious of what they *do not* allow us to do as what they do allow us to do.

The second way media exert control over us is through the social conventions that grow up around their use. The way particular tools get used is not just a matter of what we *can* do with them, but also of the ways people have used them in the past. All tools carry the history of their past use. After people have used a particular tool in certain ways to perform a particular practice for a period of time, the conventions or 'social rules' that have grown up around the tool and the practice become 'solid'. We call the process by which social practices and conventions come to 'solidify' around various technologies the **technologization of practice** (Jones 2002). The technologization of practice often leads to situations in which, directly or indirectly, the way certain things are done comes to be controlled by the dominant technologies that we use to do them.

The third way media exert control over us is through who has access to them. The distribution of tools, both technological and symbolic, in any society is always unequal. What this means is that the kinds of actions that media make possible are always only available to certain people. In other words, the use of mediational means is always tied up with economic and political systems that govern the way access to them is distributed. As a result, the ways media end up being used usually support or perpetuate these political and economic systems.

Finally, media exert control over us through how easy or difficult they are for us to use. All tools require that people learn how to use them. Some require a great deal of time and energy to learn how to use, while others are much simpler. Media that are extremely easy to use can exert control over us by encouraging us to regard them and the actions they make possible as 'natural'. Media that are more demanding exert control by requiring us to make a 'commitment' to them. The more time and energy you devote to mastering a particular tool, the more likely you are to regard the kinds of actions that that tool makes possible as valuable.

The longer we use some technologies, the harder it becomes for us to get along without them or to switch to competing technologies, either because we have organized so many of our activities around the affordances of these technologies or because so many of our friends use them that abandoning them might result in social isolation. The phenomenon by which technologies make it progressively difficult for us to separate ourselves from them is called **lock-in**. One good example of lock-in can be seen in online video game servers which ensure that owners of a particular system can only play with other owners of that system: PlayStation gamers, for instance, can only play with other PlayStation gamers and only Xbox gamers can play together. When you buy a PlayStation, you become 'locked-in' to playing with other people who have this platform, then after a while the costs of switching to an Xbox become too high, not just because of all the games you have paid for, but also because you have developed relationships with other people using your system.

Fortunately, the way media exert control over us is only half the story of mediation. Mediation also involves human agency. While media exert considerable control over what we can do with them, we also exert control over how we use media. There are at least four ways that we can exert control over the media that we use.

The first has to do with our ability to choose (or **appropriate**) the media we use. Even though we may feel we are locked in to particular media choices, there are often alternative choices available. We might choose a free open source software (see below) over a proprietary one, or an academic database instead of Google. The second way we can control media is by finding new ways to use them, which may not have been intended by their designers – that is, by **adapting** them to fit our own purposes. Facebook, for example, can be used to share personal information with our friends (and with Facebook's advertisers), or it can be adapted to do other things like mobilize people to protest Facebook's privacy settings and terms of use.

The third way we can control media is by actually changing or **modifying** ('modding') them in sometimes small but significant ways to make them more suitable for our purposes, a practice which, as we will see in Chapter 9, is common among computer gamers. Finally, the fourth way we can control media is by **mixing** two or more tools together such that the constraints of one tool are cancelled out by the affordances of another, opening up actions which neither of the tools alone could have made possible, as people do when they create remixes and mashups.

We will refer to these four ways we can control media – appropriating, adapting, modifying and mixing – as hacking. Often when people think of 'hackers' they think of cybercriminals who break into other people's computers and alter or steal data, but our use of the term harkens back to the 'hacker culture' of the early days of the internet (The Mentor, 1986). In this sense, the word 'hacker' refers to expert computer programmers, who get satisfaction from exploring the limits of programmable systems. For our purposes, what we mean by hacking is simply taking control of media and appropriating, adapting, modifying or mixing it in creative ways rather than simply going along with the agendas of those who manufactured or control the use or distribution of the media we are using.

The process of mediation, then, is not just a matter of media controlling people or people controlling media. It is a matter of the *tension* between what technology wants us to do and what we want to do with it, between the limitations it imposes on us and our ability to get around these limitations by 'hacking' it.

Media become *ideological* when they become resistant to hacking, that is, when the affordances and constraints they embody are presented as 'just the way things are' rather than as 'workable' and adaptable. They do this in two ways. One way is by becoming **transparent**, encouraging us to forget that they are standing between us and reality (Bolter and Grusin, 1999). Transparent media encourage us to regard the kinds of actions that they make possible as 'natural' or desirable and the kinds of actions that they constrain as unnatural or undesirable. Technologies tend to become more transparent to us the more we use them. A person writing with a pen, for example, is apt to forget that the pen is actually coming between him or her and the words that are appearing on the page. They think *they* are writing and forget the pen altogether. Similarly, a person chatting with a friend online may momentarily forget the mediational means and feel like he or she is communicating 'directly' with the other person.

There are, of course, a lot of apparent advantages to media transparency. The more transparent a mediational means is, the more comfortable and convenient it is for us to use. But at the same time, the more invisible its built-in limitations are to us, the more difficult it becomes for us to question those limitations. Transparent tools are resistant to hacking because they make us forget that they are even there. Many marketers of media technologies extol the value of media transparency. When Apple first released its iPad, for example, it advertised it with the assertion: 'Technology is at its best when it feels completely natural, almost like there's no technology at all'. From the point of view of critical literacy, too much media transparency is inherently dangerous because it makes us less conscious that what we are experiencing is mediated.

The second way technology becomes resistant to hacking is by becoming **opaque**. When something becomes opaque, we are unable to understand it fully; unable to figure out how it works. Despite the increased access to information made possible by digital media, very few people know much about how the technologies they use on a day-to-day basis actually work. In his book *Program or Be Programmed* (2010), the author Douglas Rushkoff points out the irony that fewer children nowadays learn computer programming than did thirty years ago. At the same time, many technologies themselves seem designed to prevent users from learning how to re-program them.

A system that does not allow anybody apart from the technology manufacturer or those with whom it has agreements to alter it in any way and usually requires that users purchase a particular device to run particular software is called a **closed system**. Apple Corporation's devices and software are examples of closed system technologies. Users cannot run their software on any devices other than those manufactured by Apple and they cannot repro-gram these devices. Microsoft's Windows and Google's Android are examples of more **open systems** which can be run on different devices, though these systems are still licensed by the manufacturers. An example of a truly open system technology is Linux, an **open source** operating system whose code is publically available to anyone who wants to change it.

The more closed a system is, the more opaque the technologies within it become. Technologies are opaque when we can't open them up and see what's inside and when the code for the software or the algorithm for the search engine is kept secret from us. Of course there are often good reasons for media opacity having to do with intellectual property, the ability of technology companies to earn money, and the protection of other people who are also using the technology. Sometimes people who hack media have less than honourable intentions (which is one reason why the whole idea of hacking has gotten a bad name). Systems that are completely open make it difficult to maintain quality and are more vulnerable to abusive practices. Systems that are totally closed, on the other hand, lock people in to certain ways of behaving and thinking and discourage innovation.

It is important to remember that what we mean by transparency is not that we can see 'inside' of something, but that we 'see through it' and forget that it's there, and what we mean by opacity is not that something becomes obtrusive or obvious, but that it becomes resistant to adaptation and modification.

And so, opacity and transparency, the way we are using the terms here, are *not oppo-sites*. In fact, the ironic thing about digital media is that transparency and opacity often go hand in hand. The more transparent a technology becomes, the less likely it is for us to understand how it works. Transparency makes the effects of media less apparent to us and discourages us from critically examining them, and opacity makes it more difficult for us to critically examine them, even if we want to.

Activity 7.1: Your experience with technology

A. TRANSPARENCY AND OPACITY

List the media that you use on a daily basis (including both hardware like mobile phones and software interfaces like Facebook) and rate them according to their *transparency* (how 'natural' they feel to use) (10 = very transparent, 1 = not at all transparent) and their *opacity* (how difficult it is to understand and alter their 'inner workings') (10 = very opaque, 1 = not at all opaque). Talk about the reasons why you rated these media the way you did and discuss the degree to which the transparency and opacity of media affect how much control you have over what you can do with them.

B. LOOKING FOR LIMITATIONS

As we have said, whereas the affordances of technological tools are often obvious to us (usually because manufacturers of those tools spend a lot of money communicating those affordances to us), sometimes the ways these technologies limit our abilities to take certain actions or engage in certain social practices is not so obvious. Choose one of the media you considered above and list the kinds of social actions, social practices, social relationships and social identities that this tool makes it *more difficult* for you to participate in.

C. ARE YOU A HACKER?

Think of some instance where you have selectively appropriated, adapted, modified or mixed technologies in order to get around their limitations or do something new with them. Describe how you did this and how it altered your relationship with these technologies.

IDEOLOGY AND THE TECHNOLOGY OF LANGUAGE

When it comes to developing critical literacy with digital technology, a good place to start is by practising it first with the analogue technology of language. Like digital media, the medium of language also tends towards transparency and opacity. We are rarely aware of language as a mediator of meaning. Instead we tend to think that we are communicating with people directly. Thus, certain ways of constructing reality with language come to be taken for granted by us, considered 'natural' or 'normal'. Furthermore, most of us are just as unaware of how language actually works to create meaning and promote ideology as we are of the workings of our personal computer or smartphone.

Anytime a person uses a semiotic system like language to make meaning they always have an *agenda*. We produce texts in order to get things done – whether that means achieving some kind of material gain, fulfilling an obligation to someone, or making someone do something or believe something. We judge how successful our texts are by how well they help us to realize our agendas. The first question to ask whenever we encounter a text is what the agenda of the person or people who produced this text is.

This is not always an easy question to answer because people are often not completely straightforward about their true intentions when they produce texts, and sometimes they even try to hide them. Sometimes it's even difficult to find out who produced a text in the first place. The text may come from an institution or group (like a company or a government) rather than an individual, or the source of the text may be a complete mystery to us. However, we can never really critically assess a text unless we have some idea about 1) who produced the text and 2) what their agenda might be.

The second important thing about language is that it is *never* 'objective'. That is to say, the 'reality' that texts depict is never 'true' reality – it is always a matter of selection, a particular 'version' of reality. We depict reality by using various words that represent *things* and *actions*. Language is basically a 'filter' (see Chapter 2) – a system of inclusion and exclusion: whenever we choose to include or emphasize one thing in our version of reality, we are also choosing to exclude or downplay something else. When we refer to the World Wide Web as 'an information superhighway', for example, we emphasize the role of the web in the exchange of information and commerce and deemphasize the role the web plays in social interaction or entertainment.

The versions of reality that we construct with our language are not just a matter of the words we choose, but also how we choose to connect up these words to form **proposi- tions** – statements about the world and how it works. The function of language in forming propositions is called the **ideational function** of language because it allows us to express our ideas about reality. We might, for example, attempt to construct propositions by assert- ing various kinds of 'logical relationships' like those discussed in Chapter 3 (e.g., part/whole, cause/effect) between things and/or actions. The problem is that these 'logical connec- tions' are not always entirely logical. For example, in an article entitled 'The Internet Helps Build Democracies' published in *Newsweek* on April 30, 2010, the authors wrote:

> The revolts in Ukraine, Kyrgyzstan, Lebanon, Burma, Xinjiang, and Iran could never have happened without the web.

The main problem with this sentence is that, although it seems to establish a cause and effect relationship, this relationship is neither logical nor scientifically verifiable. It is impos- sible to either prove or disprove. Since the web *did* exist and *did* apparently play some role in these revolts, we have no way of knowing if they would have occurred without the web. Another problem with this statement is that it confounds *association* with *causation*: just because the people involved in these revolts were using the internet does not mean that their internet use caused the revolts or even that it contributed to the revolts in any signifi- cant way.

Just because somebody constructs a proposition doesn't mean we have to accept it as the truth. There are, however, a number of linguistic tricks that people use to make their propositions more 'natural'-seeming (transparent) and more difficult to question (opaque). One of the most powerful is called **presupposition**. Presupposition is when, rather than asserting something directly, writers or speakers treat certain propositions as 'given'. When Steve Jobs, for example, said of the iPad, 'It is the best browsing experience you've ever had,' he was making a couple of assumptions: first, that the 'browsing experience' you have had in the past is somehow 'defective' or 'inferior' compared to the one you will have with his product (an assumption he made without much information about your particular past experiences with browsing); and second, that what makes a browsing experience positive is the *technology* that you use rather than the *content* that you access. This last proposition, though debatable, is very difficult to question since it is hidden deeply inside the bigger proposition about your browsing experience.

Texts promote ideologies not just through how they represent the world, but also through how they represent relationships between people, what linguists call the **interper- sonal function** of language. They do this in many different ways, one way being through adopting certain genres or styles of writing or speaking. Different kinds of texts create different kinds of relationships between their producers and the people who read them. Some kinds of texts make it easy for the reader to disagree with or debate the writer, whereas others make it almost impossible. A legal notice, for example, puts the reader in a different kind of position vis-à-vis the writer and the text than an online advice column.

One of the points we made in Chapter 3 was that web 2.0 has introduced new ways for people to 'talk back' to writers by commenting on the text, adding to the text, or even changing the text. Different tools, however, differ dramatically in the amount of power they give to readers. Blogs, for example, might allow readers to comment on what they have read, but don't have the capacity of other tools like wikis (see Chapter 11) to allow readers to alter the actual text that they have read.

Furthermore, writers can create a relationship with readers through the kind of language they use. Texts written in an informal style often create a sense of intimacy, whereas texts written in a formal style create a sense of distance. In the example above, when Steve Jobs said that the iPad is 'the best browsing experience you've ever had', he created a sense of closeness with the reader by addressing him or her directly and by using informal language ('you've').

Finally, authors of texts create relationships with their readers by adopting certain kinds of identities, projecting certain kinds of identities on to the reader, and portraying what they are doing in a certain way. For example, you might be more receptive to an opinion about a new technology product if it appears in the context of a news story or a customer review than if it appears in an advertisement. This is why technology companies spend so much money on public relations campaigns designed to get journalists and customers to express positive opinions about their products in the context of news stories and reviews.

Activity 7.2: Analyzing texts

Analyze the following two texts using the questions below as guidelines. (The URLs provided are for both the original locations of the texts and their locations in the internet archive: **http://waybackmachine.org**)

Text 1
'iPad: A magical revolutionary product at an unbelievable price', by Apple Corp (http://www.apple.com/ipad/)
(Archived at http://web.archive.org/web/20101211014634/http://www.apple.com/ipad/)

Text 2
'Why I won't buy an iPad and think that you shouldn't either' by Cory Doctorow (http://boingboing.net/2010/04/02/why-i-wont-buy-an-ipad-and-think-you-shouldnt-either.html)

(Archived at http://web.archive.org/web/20101206055212/http://boingboing.net/2010/04/02/why-i-wont-buy-an-ipad-and-think-you-shouldnt-either.html)

1. What is the source of the text? Who produced it? Is the author an individual or an institution? What is the 'agenda' of the people who produced the text? What

opportunities do you have to comment on the text or communicate with the producer?
2. How does the text construct a version of reality? What *things* and *actions* are included and excluded? How are these things and actions characterized?
3. What kinds of *propositions* does the text contain? Are these propositions logical or verifiable?
4. How does the text use presupposition to make meanings seem more 'natural'?
5. What kinds of social relationships are constructed by the text through things like genre and style? What identities do the authors construct for themselves and their readers?

IDEOLOGY AND DIGITAL TECHNOLOGIES

Just as texts promote certain versions of reality and certain social relationships and identities as 'natural' or desirable, so do media, and they often do so using similar kinds of techniques as those we have pointed out in texts.

Like texts, media are never 'objective'. They always promote a particular version of reality through the choices they require users to make, choices which, in the case of digital media, are often expressed in terms of drop-down menus or 'preference' settings. While the word 'preference' gives the illusion that the media can be truly personalized, this is rarely the case. The choices we are presented with always instantiate systems of inclusion and exclusion, which limit the kinds of actions we can take and the kinds of meanings we can make.

Perhaps the main difference between digital technologies and earlier analogue technologies lies in the nature of the choices they make available to us. While digital technologies seem to make more choices available to us, sometimes dizzying in number, these choices are always expressed as discrete alternatives. We are not, as we are with many analogue technologies, able to invent our own choices by creating fine gradations of meaning which we can control ourselves. Even when it seems we can move along a continuum of, say, brightness or volume, the underlying mechanism is always governed by a predefined set of alternatives.

The semiotician and jazz pianist Theo van Leeuwen (2012) pointed this out in a comparison of what it's like to play a digital piano as opposed to an analogue one. He writes:

On a modern digital piano I cannot do what Billie Holiday did with her voice, or what I can even do, to some extent, on an acoustic piano. I cannot make the sound rougher or tenser as I play. Instead the designers of the instrument have provided me with a choice from a wide range of piano sounds, some tenser, some mellower, some higher, some lower, some smoother, some rougher (in a synthetic kind of way) and so on. All I can do myself is phrasing.

Furthermore, these fixed systems of inclusion and exclusion can become 'locked-in' in ways that they affect the development of later technologies. Jaron Lanier (2010), author of *You Are Not a Gadget*, for example, relates the story of how the MIDI format, which was developed in the 1980s to digitally represent the sounds of a keyboard, has become the foundational technology for all digital music, including the mp3 files most people listen to today. The problem with this, he argues, is that, while it is good at representing the sounds of a keyboard, it is less accurate when it comes to representing the sounds of other instruments like the violin or the human voice. Unfortunately, this format has become such an integral part of digital music systems that it is too difficult to change it. 'Software' writes Lanier (2010: 1), 'expresses ideas about everything from the nature of a musical note to the nature of personhood . . . (it) is also subject to an exceptionally rigid process of "lock-in." Therefore, ideas (in the present era, when human affairs are increasingly software driven) have become more subject to lock-in than in previous eras'.

Not only do technologies impose upon reality systems of inclusion and exclusion based on the limited number of choices they make available, but, like texts, they sometimes present these choices as 'givens' (presuppositions) – that is, they make certain choices seem 'normal' and others seem unusual. Most software programs, for example, present users with a series of 'default settings', which inevitably influence their perceptions of normalcy and deviance. No matter how much the palette of choices is expanded, giving the impression of freedom, default settings always steer users towards a certain set of normative behaviours and normative meanings.

Most programs go even further, building in things like 'wizards', 'templates', and 'themes' which instruct users not just about design choices but also about the kinds of social contexts in which the technology is meant to be used and the kinds of social actions it is meant to be used to perform. Apple's iMovie, for example, offers themes like 'Photo Album', 'Comic Book', 'Scrapbook' and 'Film Strip', each with different kinds of title pages and transitions. Such prefabricated templates are not just there to make it easier to use the software but to *create* the contexts in which users are expected to make movies. iMovie asks its users to use it to 'have fun' and 'share memories' with friends and relatives. It doesn't invite them to make probing documentaries or film noir features.

Another way systems of inclusion and exclusion can limit our perception of the world is through the various ways technology 'filters' the data that is available to us. Google's Page Rank algorithm, for example, promotes the proposition that the value of a piece of data is best determined by how popular it is. Perhaps the most insidious ideological filters are those that shape our view of reality based on the view of reality that we already have. Examples of such filters are Google's personalized search (see Chapter 2) and the EdgeRank algorithm in Facebook, which pushes status updates and news about the friends you most frequently interact with to the top of your News Feed. The danger of such filters is that we end up essentially 'brainwashing ourselves' by limiting what we are exposed to based on our past preferences. In his book, *The Filter Bubble: What the Internet Is Hiding From You* (2011), Eli Pariser, describes the problems associated with personalized filters in the following way:

> With Google personalized for everyone, the query 'stem cells' might produce diametrically opposed results for scientists who support stem cell research and activists who oppose it. 'Proof of climate change' might turn up different results for an environmental activist and an oil company executive. In polls a huge majority of us assume that search engines are unbiased. But that may be because they are increasingly biased to share our own views.
> (2)

Finally, like texts, technologies always create particular relationships between users and producers of the technologies and between users and other users. A good example of this is Microsoft PowerPoint, which has become a fixture in many classrooms and lecture halls. While there are obvious advantages to using PowerPoint to present information, there are also biases built into the software in terms of the kinds of meanings and the kinds of social relationships that it promotes. Not only does the program encourage users to express ideas (and conceive of problems) in terms of bulleted hierarchical lists, excluding other ways of thinking, it also promotes a certain kind of power relationship between teachers and students. Although it is possible for teachers and students to have discussions in the context of a PowerPoint presentation, the way the technology is designed to be used discourages interaction. Furthermore, because the person manipulating the slideshow has access to more modes of communication than the person watching, it is more difficult for audience members to question or challenge the presenter. Embedded within these affordances and constraints is a certain *ideology* of education, one which conceives of education as a matter of presenting authoritative information in the form of discrete, 'digestible' bits, rather than a matter of encouraging inquiry and debate.

One problem with the way technologies promote certain kinds of social relationships is that the nature and purpose of these relationships are not always obvious and straightforward. Perhaps the best example of this is Facebook. The default relationship with Facebook 'friends' is to disclose as much information as possible to them. Although the interface allows these 'default settings' to be modified, the technology itself and the applications associated with it encourage greater and greater disclosure from users, which, given Facebook's business model of selling user information to advertisers in aggregated form, is good for the company.

While Facebook is in the business of encouraging users to make their relationships with other users as visible as possible, the relationship Facebook itself has with its users is rather ambiguous. On the one hand, they are providing a service, making their users their customers, but on the other hand, they are selling information about and access to their users to advertisers, making their users their *product*.

Learning how to use technological tools, then, involves not just mastering the range of choices they present, but also being indoctrinated into the social practices that have come to be *technologized* around these tools. The range of actions these tools make available not only determine how people behave and communicate with each other, but they also end up promoting particular versions of reality and making some kinds of social relationships more possible and others less possible.

Case study 7: Protecting children online

A good example of how different technological tools can promote different ideologies can be see in the design of massively multiplayer online games (MMOGs) for young children. MMOGs are digital games that you can play with a large number of other players on the internet.

Typically, the designers of such games as well as the parents of children who play them share the belief that children require protection in online settings from unwanted online interactions, such as those associated with cyber-bullies or online predators. In order to provide a safe environment, game designers provide tools that structure interaction in particular ways, and thereby promote particular beliefs about how to keep children safe.

In order to illustrate these points, we will consider three browser-based, cartoon-style MMOGs designed for children: *Poptropica* (by Pearson Education), *Moshi Monsters* (by Mind Candy) and *Club Penguin* (by Disney). All of these games are aimed at young children and have information for parents prominently linked from their home pages. Online safety for players is explicitly addressed in all three games and is clearly perceived as an important value by the game designers. What is interesting is the different ways that designers promote this value through the affordances and constraints of the communication tools they make available in their games, and how these affordances and constraints create different 'versions' of what does or does not constitute 'safety'.

The first game, *Poptropica*, is an adventure game consisting of a number of islands which players can visit. Each island is a different virtual world with its own puzzle-like adventure for players to solve. Players can also visit 'common' or 'multiverse' rooms and play a range of mini-games against other players. In these common rooms synchronous interaction with other players is possible, using a 'pre-scripted chat' system that provides players with a limited number of questions and answers. For example: 'Are you good at soccer?'; 'I am ok at it'.

Because the chat is pre-scripted in this way, the range of topics that can be explored by players is limited. This constraint on chat means that 'unsafe' conversations are technically impossible. As the developers note in the FAQ: 'There is purposely no free chat in *Poptropica* in order to make our virtual world as safe as possible for kids' (http://www.poptropica.com/Poptropica-FAQ.html). The particular choice of design in *Poptropica* reflects the belief that an effective way to provide protection for children is to greatly restrict the number of possible actions that they can take and topics they can discuss.

The second game, *Moshi Monsters*, is a social game in which players adopt and look after a pet monster. They interact with the monster by feeding it, playing with it and customizing the room that it lives in. They can also play mini-games to earn points so that they can visit shops in the virtual world and buy items for their monsters. In this game, players can interact with other players by adding each other to their buddy list. Once they have buddies, they receive 'news' about their buddies' actions and achievements, in the form of a non-interactive list of automatically generated status updates. In addition, they can visit their buddies' rooms and leave a note on their buddies' pinboards, a form of asynchronous messaging. Finally, they can connect with other players by posting comments to a community forum on the site.

Unlike *Poptropica*, the communication tools in *Moshi Monsters* are not pre-scripted, allowing users to compose freely. However, as asynchronous tools, the pinboard and forum systems are also constrained – the proximity of such asynchronous tools is lower than that of synchronous chat, and so it is possible that this reduced proximity discourages undesirable behaviour. Nevertheless, additional monitoring is necessary to promote a respectful online culture. This takes the form of a filtering system for pinboard posts and self-policing tools throughout the site, which allow players to flag content for a moderator to review (see http://www.moshimonsters.com/parents). The choice of communication tools here reflects a subtly different ideology about online safety for children, one which aims to promote 'safety' by monitoring interaction rather than restricting it.

The third game, *Club Penguin*, is another social game. Players are penguins in an icy virtual world where they can interact with other players and play a range of mini-games. Out of the three games, *Club Penguin* is the one that makes synchronous interaction with others the easiest. It is possible to interact through synchronous chat with any other player anywhere in the virtual world. Chat can be either pre-scripted or free, but the default selection is free synchronous chat and changing this setting requires a separate parent account.

The chief way safety is promoted in this more open environment is through a set of 'rules' that are posted on the homepage of the website: 1. Respect other penguins; 2. Never reveal your personal information; 3. No inappropriate talk; 4. No cheating. Players are encouraged to report other players who violate these rules. In addition, the site employs moderators who monitor activity and chat and investigate complaints about particular players. In this model, safety is seen as a matter of people agreeing to follow a common set of rules. Responsibility is given to the children themselves (and their parents) to both refrain from inappropriate behaviour and to monitor the behaviour of others and report any transgressions to the 'authorities'.

All three of the games described here are clearly committed to the value of online safety for children and take steps to promote community norms that are consistent with this value. However, the approaches taken reflect different ideologies about the level of control that is necessary in order to achieve the goal of safety. Compared to the pre-scripted chat tools of *Poptropica*, the communication tools adopted in the design of both *Moshi Monsters* and *Club Penguin* reflect the belief that children should have more freedom of expression when networking with their friends. They also reflect beliefs about the role of parents and of children themselves in helping to maintain a safe environment.

Although these are just children's games, what children are exposed to when they play them are actually potent lessons in politics and citizenship. Each game indoctrinates them into a different model of what it means to be a citizen, from the restrictive censorship of *Potropicia* to the 'self-regulation' and 'rule of law' promoted by *Club Penguin*. Although it is difficult to say how much the experiences of playing these games might affect their later civic lives and political choices, it is important to note that even something as seemingly innocent as an online game about penguins cannot avoid reflecting and reproducing ideology.

Activity 7.3: The ideology of media

Choose one of the digital tools listed below or some other tool that you are familiar with and analyse it for 'biases' using the questions provided for guidance.

- Facebook (or some other social networking site)
- Google (or some other search engine)
- Microsoft Word (or some other word processing program)
- iPhoto (or some other photo management program)

A. IDEATIONAL FUNCTIONS

What kind of 'version of reality' does the tool construct through the choices it makes available to users? What are the 'default settings' and how do they reflect the way users are expected to use the tool? How easy is it to change these default settings? What kinds of things are users *not* able to do with the tool?

B. INTERPERSONAL FUNCTIONS

What kind of relationships does the tool construct between the manufacturers and the users or between different users. Does the tool encourage users to treat other people in a certain kind of way? How clear and visible are these relationships? How easy are they to change?

CONCLUSION

If there is one lesson you are meant to take from this chapter it is that critical literacy means trying as much as possible to learn how things work, whether we are talking about the way language works to influence our opinions and view of the world or the way software works to influence our behaviour and our relationships with other people. We cannot avoid using various mediational means to take action in the world. However, the more we know about how these media work, the better we can become at 'hacking' them through selective appropriation, adaptation, modification and mixing to fit our own purposes and promote our own agendas rather than the agendas of politicians, journalists, engineers and corporations. Of course, this is not always easy as producers of texts, software programs, digital devices and other mediational means increasingly work to make their tools more and more transparent and more and more opaque, and therefore more and more resistant to hacking.

In this first section of the book, we have outlined some of the affordances and constraints digital media have introduced into our lives, and how these affordances and constraints affect how we can perform various social actions, how we can make meaning, how we can relate to others and construct our own identities, and even how we can think. To really understand the effects of digital media on our behaviour, our social relationships and our thoughts, and to understand our potential to creatively appropriate, adapt and mix these media to fit our own purposes, we must examine them in the context of actual *literacy practices* embedded in real life situations. These literacy practices will be the subject of the second part of this book.

USEFUL RESOURCES

Print

Lanier, J. (2010). *You are not a gadget*. New York: Alfred A. Knopf.
Morozov, E. (2011). *The net delusion: The dark side of internet freedom*. New York: Public Affairs.
Gee, J. P. (2010). *An introduction to discourse analysis*, 3rd edition. London: Routledge.
Pariser, E. (2011). *The filter bubble: What the internet is hiding from you*. New York: The Penguin Press.
Rushkoff, D. (2010). *Program or be programmed: Ten commands for a digital age*. New York: Or Books.
Vaidhyanathan S. (2011). *The Googlization of everything (And why we should worry)*. Berkeley: University of California Press.

Web

The Mentor, The hacker manifesto
http://www.mithral.com/~beberg/manifesto.html

List of logical fallacies
http://web.cn.edu/kwheeler/fallacies_list.html

Jay Lemke, Towards critical multimedia literacy: Technology, research, politics
http://www.personal.umich.edu/~jaylemke/papers/reinking2/htm

Video

Net neutrality
http://www.youtube.com/watch?v=I9jHOn0EW8U

TED, Eli Pariser, Beware online 'filter bubbles'
http://www.ted.com/talks/eli_pariser_beware_online_filter_bubbles.html

Jaron Lanier, You are not a gadget
http://youtu.be/T5JZFx6rIIY

PART II

Digital Practices

CHAPTER 8

Online Cultures and Intercultural Communication

In the 1960s, the scholar Marshall McLuhan prophesized that the world would soon become a 'global village' in which nearly everyone would be linked together by communication technology. He predicted that this would lead to greater political and social consensus and a heightened awareness of our common responsibility for one another. Although nobody could argue that the more utopian aspects of this vision have come true, we do now, in a sense, live in a global village. Evidence of globalization is everywhere, from the shopping mall to the evening news, and much of what is driving it is digital media.

Digital media support the trend towards globalization by breaking down barriers to communication over great distances. Cheap and reliable communication networks facilitate global flows of information, money, goods, services, and people. Digital media allow for the formation of globalized **online affinity spaces**, where people can meet, interact, and build relationships and communities. In the chapters that follow we will consider some of these online affinity spaces, including social networking sites, massively multiplayer online games, and the communities that grow up around blogs and wikis. Although not all such spaces are necessarily global in their reach, they nevertheless have the potential to bring people from very diverse cultural backgrounds into contact.

In this chapter we will be examining the kind of globalized online affinity spaces described above using theories of culture and intercultural communication. On one level, participating in such spaces means learning their cultural conventions and norms of interaction. On another level, interaction in these online spaces may be fundamentally different from offline interactions because of the way that they bring together such diverse groups of people. A 39-year-old female university professor from the United States, for example, might interact with a 15-year-old male secondary school student from Hong Kong while playing *World of Warcraft* in ways that would be very improbable in 'real life'. In such cases, successful communication depends not only on a common shared understanding of the culture of the affinity space, but also on more general awareness of the kinds of cultural assumptions that people from diverse backgrounds might bring to the interaction.

We begin the chapter by introducing the notion of culture in online affinity spaces and providing an analytical framework for thinking about individual online cultures. Next, we consider how the technological affordances and constraints of digital communication tools can have an impact on the **cultures-of-use** that grow up around these tools. Finally, we describe a number of online spaces and the kind of 'intercultural communication' that occurs in them.

ONLINE CULTURES AS DISCOURSE SYSTEMS

To understand the idea of **online cultures** we need to first clarify what we mean by 'culture' and how this notion might in turn be applied to the kinds of spaces where people interact online. The word 'culture', in its everyday use, typically refers to the traditional norms, conventions and practices often associated with particular ethnic or regional groups. For example, we might talk of 'Chinese culture', 'American culture', or 'French culture' to refer to the traditional practices of people who live in these places. However, one problem with using the word 'culture' in this way is that it suggests that the practices described are universally shared by all members of a particular ethnic group or people who live within particular geographical boundaries. In addition, by focusing our attention on ethnic and regional groupings, this use of the word 'culture' distracts us from other possible sources of norms and practices not associated with region or ethnicity.

In this chapter, we will use the word 'culture' in a rather different way. We follow Ron Scollon and his colleagues (Scollon, Scollon and Jones, 2012) in defining cultures as **discourse systems** made up of ideologies, norms of communication, ways of conducting social relationships and practices of socialization which people *participate in* rather than 'belong to' or 'live inside of'. In this sense, culture can refer not only to the practices of a regional group, but other kinds of groups as well: gender groups, generational groups, professional groups, and many other groups based on shared affinities, interests and discourse practices.

This broader view of culture highlights the fact that individuals participate in many different 'discourse systems' at the same time. For example, Christoph is affiliated with a number of different regional discourse systems: he was born in Switzerland, grew up in New Zealand, is married to a Canadian woman and (at the time of writing) lives in Hong Kong. At the same time he also participates in a variety of professional discourse systems: he trained as a lawyer, then as an English language teacher and now works as an academic in the Department of English, City University of Hong Kong. He is also a participant in discourse systems based on gender, generation and interests: for much of his life, for example, he has participated in various musical groups like orchestras and choirs. If you think about your own background, you are bound to notice similar diversity in terms of the discourse systems that you participate in.

Taking this more flexible view of culture also allows us to describe the way people participate in a much greater variety of social practices. For example, we can describe the 'culture' of a particular professional group in a particular workplace by describing the norms, conventions and practices that people who participate in that workplace share. We can also extend the notion of culture to online affinity spaces and describe the particular 'discourse systems' of those spaces, i.e. the shared norms, conventions and practices of people who participate in them.

Online affinity spaces (Gee, 2004) are the virtual places where people interact to promote a particular shared interest or common goal (i.e. a shared 'affinity'). They include a range of different online spaces, such as websites that promote particular kinds of fan fiction writing, online games, social networking sites, knowledge building sites, or sites catering to the interests of particular professions or workplaces. The participants in such online affinity spaces often come from very diverse backgrounds, including people of different ages and genders and with different regional, linguistic and professional affiliations. In addition, people may participate to varying degrees, with some participants being regular and active contributors, while others just 'lurk' or 'pass through'. In spite of this diversity, just like physical places (such as neighbourhoods in a city), these online spaces nevertheless develop their own 'character' based on the unique norms of interaction that grow up among the people who frequent them. That is, affinity spaces often develop their own 'cultures' or 'discourse systems' which include shared ways of thinking, interacting, and getting things done.

As we increasingly live our lives moving in and out of such spaces, it is important for us to develop some understanding of how the norms, conventions and practices of all of the different 'cultures' of the spaces we participate in interact. 'Online cultures' are in many respects similar to other discourse systems. According to Scollon, Scollon and Jones (2012), discourse systems can be broken down into four interrelated and interdependent components, as follows:

1. **Ideology**: what people think;
2. **Face systems**: how people get along with one another;
3. **Forms of discourse**: how people communicate;
4. **Socialization**: how people learn to participate.

As we said in the last chapter, ideology refers to people's deeply held beliefs about what is true or false, good or bad, right or wrong, and natural or unnatural. The 'ideology' of a discourse system refers to the commonly held beliefs, values and worldviews of participants in the system. These beliefs are rarely made explicit but are assumed and operate in the background of communicative interactions and surface in the form of 'values' – whether or not, for example, things like 'education', 'hard work', 'material wealth' or 'spiritual attainment' are valorised.

Among the most important of these values has to do with the nature of the self and its relationship to the group. Some discourse systems emphasize the individual, seeing the purpose of the group to promote and support individual achievement. Others emphasize the group more, with individuals being judged on the basis of their contribution to the community. Most discourse systems, however, have rather complicated ideas about the nature of the self and the nature of the group, and it is very difficult to label any particular 'culture' as either strictly 'individualistic' or strictly 'collectivistic'. It is usually the case in most discourse systems that the individual will be emphasized in some circumstances and the group will be emphasized in others.

Because we all participate in multiple discourse systems, we sometimes have to modify or adapt our beliefs and worldviews as we move from one discourse system to another in the course of our lives. The ideology we advance in the workplace, for example, might be very different from the one we advance at home, and from the one we advance when we are playing *Counter-Strike* with our gaming friends.

'Face systems' refers to systems of interpersonal relationships that govern the way that people interact and how they get along with one another. This, in turn, depends to a degree on the ideology of the discourse system. One aspect of face systems can be seen in forms of address, for example, whether you address someone by their first name, or by their title and last name, or some other honorific. In some discourse systems, the preferred face systems are more egalitarian, and in such systems people tend to address each other in a similar way and use more strategies of solidarity. In other discourse systems, the preferred face systems are more hierarchical, with people at the top of the hierarchy addressed differently to those in the middle or at the bottom, and people at the bottom expected to use strategies of deference towards their 'superiors'.

'Forms of discourse' refers to the media, languages and texts that are used in interactions between participants in a discourse system. This dimension is particularly important for 'online cultures', because of the various ways digital media can potentially influence interaction in online contexts. As we have seen in the preceding chapters, different media introduce different affordances and constraints in terms of communicative action, and so the forms of discourse used in an online interaction can both reflect and shape the values, relationships and social practices of a given 'online culture'.

Forms of discourse also include the assumptions within a discourse system about how meaning is made and what the purpose of communication is. In some 'online cultures', such as political and academic blogs, the informational function of language is valued more highly than the relational function. In other 'online cultures', however, such as those that grow up around online social networks on sites like Facebook, the relational function of language is often more highly valued. People use language not so much to convey information as to establish and maintain relationships (see Chapter 5).

Finally, 'socialization' refers to the ways that people learn to participate in a given discourse system. Some 'cultures' place value on formal processes of education, as for example in school settings. Other 'cultures' place value on more informal processes of socialization, where novices are apprenticed into the discourse system by expert members. This kind of 'apprenticeship' (Lave and Wenger, 1991) is often the kind of socialization one finds in online affinity spaces.

To get a better idea of how the concept of the discourse system (and its components) applies to online cultures, it is helpful to consider an example. One online discourse system with an explicit ideology is Wikipedia. Wikipedia's ideological commitment to collective action over individual achievement is clear: articles are written by groups of volunteers, and are owned by the community. It is difficult for individuals to take credit for their contributions because the only acknowledgement that individual editors receive is the record of their edits maintained in an article's history. In Chapter 11 we will explore in greater detail the kinds of norms and conventions that grow up around this kind of peer production.

As the 'free encyclopaedia that anyone can edit', one would expect to see egalitarian face systems at work in Wikipedia. Indeed, Wikipedia's principles make it clear that regardless of background, all editors are entitled to be treated in a polite, civil way. If you look at Wikipedia discussion pages, you can see that editors tend to refer to each other in a neutral way, by referring to the username and tend not to employ honorifics (like 'Professor'). In principle, respectful treatment in Wikipedia depends on the quality of the edits that a contributor makes, not on his or her social position. This principle is of course complicated by the fact that Wikipedia nevertheless embodies a social hierarchy with founders like Jimmy Wales (at the top) to moderators (in the middle) to editors (at the bottom).

The forms of discourse in Wikipedia, especially the choice of media, both reflect and promote the ideological values described above. First of all, the wiki is set up so that anyone (even anonymous users) can participate, in line with Wikipedia's egalitarian philosophy. Second, the wiki's discussion page provides editors with the means to collectively resolve differences, in line with its more collectivistic ideology. As already noted, other features of the texts themselves, such as a lack of individual attribution, also reflect this cultural emphasis on the good of the collective.

Finally, socialization in Wikipedia, as in many online communities, is an informal process of mentoring and apprenticeship. There are no formal qualifications that prepare Wikipedians for participation, though there is documentation that provides explicit instructions on how to write an appropriate article. Learning to contribute to Wikipedia is comparable to learning to function in a workplace, a gradual process characterized by a combination of explicit instructions and informal socialization through observation and trial and error.

Activity 8.1: The 'cultures' of social networking sites

Read the extracts from the 'About' pages of Facebook, LinkedIn and MySpace below and answer the questions.

1. What different kinds of people do you think these different social networking sites are targeting?
2. How do you think their 'online cultures' differ? Consider:

    a. Ideology: how people think, what is valued, what is devalued;
    b. Face systems: how people get along, whether or not relationships tend to be egalitarian or hierarchical;
    c. Forms of discourse: how people communicate, what they think the underlying purpose of communication is and the different kinds of tools, languages, genres and styles they use for communication;
    d. Socialization: how people learn to participate, how much of this learning is formal and how much is informal, what the consequences are for those who fail to participate in a manner deemed appropriate by the community.

Facebook (http://www.facebook.com/facebook#!/facebook?sk=info)
Millions of people use Facebook every day to keep up with friends, upload an unlimited number of photos, share links and videos, and learn more about the people they meet.

LinkedIn (http://press.linkedin.com/about/)
LinkedIn operates the world's largest professional network on the internet with more than 100 million members in over 200 countries and territories.

MySpace (http://au.myspace.com/Help/AboutUs)
MySpace, Inc. is a leading social entertainment destination powered by the passions of fans. Aimed at a Gen Y audience, MySpace drives social interaction by providing a highly personalised experience around entertainment and connecting people to the music, celebrities, TV, movies, and games that they love.

(Web sources retrieved on April 10, 2011)

'CULTURES-OF-USE' AND 'MEDIA IDEOLOGIES'

One characteristic of 'online cultures' is that the forms of discourse available for people to communicate with are mediated by digital technologies. In some cases new forms of discourse have emerged as a result of these new digital media, forms of discourse which do not always have clear antecedents in 'analogue' communication. One example of this is the

Facebook 'poke', a feature that allows users to virtually 'poke' each other. As a communicative act, pokes usually serve as a playful way to get attention, but are ambiguous as to their exact meaning. They are therefore likely to be understood in different ways by different people.

Exactly how digital media help to give rise to 'online cultures' depends on two things: 1) the technological affordances and constraints of the media, and 2) the 'cultures-of-use' that grow up around it. To return to our example of pokes: on the one hand, it's obvious that pokes afford minimal communication for minimal effort, and so one way of using them would be to say 'hello', when you don't really have that much to say. On the other hand, how you understand a poke depends on individual and collective experience of the practice. Like other computer mediated communication (CMC) tools, a poke is a 'cultural tool'. How cultural tools are used and what meanings are attached to them depends very much upon the 'culture' of the people who use them.

The applied linguist Steven Thorne suggests that over time particular 'cultures-of-use' grow up around digital media. He defines 'culture-of-use' as 'the historically sedimented characteristics that accrue to a CMC tool from its everyday use' (Thorne, 2003: 40). In the last chapter we described the way certain kinds of social practices are 'technologized' around certain tools. 'Cultures-of-use' refer to the expectations, norms and values associated with these 'technologized' practices. Thorne points out that digital media are variably understood by different individuals and often affected by the 'cultures' (or 'discourse systems') individuals participate in. In other words, the 'natural' way to use a cultural tool like the Facebook poke might vary from one person to another and from one 'cultural' group to another.

To illustrate this, Thorne uses the example of a tandem language learning project, in which language students from two universities (one in France, one in America) were paired up over email for communicative practice. He demonstrates that the expectations of the American students were very different from the expectations of the French. The Americans expected to develop a relationship of trust and solidarity with their French counterparts by using this medium, which they were heavily engaged with in their everyday lives. The French students, however, were less likely to use email in their day-to-day social lives and treated the exchange as a purely academic exercise. Thus, for the Americans, email was seen as a *relational* form of discourse, whereas for the French it was seen primarily as an *informational* one. Thorne suggests that the mismatch occurred partly because of the students' different historical experiences of the medium.

Thorne also describes how different groups have differing attitudes towards media like email and chat. Both of these media afford communication through text over a distance, but chat is synchronous, whereas email is not. Thorne reports the perceptions of American students in another tandem learning project. The students indicated that, while they were excited to interact with French speakers, they felt that the use of email constrained their interaction. One characterized email as 'inconvenient', and 'an effort' (56). Thorne concludes that for these students: 'Email is a tool for communication between power levels and generations (for example, students to teachers; sons/daughters to parents) and hence is unsuitable as a medium for age-peer relationship building and social interaction' (56).

The point of these studies is not that 'French' are different from 'Americans', or that people who use email belong to a different 'culture' from people who use chat. The point is that certain norms, conventions and values tend to grow up within different groups of media users over time. The practices that grow up within what Thorne calls 'cultures-of-use' are not solely determined by the affordances and constraints of media, and not solely determined by the 'cultures' of users, but rather the result of an interaction between the 'biases' inherent in the media (see Chapter 7) and the values, experiences and predispositions of users.

The idea that media have different meanings for different people is one that is also developed by the linguistic anthropologist, Ilana Gershon. According to Gershon, the way that individuals understand and use media is shaped by their **media ideologies**, the 'set of beliefs about communicative technologies with which users and designers explain perceived media structure and meaning' (2010: 3). Her work shows how different people develop different beliefs about when and how to use media based on their perceived affordances and constraints.

In her 2010 book, *The Breakup 2.0*, Gershon examines media ideologies in the context of mediated breakups, for example breakups through email, Facebook, instant messenging, and SMS text messaging. She describes how texting is often used by people at the beginning stages of relationships when they are first getting to know each other. Texts, which are limited in length, afford a medium to briefly catch attention without expending great effort. Because they are short, the messages also tend to be ambiguous with respect to any underlying feelings. People often perceive the medium as informal, low stakes, and not very serious: a good alternative to a phone call which would express too much interest (see Chapter 5). However, as Gershon notes, 'it is this very casualness that makes texting a problematic medium for breaking up' (24).

Another point that Gershon makes is that media ideologies cannot be understood in isolation. This is because people's media ideologies change when they begin regularly using a new medium. For example, your beliefs about email (how formal or informal a medium it is for example) might change if you begin to use text messages. Thus, to understand the media ideologies of a particular person or group of people, you have to consider all of the media that they use, because of the way that these ideologies influence each other. Similarly, because different generations have grown up with different media, media ideologies can differ across generational discourse systems. Gershon (75–77) notes that many of the young people in her study considered the telephone to be an acceptable medium for breaking up, which would not have been the case when she and her generation were at university. She explains this observation by pointing out that the younger generation have grown up with a much wider range of media, and compared to text-based digital media, the telephone constitutes a relatively rich medium.

From this discussion it should be clear that choice of media can have a profound effect on the forms of discourse that are available in any given online discourse system. The affordances and constraints of a particular digital medium have an obvious effect on the kinds of message that can be constructed (for example, whether synchronous or asynchronous, long or short). In addition, cultures-of-use develop around media which shape how people understand and use them (for example, whether they associate it with formal or informal, serious or casual interaction). Because communication in online discourse systems is always mediated by technological tools, the range of meanings that can be made depends heavily on the kinds of tools available. At the same time, people bring to their use of cultural tools their own values, knowledge, relationships and experiences and those associated with the various groups they participate in. It is in this tension between the affordances and constraints embodied in cultural tools and the 'cultures-of-use' that develop around these tools that 'online cultures' are formed.

Case study 8: Massively multiplayer online games as online discourse systems

In the last chapter we examined how massively multiplayer online games (MMOGs) designed for children both reflect and promote different ideologies about play and safety and the extent to which the actions of children online need to be constrained. We defined MMOGs simply as 'digital games that you can play with a large number of others on the internet'. In this case study, we return to MMOGs in order to consider the way that participants interact in the persistent worlds that such games create. We consider the virtual worlds of MMOGs as online affinity spaces with their own discourse systems, where a diverse range of individuals interact according to the shared cultural norms of these spaces.

The virtual worlds of MMOGs are populated by individuals from a diverse range of backgrounds. While you might at first think that such games appeal mainly to teenage males, the research shows that this is in fact not the case. For example, Williams, Yee and Caplan (2008) surveyed 7,000 players of the popular role-playing game *Everquest II* (Sony, 2004) about their background and motivation. The results showed considerable diversity in the player population on all demographic measures except for gender (where the distribution was 80.8 per cent males, 19.2 per cent females). Players ranged in age from 12 to 65 years old (average 31.16), with more players in their 30s than in their 20s. The player population was also found to be diverse on other demographic measures, such as ethnic background, income and education, and religious beliefs. One would also expect to find players from diverse regional and linguistic backgrounds coming into contact in such MMOGs.

Because of this diversity, MMOGs provide players with the opportunity to come into contact with others from cultural and linguistic backgrounds very different from their own. In the virtual world, players may find themselves interacting with people whom they would normally have nothing to do with in the 'real' world. What unites players in such a multicultural and multilingual space is their common affinity for the game and their common desire to advance in it. Often, in order to achieve the objectives of the game, players must work together, drawing on each other's complementary strengths in order to successfully complete 'quests' or go on 'raids'. Players of the game can be seen as participating in an online discourse system, with its own ideology, forms of discourse, face systems and socialization processes.

One feature of these discourse systems is the organization of players into social groups. For example, in many role-playing games players can band together and form a 'guild', i.e. a persistent group of like-minded players who meet online more or less regularly to play the game together. Over time such guilds develop social norms that regulate the behaviour of group members, and some of these norms are made explicit in the form of guild rules posted online. Such rules are one example of a specialized form of discourse in the discourse system of particular MMOGs. In part, they reflect the specific values and practices of the guild that created them. In part, they reflect more general values and practices common to the online culture of the MMOG to which the guild belongs.

Johansson and Verhagen (2010) analysed guild rules and found that they address issues related to: 1) group membership; 2) commitment to the group; 3) code of conduct; 4) distribution of resources (for example 'loot'); 5) cheating; 6) strategies; 7) 'griefing'. Many of these categories reflect underlying collectivist values, which promote the interests of the group above the individual. It's not surprising to see this value in many online games in which players working together for the benefit of the group are able to achieve much more in the game than individuals acting alone. Indeed, one of the largest guilds on *Everquest II* (*Virtue, Guild of Honour*), provides a code of conduct with the following rule at the top of the list:

> Thou shalt love thy guild mate by helping them complete tasks and quests and expecting nothing in return.
>> (Retrieved 6 July, 2011 from: http://virtue.everquest2guilds.com/
>> en/twopage.vm?columnId=10520)

The guild rules also identify another interesting cultural practice, found in a range of online virtual worlds: 'griefing' or 'grief play'. This refers to a kind of play which is intended to disrupt the experience of other players, for example by harassing them, deceiving them, unfairly 'killing' them, and/or behaving in other ways that violate the 'spirit of the game' (Foo and Koivisto, 2004). It is interesting to note that the word 'griefing' itself is a specialized term of players of MMOGs, and therefore in order to understand what constitutes 'griefing', insider status or some knowledge of a particular MMOG or the conventions of a particular guild is required. Analysing such disruptive behaviour is particularly useful because it helps to highlight the norms of particular gaming cultures and what happens when those norms are breached.

The practice of griefing is one which is hotly contested. Firstly, what players consider to be griefing varies from one kind of virtual world to another, depending on the aims and goals of the virtual world in question. For example, killing another player's character may be acceptable in MMOGs that permit player versus player combat, but not in a virtual world like *Second Life* (Linden Lab, 2003), where such combat is not allowed. Secondly, in some contexts players might argue about the status of griefing itself, with some suggesting that griefing is a legitimate form of activity in the game world.

Fink (2011) describes how the practice of griefing is interpreted by residents of *Second Life* (referred to below as SL – a well-known virtual world which we discuss in more detail in Chapter 9). He identifies three different frames (see Chapters 4 and 5) that residents use in order to make sense of the activity: 1. The 'lawbreaker' frame; 2. The 'misfit' frame; 3. The 'jester' frame. Here's how he describes them:

1.   The 'lawbreaker' frame: Griefing is interpreted as a crime and griefers are seen as criminals who violate the 'right of quiet enjoyment' of other residents of the virtual world.

2. The 'misfit' frame: Griefing is interpreted as unacceptable behaviour related to some kind of personality disorder, and griefers are seen as sociopaths in need of psychological care.
3. The 'jester' frame: Griefing is interpreted as play or performative critique of the prevailing norms of the virtual world. Griefers adopt this frame to justify their actions, saying that their activity is aimed at residents who treat the virtual world too seriously.

Fink's analysis highlights the dominant norms of the SL discourse system, as they emerge through the practice of griefing and the interactions and conflicts between SL residents that surround it. Those who adopt the lawbreaker and misfit frames cast griefers as socially unacceptable outsiders whose behaviour threatens the norms of the SL community. The interactions suggest that these SL residents view behaviour which causes harm to others or interferes with a right to 'quiet enjoyment' of the virtual world as unacceptable or wrong. They often go further to suggest that such behaviour should be dealt with through rules and sanctions imposed (for example, when a resident files an 'abuse report' with Linden Lab, the creators of SL).

Residents who adopt the jester frame do not deny that griefing in some sense violates the norms of the SL discourse system. Indeed, they openly acknowledge that griefers are testing and breaking the 'rules of the game'. However, they justify these actions by casting the griefing activity as a legitimate form of expression, which deliberately disrupts the experience of others in order to provide a playful commentary or critique of SL culture. Considering the two sides of the conflict around the social practice of griefing in SL, we gain some insight into the way that online culture develops in this online affinity space: social norms and values are created and contested through the online discussions of participants in the space. As participants discuss the practice of griefing and whether it ought to be sanctioned, they negotiate which values should take priority: the right to 'quiet enjoyment' of the virtual world or the right to complete freedom of expression in that world.

INTERCULTURAL COMMUNICATION ONLINE

The case study shows how participants in online affinity spaces like MMOGs develop discourse systems with shared norms and practices. In such online spaces we are increasingly likely to come into contact with and need to communicate with people from a wide range of diverse backgrounds. Thus, another feature of these spaces is the possibility for 'intercultural communication', where participants in different discourse systems (and often from different linguistic backgrounds) communicate with one another, and accommodate to one another's communicative assumptions and expectations. Such accommodation leads to the possibility for developing innovative new forms of communication, and the opportunity to engage with and learn about the diverse languages and cultures of participants in the space.

In the early days of the internet, there might have been some cause for concern that the English language would come to dominate such intercultural communication. At the time, technical limitations such as input hardware and internet protocols made it impossible to write with non-Roman sign systems like Chinese characters, and even some languages based on Roman scripts were difficult to write, because diacritics and accents were not available in the standard character set. Fortunately, much has changed since those days, and more recent studies of language on the internet describe a range of multilingual and multicultural practices (see, for example, Danet and Herring, 2007).

Much of the research on intercultural communication in online affinity spaces has focused on the out-of-class learning experiences of language learners. For example, education researcher Eva Lam (2000) describes how 'Almon', a Hong Kong Chinese teenager living with his family in the US, designs a J-pop (Japanese pop music) website. Through the website, he develops a number of online friendships with others who share his affinity for J-pop, and communicates with them using online chat and email. His online friends come from diverse locations, including Canada, Hong Kong, Japan, Malaysia and the US.

Lam describes the language used by Almon and his online chat mates in this intercultural space as 'the global English of adolescent pop culture rather than the Standard English taught in ESL classes' (475–476). She characterizes this global English as an innovative form, which is highly relevant for use in the kind of online community that developed in this case. Indeed, such innovative use of language is typical of online settings (see Chapter 5). One feature of intercultural communication online is the way that participants draw on a variety of cultures in order to create a hybrid, 'third space' with norms and conventions of its own.

Lam argues that, in the case described, successful participation in this cultural space was beneficial to Almon. She notes that 'the English he controlled on the internet enabled him to develop a sense of belonging and connectedness to a global English-speaking community' (476). This contrasts with his identity as a somewhat marginalized ESL speaker in the school system. Similar claims are made by Rebecca Black, who studies English language learners participating in fan fiction websites (see also Chapter 2, where we described these affinity spaces as 'online writing communities'). For example, she describes how one learner negotiates a strong identity as a multilingual and multicultural fan fiction writer in FanFiction.net (Black, 2006).

Another example of intercultural communication online is Thorne's (2008) study of interaction in the massively multiplayer online game *World of Warcraft* (Blizzard, 2004). Thorne reports the experiences of an American university student who chats with a Russian player. The study shows how chat in *World of Warcraft* can present opportunities to interact with and learn about people from different cultural backgrounds. Here is how their interaction begins (presented as in Thorne, 2008: 319):

1. Zomn: ti russkij slychajno ?
2. Meme: ?
3. Zomn: nwm :)) sry [sorry]
4. Meme: what language was that?
5. Zomn: russian :)
6. Meme: was going to guess that
7. Meme: you speak english well?
8. Zomn: :)) where r u [are you] from ?
9. Meme: USA, Pennsylvania
10. Zomn: im from Ukraine
11. Meme: ah nice, do you like it there?
12. Zomn: dont ask :)))) at least i can play wow :))

After an initial case of mistaken identity, when Zomn asks Meme a question in Russian, the participants take the opportunity to quiz each other about their respective backgrounds. In the ensuing interaction Meme goes on to tell a story about a friend from Ukraine as well as finding out from Zomn that he is a law student. In the interaction there are some signs of the innovative use of language that one would expect in an intercultural interaction online, including code-switching and use of text abbreviations and emoticons (see Chapter 5).

What is interesting is the way that, a bit later in the interaction, Meme (the American) begins asking questions in Russian. Using his AOL Instant Messenger he has contacted his Ukrainian high school friend and asked him to provide some Russian phrases. Here is an example (320):

24. Meme: kak dela?
25. Zomn: :))) normalno :)))
26. Meme: if I may ask, what did I say haha, I'm not quite sure
27. Zomn: how r u :) ///

These informal language lessons illustrate the positive potential of this kind of intercultural communication. As Thorne notes, 'in an uncorroborated but interesting follow-up to this episode, during an informal conversation with the American student, he mentioned a strong interest in Russian language courses' (322).

WHERE TO NOW FOR THE GLOBAL VILLAGE?

To a certain extent, the kind of intercultural interactions described in the previous section accord with McLuhan's optimistic vision of the global village. Through online communication, the participants in these interactions developed their awareness of and affinity for others from different cultural groups. However, there is clearly a question as to how typical such interactions are. Others (see, for example, Gee and Hayes, 2011; Sunstein, 2002) have suggested that the internet has failed to deliver on its promise of providing an open forum where people are able to interact with and learn about a variety of different worldviews. Instead, people are much more likely to use it as a tool to seek out other like-minded people.

It is certainly the case that the internet has provided a venue for different affinity spaces to flourish. The internet allows people who share an affinity to find one another and connect, no matter how unusual the affinity is. This is a good thing in cases where people who would otherwise have been marginalized are able to find support in an online forum. However, it also has a negative side, with people sometimes retreating into their own affinity spaces and hanging out with like-minded others who just reinforce their existing biases and prejudices (see Chapter 7). Seen this way, the internet is becoming increasingly ghetto-ized, with people rarely challenging themselves by venturing away from their habitual hangouts.

Activity 8.2: Your media ideologies

A. EVALUATING TOOLS

Consider the media/communication tools below and answer the questions:

Letter	Telephone	SMS text message
Instant messenger	Email	Social networking site

1. What different communicative situations do you use these tools for? Why?
2. Are some tools better suited to some situations than others? Why?
3. Are some tools more personal than others? Why?
4. Are some tools more formal than others? Why?

B. EVALUATING SITUATIONS

Consider the following situations and explain which of the media/communication tools listed above you would use in each context. Do any of these situations call for unmediated (face-to-face) communication? If so, why?

- You are meeting some friends at a party and you want to let them know that you are running late.
- You have been dating your boyfriend/girlfriend for about a year and you want to break up with them.
- You are writing an assignment and you want to ask your professor for an extension of the due date.
- You are learning a foreign language and you want to practice by doing a language exchange with some native speakers.
- You want to apply for a job over the summer vacation period.

CONCLUSION

In this chapter we have considered the concepts of online cultures and intercultural communication online. Online cultures can be seen as the discourse systems that develop in online affinity spaces, and are made up of four components: 1. Ideologies, or how people think; 2. Face systems, or how people get along with each other; 3. Forms of discourse, or how people communicate; 4. Socialization processes, or how people learn to participate. Media play an important role in these online cultures with specific cultures-of-use developing around different media as a result of individual and collective experience over time. Online affinity spaces are often multilingual, multicultural spaces with participants from a wide range of different backgrounds who must accommodate to one another's communicative expectations. Such intercultural communication can lead to the development of innovative forms of expression and provide participants with the potential for positive intercultural exchange. In the following chapters we will elaborate on the general principles introduced here by describing a number of specific digital literacy practices and their associated online affinity spaces. In particular, we will consider literacy practices related to digital video games (Chapter 9), social networks (Chapter 10), collaboration and peer production (Chapter 11), and the workplace (Chapter 12).

USEFUL RESOURCES

Print

Black, R. W. (2007). Digital design: English language learners and reader reviews in online fiction. In M. Knobel and C. Lankshear (eds.) *A new literacies sampler.* New York: Peter Lang, 115–136.

Lam, W. S. E. (2000). L2 literacy and the design of the self: A case study of a teenager writing on the internet. *TESOL Quarterly 34* (3): 457–482.

Scollon, R., Scollon, S. W., and Jones, R. H. (2012). *Intercultural communication: A discourse approach,* 3rd edition. London: Wiley-Blackwell.

Steinkuehler, C. A. (2006). Massively multiplayer online video gaming as participation in a discourse. *Mind, Culture and Activity, 13* (1): 38–52.

Thorne, S. L. (2003). Artifacts and cultures-of-use in intercultural communication. *Language Learning and Technology, 7* (2): 38–67.

Thorne, S. L. (2008). Transcultural communication in open internet environments and massively multiplayer online games. In S. Magnan (ed.), *Mediating discourse online.* Amsterdam: John Benjamin, 305–327.

Web

Rebecca Black, Publishing and participating in online affinity spaces
http://newlits.wikispaces.com/Publishing+and+Participating+in+Online+Affinity+Spaces

The Washington Times, Gamers: Women not allowed?
http://communities.washingtontimes.com/neighborhood/60-second-attention-span/2011/aug/3/gamers-women-not-allowed/

Opensource.com, Inside the culture of Wikipedia: Q and A with the author of 'Good Faith Collaboration'
http://opensource.com/business/10/9/inside-culture-wikipedia-qa-author-good-faith-collaboration

Video

TED, Christopher 'moot' Poole, The case for anonymity online,
http://www.ted.com/talks/christopher_m00t_poole_the_case_for_anonymity_online.html

TED, James Surowiecki, When social media became news
http://www.ted.com/talks/james_surowiecki_on_the_turning_point_for_social_media.html

Michael Wesch, An anthropological introduction to YouTube
http://youtu.be/TPAO-IZ4_hU

CHAPTER 9

Games, Learning and Literacy

Compared to other media like print and film, digital video games are a relatively recent invention. These games can be played on a range of devices, including personal computers, arcade machines, consoles, smartphones and media tablets (we use the term 'video game' to refer to all such digital games). Early video games were simple affairs, with basic graphics and simple goals. For example, one of the first commercial video games was an arcade game called *Pong* (Atari, 1972), a kind of virtual tennis in which each player controlled a stick-like paddle and hit the virtual 'ball' from their side of the screen to their opponent's side.

Video games have come a long way since those early days. The games themselves have become more demanding, often challenging players to solve complex problems as part of a developing narrative. Advanced 3-D graphics have made it possible to create intricate and compelling game worlds for players to act in. With the advent of the internet it has also become possible for players to interact in real time with other players and work together in the game world. In addition to these technological advances, there have been important social developments as well. Online affinity spaces (see Chapter 8) have emerged where video game fans can congregate and discuss their favourite games, share tips and modifications of games and watch gameplay videos called 'machinima'.

Perhaps more than any other digital media, video games have attracted criticism from parents, teachers and the media. Critics point to issues of gender stereotyping and violence in video games, as well as to the problem of video game 'addiction'. Video games are often dismissed as a corrupting influence, or, at best, a waste of time that should be avoided. At the same time, however, there is also a growing recognition of the potential of video games to promote positive values and practices, among them active and critical learning. In this chapter we will explore and critically evaluate the affordances and constraints of video games, what makes them so compelling, and the kinds of literacy practices that have grown up around them.

In his book, *Everything Bad Is Good for You*, the author Steven Johnson (2006) points out that video games have gradually become more and more demanding over time. Obviously, there are still a good number of mindless video games out there, but in this chapter we will be focusing more on the kinds of complex video games that Johnson has in mind. These are games that: 1) are situated in some kind of virtual game world; 2) tell a story in that world with the player as a central, active participant; 3) involve the player in various kinds of problem-solving activities in order to achieve the goals of the game; 4) may involve the player in collaborating with others in order to achieve the goals of the game; 5) may offer the player the possibility to customize the game in a major way, for example by 'modding' the game and designing new levels.

We will be discussing these games in terms of both technological affordances and literacy practices. We begin by considering 'reading' and 'writing' in video games and how games open up new ways of meaning, both within games themselves, and outside games in wider fan communities. Then we discuss video games and identity, and how video games allow us to adopt new ways of being in the world and relating to other people. Finally we consider the topic of games and learning, exploring the potential of games to promote new ways of thinking.

Activity 9.1: The games people play

Think about a video game that you have played, or one that you know of. Describe and evaluate that game by answering the questions below.

1.   What kind of game is it? Is it a:

    a.   Shooter?
    b.   Arcade game?
    c.   Adventure game?
    d.   Role-playing game?
    e.   Simulation game?
    f.   Strategy game?
    g.   Puzzle game?

2.   How would you describe the visuals? Sound? Music? Are they:

    a.   Realistic?
    b.   Stylized?

3.   Does the game tell a story? How?
4.   Does the game involve problem solving? How?
5.   Does the game allow you to interact with other players? How? Is it:

    a.   Competitive?
    b.   Co-operative?

6.   Does the game allow you to share your achievements? How?
7.   How similar or different is the experience of playing this game compared to other literacy practices like reading or writing in print-based media or on the screen (for example, websites)?
8.   Would you describe this as a good game? Why? Does the game motivate you, challenge you, reward you and hold your interest? How?

'READING' AND 'WRITING' IN GAMES

If you have ever read a game review, you'll know that the language gamers use to talk about games is often very similar to the language of book reviewers or film critics. Games are 'titles' that can be described in terms of their 'setting', 'backstory', 'plot', 'action' and 'characters'. Like books or films, they usually tell a story. However, the stories that games tell are always interactive ones in which players play a central role and make important decisions about the plot. Games also tell their stories through a range of visual, verbal, aural and textual modes. These elements are combined in complex ways that both represent the unfolding action in the world of the game, and provide an interface through which the player can interact with that world.

What we are suggesting here is that a video game can be seen as a complex kind of text, one that encourages new forms of 'reading' and 'writing'. We considered some aspects of this new form of reading and writing in Chapters 3 (Hyperreading and hyperwriting) and 4 (Multimodality). Like other forms of digital media, video games draw upon the affordances of new media. Here we will consider the way in which video games utilize interactivity and multimedia in order to make meaning with multimodal texts *in the game*. We will also consider the way literacy practices of video games extend to texts *outside of games*, including game manuals, walkthroughs and fan websites.

Texts within games

In order to illustrate interactivity and texts within games we will use the example of *Spore* (Electronic Arts, 2008). *Spore* begins with an asteroid collision on an alien planet far away in space. The player is a microscopic organism on that asteroid, and the game is about the player's evolution into more and more complex life forms. The game has five stages: cell, creature, tribe, civilization, space. In the course of the game, the player evolves from a single-celled organism to a complex life form to a member of a space-age civilization.

When players begin, they have to make a number of choices that affect their future evolution. The very first thing that they do in the game is to decide whether to be a herbivore or a carnivore, though they can later evolve into an omnivore as well. This choice has an impact on the options that become available to them later. For example, if they decide to be a carnivore in the cell stage, then in the creature stage they play a predator that is only able to eat meat (fruit will make them ill). In the tribal stage they play members of an aggressive tribe, in the civilization stage they play members of a military civilization, and in the space stage they play warriors. As warriors they have access to cheap weapons, so military conquest is an attractive option. However, the tools needed for economic and religious conquest are expensive, making these strategies harder to pursue.

As players progress through the game, they are constantly developing and building on to their creatures and the social groups that they live in. With every successive generation in the cell and creature stages they make changes to their organisms, using a 'creator' to add various limbs and organs. In the tribal stage they discover fire and create distinctive, tribal clothing, and in the civilization and space stages they create buildings, cars, boats, planes and space ships that they will use to conquer first the world and then the universe.

The story of *Spore* is the story of a journey from primitive life form to master of the universe. The choices that players make as they interact with the game directly shape the plot of that story and the character of the virtual environment that evolves. The player thus assumes a centrally important role as main character and storyteller, in a manner that is not possible in other media such as books and films. The education scholar James Paul Gee calls the stories of video games **embodied stories** because of the way that they are 'embodied in the player's own choices and actions in a way they cannot be in books and movies' (Gee, 2003, p. 82). Note that such embodied stories are not necessarily better than traditional stories, just different.

In *Spore*, each stage (cell, creature, tribe, civilization, space) is progressively more complex than the last, both in terms of the tools and technologies that you have at your disposal and in terms of the goals that you have to achieve to advance in the game. Even at four years old, Christoph's son was able to happily play the cell stage, even without being able to read any of the texts that appear on screen. By the time he got to the space stage, however, he had to recruit the assistance of his 6-year-old sister and other family members in order to decipher the written texts and understand the missions that he had to go on.

This increasing complexity is reflected in the game's interface, which slowly but surely becomes cluttered with the tools that players need in order to succeed in the game. It's interesting to compare the interface from the cell stage (where it is the simplest) to the interface from the space stage (where it is the most complex). Screenshots of these different interfaces can be seen in Figures 9.1 and 9.2.

At the cell stage, the player has a view of the primordial ooze in which his cell is hunting for food. At the bottom of the screen is a control panel, with 10 items. From left to right these include: a zoom button (A), an options menu (B), a pause button (C), the 'Sporepedia' (D – lists all of the creatures that the player has encountered), 'My Collections' (E – lists all of the cell parts that the player has unlocked), DNA points (F), progress bar (G), a 'Call mate'

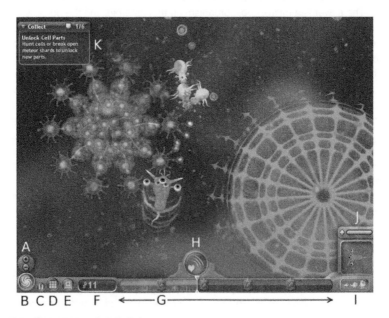

Figure 9.1   Spore screenshot: Cell stage
(Electronic Arts, used with permission)

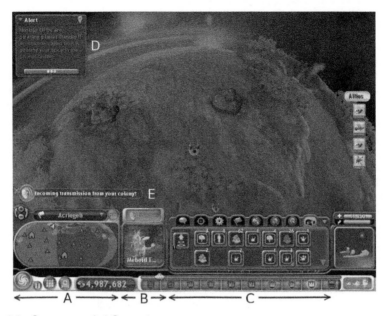

Figure 9.2   Spore screenshot: Space stage
(Electronic Arts, used with permission)

button (H), a history button (I – shows a player's evolution) and a health bar (J – shows damage). Of these, the only button that is regularly used is the 'Call mate' button. Goals appear in the top left of the screen (K).

In the space stage, the 'Call mate' button is gone (having served its purpose) and is replaced by three control panels. The first is a map of the planet (A), indicating cities, other spaceships, and so on. The second is a communicator (B), which can be used to talk to the aliens on different planets. Selecting the communicator provides a range of options: trade, repair, recharge, take on a mission, engage in diplomacy. Next to the communicator is a control panel (C) with eight different kinds of tools (maximum 18 tools per category): socialization, weapons, main tools, colonization, planet atmospheric tools, planet sculpting tools, planet colouring tools, cargo. Again, goals (D) appear on the top left, and incoming communications from other aliens (E) appear below them.

Both stages adopt an organization that is commonly seen in video games, dividing the screen into two main parts (Beavis, 2004). One part of the screen graphically displays the game world that the player can act on. The other part is an iconic display of the tools that the player can use (at the side or bottom of the screen). When playing the game, players mediate and move between their toolset and the unfolding action of the game. In networked multiplayer games, these tools include a chat tool, which allows players to send each other messages in real time.

Comparing the interface of the cell stage with that of the space stage, one is struck by two main observations. The first is how much more a player must attend to in the space stage of the game. The player has a much greater range of options open to him or her. The second thing is that the role of written text in the space stage has become much more important. In order to progress, the player must take on missions assigned by the leaders of their own or other civilizations (these are non-player characters simulated by the computer). These missions are described in written text primarily in the form of pre-scripted conversations that allow the player to negotiate the terms of the missions with the alien leaders.

That's why Christoph's son at four years old had a difficult time of it in space. In earlier stages, understanding written text was not so crucial to success: he was able to 'read' the game without being able to understand the written texts. In fact, when offered help, he confidently claimed, 'I can read'. As well as the written text, he attended to a range of multimodal cues: things like the kinds of icons and the kinds of sounds that accompanied textual messages. For example, in the tribal stage, a message warning that his village was under attack was always accompanied by a yellow 'alert' icon and a particular sound effect.

Thus, meanings in video games are highly multimodal. In addition to the visual and iconic elements of screen layout already described, subtle cues about the game world can be conveyed through colour and sound (including sound effects and music). Colour and sound do not just contribute to the overall atmosphere of the game. They also convey meaning. For example, in the space stage of *Spore*, the basic environment of a planet can be deduced from a distance by looking at its colour. If the planet is red, then the environment is likely to be hostile, with lots of volcanic eruptions that could damage your ship if you fly too close. In addition, in many online multiplayer games, colour (along with dress) is one resource that players may draw upon in order to construct identity and convey a particular impression to others. In a typical fantasy role-playing game, for example, a wizard wearing white robes suggests a different kind of character than one wearing black.

In summary, video games provide a range of ways of making meaning. On one level, video games can be seen as new kinds of texts, which tell new kinds of interactive, embodied stories. These stories are created from the choices made by the game designer on one hand, and the player on the other. As we have seen, the visual representation of the game reflects this interactive quality, by combining two main elements: 1) a representation of the game world; 2) an iconic interface, which allows players to direct action in that world. On another level, the texts in the game themselves draw on the affordances of digital media by combining a variety of modes: visual, verbal, aural, textual. In order to make sense of the game, players must attend to this combination of modes and interpret a range of cues that are often quite subtle.

Texts outside of games

So far we have been considering the kind of texts and literacy practices that can be identified in the world of the video game. However, much of the literate activity associated with video games extends to texts and practices outside of games themselves. As an example, consider the many game reviews that appear in gaming magazines and websites. In this section we will explore some of those outside texts and practices, including game manuals, walkthroughs, **fan modifications**, and **fan machinima**.

As an initial observation, it is important to point out that this web of outside texts is linked to the group of people who share an affinity for a particular game, kind of game, or even video games in general. The group of people who enjoy playing *Spore* would occupy one such 'affinity space' (as described in Chapter 8). Members of the group would create and share texts that serve to improve their own and others' enjoyment of the game. These texts then act as resources that other members of the group can draw upon if necessary.

One such resource is the game manual. As part of the package, video games are typically sold with a game manual, which provides a basic guide to playing the game. For example, the 'galactic edition' of *Spore* comes with a 100-page 'Galactic Handbook' which provides instructions on everything from installing the game to uploading creations to the Spore community. However, even this handbook does not provide exhaustive information about how to play the game. Players who encounter unexpected obstacles that they are unable to overcome on their own, can refer to player-generated 'walkthroughs'. These usually take the form of written guides that describe in detail how to advance through the game.

Game manuals and walkthroughs tend to be densely packed, specialized texts, which players consult when they get stuck and need help to advance in the game. Without first experiencing the game, these texts can be very difficult to understand. Gee (2003) compares them to the specialist literature in domains like science and law, which also presuppose extensive background knowledge as well as a shared, specialist worldview. From the point of view of digital literacies, what is interesting here is that these resources are created not just by the game designers, but also by players. In Chapter 11 we will further discuss how, not just in gaming, but in a wide variety of digital literacy practices, the role of the media consumer has shifted from passive recipient to active participant.

In the context of gaming, this more active role is illustrated by two new literacy practices: 'modding' and 'machinima'. Modding or fan modification is the practice of modifying a game either by adding content (like a new level or new items) or by creating an entirely new game. Many video games, such as *The Elder Scrolls* series (Bethesda Softworks, 1994–2011) provide fans with the tools to create these **mods**. In some cases, mods can lead to a new commercial release. For example, the popular game *Counter-Strike* (Valve, 2000) is a mod of the earlier game *Half-Life* (Valve, 1998).

Creating an interesting mod requires not only a good understanding of the technological tools, but also an understanding of elements of representation in games, like plot and character, as described above. It also requires an appreciation of the ludic qualities of games, those qualities that make the game fun to play. In their study of students designing games, Buckingham and Burn (2007) stress the importance of understanding games as rule-based systems that both challenge players and reward them when they follow the rules correctly. They also point out that game designers create economies of resources, such as health, hunger, point scores, and so on, which players must utilize strategically in order to achieve their goals.

Machinima is another emerging literacy practice in the context of gaming. The word is a combination of 'machine' and 'cinema' and refers to the use of a video game's real-time 3-D animation engine in order to create a cinematic product. The creation of machinima is in many ways similar to the creation of fan fiction, discussed in Chapter 3. It draws on the characters and settings in a game but combines them in a way that is new and original, whether that be as a drama, comedy, music video or whatever.

As we suggested earlier, these new literacy practices often take place in the context of online affinity spaces where fans of games can interact and share their creations. These spaces provide fans with a venue where they can create and share a range of texts: walkthroughs and guides on how to get the most out of the game; mods that extend the game with new levels; machinima that build on the game's resources to create new stories. All of these practices allow fans to adopt new, more active roles in the creation and distribution of culture.

Case study 9: Virtual game worlds

The idea of a virtual game world that you can interact with has been around for a long time. It goes back to interactive text-based adventure games, which peaked in popularity in the 1980s and 1990s. In these games, the player assumes the role of the central character and has to use problem-solving techniques to navigate through the world and progress in the story. This world is described using text and players type simple commands (for example 'go west', 'open door', 'get key') into their computer to interact with the world. A well-known example of this kind of game is *Zork* by Infocom (1980). In this game, the player becomes an adventurer whose goal is to collect twenty treasures. The game opens with the following text:

> West of House
> You are standing in an open field west of a white house with a boarded front door. There is a small mailbox here.

If the player types 'open mailbox' more text appears: 'Opening the small mailbox reveals a leaflet'. By responding to these textual descriptions the player gradually uncovers clues about the location of the twenty treasures, progressing through the story in an interactive way. Of course, now adventure puzzle games like this have been replaced by games with more advanced graphical user interfaces.

It has also become possible to interact with other players in the game world, forming alliances with them and working together to achieve the goals of the game. This kind of interaction first became possible with **MUD**s (Multi-User Dungeons, later known as Multi-User Domains) and **MOO**s (MUD Object Oriented). Again, these were text-based spaces that simulated a virtual world by using textual descriptions. Unlike the adventure games considered above, MUDs and MOOs were created for networked computers, so that it was possible for people on the network to interact and collaborate. People interacted in this way by using text.

The virtual game worlds of today's massively multiplayer online games (MMOGs, see Chapters 7 and 8) are far more sophisticated than those of the early adventure games, MUDs and MOOs described above. In MMOGs, large numbers of players meet in online virtual worlds dedicated to a range of different kinds of games: from first person shooter games like *Counter-Strike* (Valve, 2000) where players team up and go on military missions, to fantasy role-playing games like *World of Warcraft* (Blizzard, 2004) where groups of players enter dungeons and do battle with mythical monsters. The virtual worlds of these MMOGs can be very compelling, often drawing on advanced 3-D graphics in order to simulate a life-like setting, which includes a graphical representation of the player, called an **avatar**. Players can control this avatar's actions and can usually communicate with each other through a range of channels, including both text and voice options.

The idea of the virtual game world has been taken one step further with the development of *Second Life* (SL), launched by Linden Lab in 2003 (http://secondlife.com).

Like MMOGs, SL has a persistent online virtual world where people (the 'residents' of SL) can meet and interact. But unlike the kind of MMOGs mentioned above, there are no clearly defined goals or problems to be solved, and players don't 'level up', so talk of 'winning' or 'losing' doesn't make much sense. Instead, SL provides its residents with a virtual environment which they themselves can design, using modelling tools to construct virtual islands, buildings, gardens, and objects like cars, motorbikes, clothes and so on. The resulting virtual world often bears an uncanny resemblance to 'real life'.

In order to participate in SL, players must create an account and download client software, which enables them to experience the virtual world. Players begin at a 'Welcome Island' where they are walked through the basics: how to walk, how to fly, how to customize appearance, how to interact with objects, how to interact with people. If the information provided here is not enough, there is plenty of support available in websites dedicated to SL.

As mentioned above, the 3-D virtual world of SL is itself entirely created by residents, using the modelling tools that are built into the client. Residents can design accessories for their avatars, or buy property and create virtual buildings. This kind of creative activity is not limited in the same way that it is in the real world. As a result players can experience a range of virtual recreations and simulated environments, which might be difficult or impossible to access in real life. Some of the things that players can do and experience in SL include:

• Visit a historical place like Ancient Greece or Renaissance England;
• Visit major cities like London, Paris and New York;
• Visit the White House oval office;
• Land on the moon or visit a space station;
• Step inside a giant Dell Computer;
• Enter the human body and perform surgery.

Because of the ability of the virtual world to create compelling simulations like those listed above, it has attracted the attention of educators who want to provide an immersive experience for their students. In one instance, Peter Yellowlees, a Professor of Psychiatry at University of California, Davis, created an environment that simulated the hallucinations suffered by a schizophrenic. By visiting SL, Yellowlees' students could experience first-hand the kind of disorientation that their patients feel (Virtual Online Worlds: Living a Second Life, 2006).

SL also allows residents to adopt new identities, new ways of being in the world. One of the first things that you do is customize your avatar, and, unlike in real life, you can be as fat or thin as you like. Whether to create an avatar that resembles your real life self is completely up to you, though it's interesting that quite a few people choose to do just that.

Other people deliberately create an avatar that is at odds with their real life selves in order to project a different kind of person onto the virtual world. One striking example of this is the case of the physically disabled, who can adopt a 'normal' body in SL, and walk, fly and teleport around SL, just like everyone else. In their interactions with other residents, these people learn what it is like to be treated 'normally' (Lessig, 2008). Of course, we are not here saying that SL solves the problem of social stigma for disabled people. It's important to recognize that many disabled people in SL do in fact choose to have wheelchairs. From their perspective, 'able' people should learn to treat them 'normally' even with their disability (Jones, 2011). Other physical characteristics like age, race and gender can be similarly 'masked'. As a result a wide range of people who might otherwise not give each other a second glance can interact and form relationships in SL.

The virtual world of SL is one that is compelling. The line between real and virtual can become blurred in a way that challenges us to rethink notions about the real and virtual world, and what it means to 'play' a game. Although the world of SL is a virtual one, it is far from trivial. Like many other MMOGs, SL has a booming economy, with SL residents trading virtual goods and services for so-called 'Linden dollars' (the SL currency). In 2006 the GDP of SL was estimated at around 64 million USD (Newitz, 2006), which at the time of writing would rank it 64th out of all of the countries in the real world. Thus, while in the past we might have thought of play in virtual worlds as activity that is 'not real', it is now clear that what goes on in these spaces can carry over to the real world in significant ways. Another example of this is the way that people can meet one another in a virtual world like SL and form lasting relationships in the real world.

GAMES AND IDENTITY

One thing that we can learn from the case study above is that video games like the MMOGs discussed provide a range of new opportunities for the construction of identity. In the virtual worlds of video games it is not necessary (sometimes not possible) to 'be yourself'. Instead, you choose a virtual identity, which as we have seen, can be more or less similar to your real identity. The degree to which you can customize this virtual identity varies from game to game. In SL a great deal of customization is possible, but in a game like *SuperMario Galaxy* (Nintendo, 2007), there is only one character you can play (Mario).

In his 2003 book, *What Video Games Have to Teach Us about Learning and Literacy*, James Paul Gee describes three different identities that come into play in video games. According to Gee, the real identity (of the player in the real world) and the virtual identity (of the character in the virtual world) are mediated by a 'projective identity' – the interface between real and virtual. In this identity players project their own values, hopes and aspirations onto the virtual character, shaping that character through the decisions that they make and the actions that they perform.

So, for example, if you, the player, have certain beliefs about 'fighting fair' then you might try to make sure that the actions of your virtual character conform to those beliefs.

You adopt a projective identity that places limitations on the way that your virtual character can act. Gee argues that such a projective identity opens up a space to critically reflect on the values that you are required to enact as you progress through the game.

Gee goes on to describe how video games can serve to develop an understanding of cultural models, by immersing players in a particular cultural worldview. He points out that video games make implicit cultural assumptions, which players are unable to influence. For example, in American first person shooter games, the cultural model puts the Americans in the role of the 'good guys' who face off against 'bad guys' like the Germans, the Russians, and Islamic 'extremists'. Gee points out that a game which pits Palestinian militants against Israeli military forces and civilian settlers is operating according to a completely different cultural model. In this model, the militants are viewed as justified in attacking civilian settlers because they are seen as enemy advance forces. This is not to say that the ideology underlying and implicitly legitimated by such a game should be accepted, but rather that video games (like literature) provide a means to experience, understand and critically evaluate alternative cultural models.

Video games that reverse commonly held cultural models in the manner described above are likely to be highly controversial. In part this is because of the way that video games involve the player so actively in the development of the story. A recent example is the latest in the *Medal of Honour* series of first person shooter games (Electronic Arts, 2010). This release is set in modern day Afghanistan and in its multiplayer version initially included the possibility for players to play the game either as NATO forces or as Taliban militants. After a storm of criticism, the game designers reacted by removing the Taliban option, renaming the opposing team 'Opposing Force'. However, the game remained controversial, with the U.S. Army and Airforce Exchange Service refusing to sell the title on its bases.

The concern with video games like *Medal of Honour* is that the immersive experience of the game will lead players to identify strongly with the political objectives of the groups that they role-play in the game. Commenting on the *Medal of Honour* controversy, the Canadian Minister of National Defence, Peter Mackay gave voice to this concern, saying: 'I find it wrong to have anyone, children in particular, playing the role of the Taliban' (Wylie, 2010). Nevertheless, Gee argues that in spite of such concerns, it is important to engage with such games, even if we do not agree with the cultural values that they represent. According to Gee, such games, and the identities and cultural values that they promote, should be subjected to a critical evaluation, rather than dismissed out of hand.

Another aspect of identity in video games has to do with the kind of relationships that can form in virtual spaces like MMOGs. Because people in these spaces interact with each other's virtual identities rather than real identities, relationships that we might find unlikely in the real world can form. For example, a teenage student might regularly play a game like *World of Warcraft* with a group that includes young professionals in their 20s and 30s (see Chapter 8).

In the make-believe world of the role-playing game, the 'physical' characteristics of the player's avatar (such as race, gender and age) may not correspond to the 'real-world' characteristics of the player, and in many cases these 'real-world' characteristics may not be relevant. Instead, what counts is the player's ability to perform their virtual identity (for example as a fighter, or thief) and contribute expertly to the in-game fortunes of the group. In this way MMOGs provide opportunities for individuals to take on roles that would not be possible in the real world. For example, with sufficient expertise, the hypothetical teenager that we mentioned above could perform the role of teacher and mentor to other players who, in 'real life' might be much older.

GAMES AND LEARNING

One way of looking at video games is as learning experiences. If this is true, then what exactly is it that people are learning? Marc Prensky, author of *Digital Game-based Learning*, points out that learning occurs at two different levels. He says:

> On the surface, game players learn to do things – to fly airplanes, to drive fast cars, to be theme park operators, war fighters, civilization builders, and veterinarians. But on deeper levels they learn infinitely more: to take in information from many sources and make decisions quickly; to deduce a game's rules from playing rather than by being told; to create strategies for overcoming obstacles; to understand complex systems through experimentation. And, increasingly, they learn to collaborate with others.
>
> (Prensky, 2003: 21/2)

As we have already argued, video games have become progressively more sophisticated over time. As a result many games now give players the opportunity to practice complex problem-solving skills. In addition, with MMOGs players can also learn important social skills by interacting with the large number of other players in the gaming environment. In some cases, what you do in the game world might not seem particularly important or useful, and this leads some people to suggest that video games are a waste of time. However, most people would agree that the kind of collaborative problem-solving skills, innovation and creativity fostered in games are just the kind of skills that twenty-first-century citizens are increasingly going to need (see Chapter 12).

As well as the question of *what* you learn, there is also the question of *how* you learn. As Gee (2003) points out, the best (most popular) games are usually difficult and complicated to learn, so if video game designers want to make money, they have to somehow make learning how to play their games fun. Gee argues that this commercial necessity has turned video game designers into expert teachers and motivators. He goes on to suggest that we can learn a great deal by understanding the principles of learning that are used in good video games. In total, Gee (2003) identifies 36 such principles of learning; here, we will try to distil some of the main ideas.

First of all, learning in games is always experiential and active. You are placed in a world that you can experience first-hand through seeing, hearing and feeling (not just thinking). Moreover, as already discussed, players can exert an influence on that world through their actions, as well as take on identities that they are willing and able to invest in emotionally. The result is that the player feels like an active agent in the game, playing an active role in co-creating the game world.

Second, the learning itself is carefully staged, so that players are always operating around the edge of their level of competence. As a result, the activities that players engage in are challenging but do-able. When players need to learn new skills and new routines, these are introduced gently and in a non-threatening way. For example, many games have a kind of sandbox or tutorial area where players can practice basic skills (running, jumping, attacking, defending) without consequences (like physical injury) if they make mistakes.

Gee contrasts the learning in video games with the learning in formal school-based contexts, which he finds lacking. He points out that learning in video games is always situated in experience of the game world: information is provided 'just-in-time' when it is needed to solve a problem in the game. In contrast, much of the learning that children do in schools is abstract and decontextualized. Gee argues that school contexts, with their emphasis on standardized skills, too often adopt a 'just-in-case' model of learning. In this model, the curriculum is covered without any strong connection to the experiences of the students, 'just-in-case' they need it at a later point in their lives.

Game designer Jane McGonigal takes Gee's argument a step further in her 2011 book, *Reality Is Broken*. She observes that increasing numbers of people are spending an increasing amount of time playing digital video games and concludes that 'in today's society, computer and video games are fulfilling *genuine human needs* that the real world is currently unable to satisfy' (4). She foresees a possible future where people retreat from reality into the relative comfort of the virtual worlds of games. However, she goes on to suggest that the power of games to engage such vast numbers of people is not something that should be wasted on escapist entertainment. Accordingly, she challenges game designers to come up with games that are able to 'fix' reality and engage people in solving 'real-world' issues and problems.

One example of such a game is *Evoke* (World Bank Institute, 2010). The trailer for this **alternate reality game** claims that it will teach players 'collaboration, creativity, local insight, courage, entrepreneurship, knowledge networks, resourcefulness, spark, sustainability, vision'. Players are 'agents' who are tasked with tackling social issues, with 10 missions over a 10-week period, each mission focusing on a potential future crisis related to issues like poverty, hunger, disaster relief, and so on. Players respond to each crisis with a creative solution, including a project which they try out in the real world. They report on their projects each week by sharing blog posts, videos, and photos. The game is designed so that by the end players will develop an idea for a larger project or business, with top players awarded online mentorships, travel scholarships or seed funding for their projects.

Activity 9.2: Boon or bane?

Consider the quote from Michael Highland's (2006) short film 'As Real as Your Life' and discuss the questions.

> But maybe brainwashing isn't always bad. Imagine a game that teaches us to respect each other, or helps us to understand the problems we are all facing in the real world. There is a potential to do good as well … It is critical, as these virtual worlds continue to mirror the real world that we live in, that game developers realize that they have tremendous responsibilities before them.

1. Do you know/Can you imagine any games designed to teach players to respect each other, or help them to understand the problems we face in the real world?
2. What does it/would it look like?
3. How do you/would you play?

CONCLUSION

In this chapter we have considered the potential of the medium of digital video games to provide a space for new literacy practices. Video games open up new ways of making meaning by drawing on the affordances of digital media described in earlier chapters of this book, which include hypertext, interactivity and multimedia. In particular, games provide for a new kind of embodied storytelling, with the player positioned as active co-creator rather than passive recipient of information. In addition, the literacy practices associated with video games extend beyond the game itself into online affinity spaces, where fans interact, creating and sharing a range of texts: walkthroughs, mods, machinima. The interactions that players experience both within and outside of games provide them with various opportunities to adopt alternative identities, often very different from the ones that they are able to play in other parts of their lives. In the next chapter we will further explore this aspect of identity in digital media by examining how people present themselves in online communities and social networking sites.

USEFUL RESOURCES

Print

Buckingham, D., and Burn, A. (2007). Game literacy in theory and practice. *Journal of Educational Multimedia and Hypermedia 16* (3): 323–349.

Gee, J. P. (2003). *What video games have to teach us about learning and literacy*. New York: Palgrave Macmillan.

Gee, J. P. (2007). *Good video games + good learning: Collected essays on video games, learning, and literacy*. New York: Peter Lang.

McGonigal, J. (2011). *Reality is broken: Why games make us better and how they can change the world*. New York: Penguin Press.

Prensky, M. (2001). *Digital game-based learning*. New York: McGraw-Hill.

Web

Machinima
http://www.machinima.com/

Second Life, destinations guide: Editor's picks
http://secondlife.com/destinations/editor/1

Jane McGonigal
http://janemcgonigal.com/

Video

Edutopia, big thinkers: James Paul Gee on grading with games
http://www.edutopia.org/james-gee-games-learning-video

Southpark Studios, Make love not warcraft
http://www.southparkstudios.com/full-episodes/s10e08-make-love-not-warcraft

Al Jazeera, 'Medal of Honour' game sparks anger
http://www.youtube.com/watch?v=NxGlJHHAkrA

CHAPTER 10

Social Networking

Until recently, the internet was not so different from old media networks: it connected many things together, but most users like you and me had little control over those connections beyond being able to navigate through them. This has changed with the rise of social networking sites like Facebook and Twitter. Now ordinary users of the internet are involved in creating and maintaining connections within the network. In Chapter 3 we noted that one of the main affordances of the 'read-write' web (or web 2.0) was that it allowed users to create content. Perhaps a more profound affordance that has come from social networking is that it has given internet users the ability to create *the connections* between the content based on social relationships.

The internet scholars dana boyd and Nicole Ellison (2008: 211) define a 'social networking site' as a 'web-based service that allows individuals to: 1) construct a public or semi-public profile within a bounded system, 2) articulate a list of other users with whom they share a connection, and 3) view and traverse their list of connections and those made by others within the system'. The key aspect of such sites is not just that they allow users to create profiles and share things like texts, pictures and videos, but that they allow them to do so within bounded systems of social connections which they define themselves.

In this chapter we will explore the literacy practices that have developed around social networking sites like Facebook, Twitter and Google+. First we will consider how social networking sites exploit the affordances of digital media and contrast them to the 'online communities' that dominated the early days of the internet. We will then go on to explore how people use the expressive equipment provided by social networking sites to manage their social identities and their social relationships.

WE ARE NOT FILES

The capacity for social networking sites to facilitate the formation and maintenance of complex links among people is akin to the internet's capacity to facilitate the formation of complex links among different pieces of information which we discussed in Chapter 2. Some scholars, in fact, see the development of social networking sites as a natural outcome of the web's inherent capacity for *connecting things*, 'an evolution from the linking of information to the linking of people' (Warschauer and Grimes, 2007: 2).

Of course, the idea of digitally connecting people is not new. The internet actually started primarily as a way for people to connect with others. As early as 1979, Tom

Truscott and Jim Ellis from Duke University conceived of a worldwide discussion system called Usenet that people could use to talk about things with others who were interested in the same topic. For example, users could go to rec.pets.dogs to talk about dogs, or misc.invest.real-estate to talk about investing in property. These were the earliest 'online communities'.

In the early 90s, other kinds of places for people to meet and form online communities became popular, such as bulletin board systems (BBS), MUDs and MOOs (see Chapter 9), and America Online chat rooms. Coming at a time, at least in the United States, when involvement in 'real life' communities and social organizations seemed to be on the decline (see Putnam, 1995), many people extolled the virtues of these online communities in which strangers thousands of miles away could come together around common interests and goals.

Most of these groups, however, were formed based on a system of social organization that was not much different from the file system for organizing information we discussed in Chapter 2: one which facilitated the grouping of people with similar interests into categories, but worked against the formation of connections between categories. People could go to Usenet groups, for example, and either hang out with the dog lovers or the real-estate investors, but dog lovers and real estate investors rarely hung out together. At the same time, the rhetoric around online communities in that era was not entirely optimistic. There were those who worried that online communities lacked the strong social ties and opportunities for joint action that characterized 'real-world' communities, and, even worse, that by participating in them, people were becoming even more alienated from their 'real-world' friends, colleagues, and family members. Others pointed out how the anonymity of such groups sometimes encouraged inappropriate behaviour like **flaming**, a form of digitally-mediated verbal abuse.

But then something began changing in the mid-1990s. In 1996, a company called Mirabilis released a free instant messaging client called ICQ, later followed by similar clients from AOL and MSN. These tools gave people the ability to talk in real time to all sorts of people, including people from their offline social networks like friends, relatives and colleagues whom they had rarely interacted with online before.

In the late 90s the first social networking sites like Classmates.com and SixDegrees.com, began to appear, along with a number of online journaling services like Open Diary and Live Journal. The social networking sites allowed people to contact old friends and acquaintances, and the journaling services allowed users to post their thoughts and ideas online, and to comment on the writing of others.

These developments brought about a number of changes in the way people conceived of the social organization of online groups. First, people's online interactions began to focus more on people that they already knew offline than on anonymous 'net friends'. Second, people were now able to organize their friends into groups not just according to interests but according to connections and to expand their social networks and those of their friends by introducing friends to one another. Finally, people began to see the internet as a tool for presenting and promoting their 'real selves' rather than for taking anonymous action.

Today the growth of social networking sites like Facebook has by far outpaced that of any other kind of website. In fact, there are more than twice as many people on Facebook as there are in the entire nation of Germany. The main difference between the 'Usenet' way of organizing people and the 'Facebook' way is that previously people were organized into interest groups like files in folders, whereas now people are linked to other people in complex networks based not on interests but on relationships. Just as web 2.0 tools now allow us to organize information based on its relationship with other information rather than based on fixed topics and rigid hierarchies, they also allow us to organize our connections online based on *relationships* rather than on fixed interests or roles. In other words, we are no longer like files that are put into different folders. We are like nodes in a vast network of relationships that allows us to be connected to a whole lot of people whom before we might never have shared a folder with.

WHO ARE THESE PEOPLE ON MY FACEBOOK?

There is a popular misconception about online social networks, which is mostly perpetuated by people who don't take part in them, that they are somehow fundamentally changing the nature of friendship. Some think that friendship is becoming more important because people are accumulating more 'friends' on sites like Facebook. Others declare that the notion of friendship is becoming devalued since you could not possibly be 'real friends' with all of the people in your online social networks. They go to the opposite extreme and declare that relationships formed or maintained through such sites are 'trivial'.

People who are experienced in using such services, however, are mostly aware that, although they may use the word 'friend' for all of the people in their network, these people exist in many different kinds of relationships with them. Some are close friends, some are relatives, some are acquaintances, some are friends of friends, etc. In other words, we are connected to the people in our social networks in many different ways, and part of what makes social networks so useful is the *variety* of connections they make possible.

Online social networks are characterized by a combination of what are known as **strong ties** and **weak ties**. They include your best friends as well as people you know only indirectly through your friends, including some you hardly know at all and may have never met. It turns out, however, that all these people can end up being very useful. In the event that you need help with something outside of the expertise of your close circle of friends and relatives, chances are there will be someone in this extended network who will be able to help you, eliminating the necessity to rely on complete strangers. Moreover, you are likely to trust these people more because they are 'friends of friends'. When people with whom we have weak ties become helpful to us in this way, we refer to the ties we have with them as **strong weak ties**.

The idea of 'strong weak ties' comes from an article called 'The Strength of Weak Ties' published in 1973 by sociologist Mark S. Granovetter, who was interested in why some people had an easier time finding a job than others. The answer he came up with was, in the case of most professions, those who had an easy time were those who had acquaintances who could introduce them to people who they didn't know in groups different from their own. In other words, the weak ties between such people and their acquaintances became crucial bridges to other communities. People who had only close friends and few acquaintances, on the other hand, were deprived of information and help from groups other than their own which not only put them at a disadvantage when it came to job hunting but also tended to insulate them from new ideas and make them provincial and inflexible in their thinking.

Of course, what Granovetter's work, done well before the invention of the internet, shows is that 'strong weak ties' have always been a feature of social life. Online social networks, however, have a way of facilitating the formation and maintenance of 'strong weak ties' first because they make 'weak ties' more explicit and visible to us, and second because these ties attain a kind of permanence and durability they didn't have before. Before when people swapped phone numbers or email addresses at parties, this often did not lead to the formation of any enduring connection. Now, when people exchange Facebook IDs, the chances that they will establish a more durable connection are much greater. It is much easier to communicate with someone who is already part of our online social network than it is to call someone we met at a party on the telephone. Furthermore, it is easier to make these weak ties stronger because the transaction costs of sharing information (such as photos, links, opinions and 'status updates'), even with people at the periphery of our social network, are relatively low.

The real advantage of online social networks, then, is not that they improve our relationships with our core group of close friends with whom we already have strong ties, or that they necessarily help us to meet 'new friends' that we might never have met before. Rather it is that they facilitate the strengthening of weak ties. You might not be any more likely to communicate and share information with your best friends because they are on your Facebook – you would have communicated with them anyway – but you are more likely to communicate and share information with your casual acquaintances.

This strengthening of weak ties has the result of connecting people, at least in indirect ways, to people and groups which they previously may not have had much contact with. The value of the different people in our social networks has as much to do with the functions that they serve in the network as they do with the strength of the relationships they have with us personally. According to author Malcolm Gladwell (2000), the two most important functions that people in social networks fulfil are those of **connectors** and **mavens**. 'Mavens' are people in possession of or with access to things that are beneficial to other people, such as goods, services, knowledge, information as well as emotional 'commodities' like friendship, loyalty and a sense of humour. Connectors are people who act as bridges, facilitating the flow of information, goods and services between different groups or **clusters** of people. Of course some people play both roles or play different roles at different times. The sociologist Robert Putman (1995) calls the two kinds of relationships in social networks **bonding** and **bridging**. Bonding is what occurs when you interact with your close friends. Bridging occurs when people with contacts in more than one cluster act as links between the people in those clusters (see Figure 10.1).

The first step to understanding how to manage connections in social networks is understanding the nature of those connections – whether they constitute strong ties, weak ties, or strong weak ties, understanding the different groups or 'clusters' that make up the network, and understanding the roles different people in the network play – whether they are 'mavens' – people who provide others with things like knowledge, information, support or attention – or connectors – people who act as bridges between different clusters – and whether the relationships between people are relationships of bridging or bonding or both.

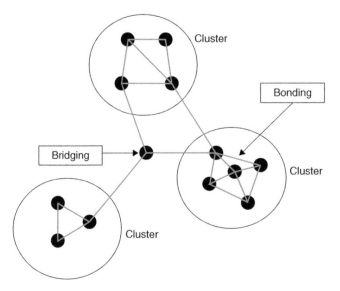

Figure 10.1   Bonding and bridging

Activity 10.1: Mapping your social network

Choose an online social network that you belong to and use one of the visualizing tools listed below to analyse it. Try to identify:

1. The different clusters that make up the network;
2. The people with whom you have strong ties;
3. The people who act as connectors among people in the same cluster;
4. The people who act as connectors between different clusters;
5. The people who act as providers ('mavens') and the kinds of things they provide to you and other members of the network;
6. The people with whom you think you have 'strong-weak' ties (and why).

Touch Graph: Allows you to visualize your network as a collection of 'clusters' with friends ranked based on who is a connector between clusters.
http://www.facebook.com/apps/application.php?id=3267890192

Social Graph: Allows you to check the connections of each of the nodes in your network and to rate your 'popularity'.
http://www.facebook.com/apps/application.php?id=67692068407

Friend Wheel: Allows you to visualize your network in the form of a wheel with clusters of linked nodes forming along the circumference.
http://thomas-fletcher.com/friendwheel/index.php

Facebook Visualizer: Allows you to filter the visualization based on gender, relation-ship status and node distance.
http://vansande.org/facebook/visualiser/

Mention Map (for Twitter): Maps conversations as a network.
http://apps.asterisq.com/mentionmap/#

InMaps (for LinkedIn): Creates an interactive visual representation of your network.
http://inmaps.linkedinlabs.com/

YT Visualizer (for YouTube): A tool for visualizing the connections between a YouTube user, his or her subscribers and his or her 'friends'.
http://www.lococitato.com/ytvisualizer/

Case study 10: Social networking and civic participation

Many people have extolled the potential of social media sites like Facebook and Twitter to facilitate political activism and increase civic participation, and there are plenty of well-publicized examples of this. One well-known case is the use of MySpace by U.S. students in 2006 to organize a national protest for immigration reform (boyd, 2008). Another is the use of Facebook by the citizens of Columbia to protest and resist the violence and kidnappings perpetrated by the revolutionary organization FARC (Kirkpatrick, 2011). It is widely believed that social networking sites played a key role in the victory of President Barack Obama in 2008, helping him to solicit small campaign contributions from a large number of people and helping his supporters organize local campaign events. Social networking has also been credited with helping to make possible the protests against Iranian President Mahmoud Ahmadinejad in 2009 as well as the protests that spread across the Middle East in 2011 (for an alternate view see Chapter 7). There is even some evidence that users of social networking sites are more likely to get involved in a political cause. In a study of Facebook use and civic engagement by university students, Sebastián Valenzuela and his colleagues (2009) found a weak but sig-nificant correlation between the intensity of students' Facebook use and their civic participation.

Social networking sites provide users with a number of affordances for the coordina-tion of joint action. First, they facilitate the wide and efficient distribution of informa-tion. It is not just that information is broadcast to a large number of people, but that this distribution network makes use of already existing social relationships.

The main difference between the groups of people that come together on social networking sites and those that formed in the online communities of the past is that, while online communities made it possible for people with similar interests to connect with one another and discuss their interests, many of these people often remained anonymous to one another and shared very little 'off topic' information about themselves. As a result, these communities usually did not facilitate much more than just discussion (which was sometimes characterized more by internal dissent than cooperation), and these discussions couldn't easily go beyond the insulated online communities where they started.

People in online social networks, on the other hand, are joined together not just by an interest in a particular topic, activity or cause, but also by *social relationships*. Bonding between friends with strong ties increases motivation and commitment to the cause, and bridging relationships help spread this commitment to other groups linked to one another through weak ties. This combination of bonding and bridging is one reason social networking sites are such effective tools for memeing (see Chapter 6). Online social networks combine the bandwagon effect associated with 'strength in numbers' (the more people that are supporting a cause, the easier it becomes to support), with the power of peer pressure (the more your friends support a cause, the more likely you will also support it).

Another reason these sites can encourage participation in political activism is that the transaction costs (see Chapter 5) of participation are often quite low, sometimes involving little more than clicking a link to join a Facebook group, sign an online petition, or make a contribution with your credit card. For those causes that require more effort, social networking sites help people to break tasks into manageable segments that can be shared among many participants so that people can make meaningful contributions without spending too much time and energy. Moreover, the loose organization of social networks makes them more flexible and more able to adjust to unforeseen circumstances.

As we mentioned in Chapter 7, however, there are people who are sceptical of the power of online social networks to help bring about political change. Among them is Evgeny Morozov, whose book *The Net Delusion* contains a detailed critique of the 'media-hype' surrounding the contribution of social networking sites to the Iranian protests in 2006.

Another prominent sceptic is the author Malcolm Gladwell. Gladwell argues that it is to some degree the very affordances we discussed above, including the low cost of participation, that make social networking sites unsuited for serious political activism. For most effective social movements, such as the marches and organized acts of civil disobedience of the U.S. civil rights movement in the 1960s, participation has tended to be high stakes, requiring people to be willing to 'stick their necks out' by, for example, risking arrest. Recruiting participants for such activities requires strong ties and a kind of 'band of brothers' mentality which social networking sites, built mostly around weak ties, do not usually foster. Social networks are effective in increasing participation by requiring a lower level of the very sort of commitment that makes social movements successful. As Gladwell puts it, 'While online social networks make it easier for activists to express themselves', they make it 'harder for that expression to have any impact'.

William Davidow, in his book *Overconnected: The Promise and Threat of the Internet* (2011), goes even further, claiming that the strengthening of weak ties, instead of helping people to organize to solve problems, can actually create problems. He uses as an example the worldwide economic crisis of 2008, which he argues would not have been so severe without the accelerated spread of rumours and fear made possible by social networking sites. Strong weak ties have the capacity to carry not just useful information and 'positive memes', but also mass confusion and what Davidow calls 'thought contagion'.

PRIVACY AND PROFIT

As we said above, an important difference between many of the online communities of the past and today's most popular social networking sites is that, while in online communities people were often anonymous, social networking sites encourage people to reveal their 'true' identities. In fact, in many online social networks anonymous participation is pointless, going against the whole purpose of joining the network.

This difference represents a dramatic change in the way people think about online communication. In the early days of the internet anonymity, role-playing, and pseudonyms were features that almost defined the medium, and there were some distinct advantages to this. For example, anonymity allowed marginalized or politically oppressed people to express their opinions without fear of being identified and persecuted, and role-playing allowed people to expand their horizons by 'trying on' different kinds of identities. Now, although opportunities for anonymity, role-playing and impersonation still exist, the ethos of the internet has changed to favour the disclosure of one's 'real' identity. Rather than a medium that helps people interact behind a cloak of anonymity, the internet is now seen first and foremost as a tool for self-promotion.

With this change of ethos have come inevitable concerns about privacy. On social networking sites it is common for hundreds of 'friends' to have access to our personal information, photos and status updates. Often the 'audience' for one's online behaviour extends far beyond one's immediate network to the networks of friends and friends of friends. Moreover, because of the 'sharability' of online content, it is more difficult for people to maintain control over what they post and what might happen to it in the future. The internet is full of anecdotes of people who have lost their jobs, ruined their reputations or wrecked their marriages because of something they posted on an online social networking site.

Social networking sites themselves – like Facebook – have played an important role in promoting this ethos of radical self-disclosure. The more people share information about one another, the argument goes, the better people will understand one another, increasing cooperation and decreasing things like corruption and political oppression. Transparency breeds freedom and democracy. Critics and sceptics would answer that what the transparency fostered by such sites actually breeds is advertising. By encouraging people to share information about themselves with more and more people, such companies have created sophisticated 'business models' in which information about people has become a valuable commodity to assist other companies in marketing their products.

Many users of such sites suffer from the illusion that they are getting a free service, when actually they are paying for their participation with information about themselves. In fact, as much as the functions that encourage 'sharing' (like soliciting information about your favourite book, your favourite movie, even your favourite people) are designed to strengthen social ties, they are also designed to encourage users to give up just the kind of information about themselves that advertisers find most useful. One aspect of the new economy, which we touched briefly upon in Chapter 6 and will discuss further in Chapter 12, is that we ourselves are becoming commodified, and social networking sites play a big role in this. Our behaviour on sites like Facebook is constantly tracked, mined and sold to outside parties, usually without our explicit knowledge, in order to direct more targeted advertising our way. That's why those ads you see on Facebook often seem eerily relevant to you.

Critics of such sites have pointed out that this creates a kind of imbalance of power in which we have less access to and control over information about ourselves than do companies like Facebook. Some, like Erik Rothenberg (2010), advocate the development of technologies which would give users of social networking sites the opportunity to track and trade their own information. Rothenberg envisions a 'personal tracking widget' which would allow users to compile statistics about their online behaviours, preferences and affinities and then sell this information to companies that are interested in advertising to them.

Whether or not such technologies are on the horizon, anyone who uses social networking sites is inescapably a participant in the 'attention economy' (see Chapter 6), with successful participation dependent on being able to manage information about oneself, to effectively engage in self-promotion and to figure out how to protect one's privacy when necessary. Some believe that in this new economy, the whole idea of personal privacy is changing, with members of the younger generation more willing to disclose personal details about themselves to large numbers of people than generations before them. While this may be true, the definition of privacy does not so much hinge on how much information you are willing to disclose, but how much *control* you have over where, when, how much and to whom you disclose it. Although many people today spend a great deal of time revealing information about themselves using digital media, these media also come with considerable affordances for controlling and 'fine-tuning' these disclosures.

THE PRESENTATION OF SELF ON SOCIAL NETWORKING SITES

Perhaps the most important digital literacy associated with social networking sites is being able to engage in effective practices of self-presentation and **impression management** in different situations and with different people. This includes understanding how to use the tools available in social networking sites to attract some kinds of attention and deflect other kinds.

Despite Facebook founder Mark Zuckerberg's insistence that 'you have only one identity', and that 'the days of you having a different image for your work friends or co-workers and for the other people you know are probably coming to an end pretty quickly' (Kirkpatrick, 2011: 199), people still, to a large extent, *perform* social identities, and they perform different identities for different people.

The idea that social identity is a kind of performance was developed by the sociologist Erving Goffman in his classic 1959 book *The Presentation of Self in Everyday Life*. When we are in public, Goffman said, we cooperate with one another in performing various roles. A large part of these performances consists of managing our 'information preserves': deciding what information about ourselves we want to reveal to others and what information we want to hide from them. This does not mean that we are dishonest. What it really means is that we are complicated. We have many different sides to our personalities and there are many different kinds of information about us that we might choose to reveal to other people. And so, even 'being yourself' is a kind of performance.

We accomplish performances of identity, according to Goffman, by making use of the various kinds of 'equipment' different settings make available to us. Actors use a stage, props, costumes and make-up. People in 'real life' also use equipment like the physical setting, various objects, clothing and make-up. Just as different physical settings make available to us different kinds of equipment for self-presentation, so do different online settings. Different social networking services, for example, make different demands regarding authenticity and identity verification. On Facebook, one's identity is verified by one's friends, and so concealing or lying about it is counterproductive. On MySpace, on the other hand, more opportunities are given for people to construct 'fake' identities. Most online dating services depend on people being truthful about themselves, and there are strong norms in such contexts against deception. At the same time, such sites often give users the opportunity to choose pseudonyms, hide some of their information in 'private' places like 'photo vaults', and to protect themselves against unwanted contact (Jones, 2012b).

The equipment made available in online social networks for identity management generally consists of two kinds: there is equipment for *displaying* information and equipment for *concealing* information. Such equipment always has *affordances* and *constraints* associated with it. Interfaces that allow users to choose different information for their profiles from drop down menus, for example, make it easier for people to display information about themselves, and, since everyone displays the same kind of information in the same format, also make it easier for users to search for other users based on the set criteria. On the other hand, such 'multiple choice profiles' also constrain self-expression by making it difficult or impossible for users to display information that does not fit into the prescribed categories.

Equipment for displaying information in online social networks consists of things like profile information, profile pictures and photo albums. Such sites also make an important part of self-presentation the display of one's relationships with other people. Lists of 'friends' and other information about one's position in the social network have become an important part of displaying one's identity. Some sites also allow users to make explicit statements about their 'relationship status' with other people or to communicate relationships through actions like tagging their friends in photos.

Such sites also make available a host of other ways for people to reveal information about themselves through, for example, taking quizzes, downloading applications through which they keep track of books they have read or movies they have seen, playing games, and answering questionnaires like '25 random things about me'. These structured exercises in information display serve an important function, giving people a reason for sharing more about themselves. Sometimes sharing information with other people can be awkward. The norms of self-disclosure in most cultures, in fact, work against people sharing unsolicited information about themselves with large numbers of people, and people who make a habit of such unsolicited disclosures are often considered conceited, self-promoting, or simply odd. Organized tools for sharing information make this process less threatening by providing a framework for it.

Identity in online social networks, however, is not static. The work of performance is not complete after one has finished designing a profile and revealing one's favourite books and 25 random pieces of personal information. One's identity must be constantly updated with even more information through things like 'status updates' and new profile pictures. In this way, more than with the personal web pages of the past, social networking sites mimic the dynamic and contingent nature of identity in the physical world.

Some sites like Facebook facilitate this constant maintenance and reinvention of the self with features like the 'news feed' which alerts people in your network when you update your status, post new information or change something in your profile. At first this was a controversial feature among users, making them feel that too much information about their actions was being broadcast to other people. The clever and oddly attractive part of this feature, however, is that it encourages the performative aspect of identity: our own lives and the lives of others become like dramas that are played out before different audiences in our social networks. Even the network itself, with its changing ties and relationship statuses, takes on a dramatic feel.

It is chiefly though interaction in the network, therefore, that we display our identities. People's Facebook walls are like stages on which they act out conversations with their friends for other people to witness. What this means is that we are not alone in constructing our online identities. Others in our social network also contribute by doing things like commenting on our posts and tagging us in pictures.

This interactive and cooperative aspect of self-performance also makes it more difficult for us to manage our information preserves. While we have control over what we want to reveal and what we want to conceal, we do not have control over what other people reveal about us or the kinds of comments they make about our information. Moreover, many social networking sites include algorithms that automatically share information about users whenever they do something like upload a new photo or change their relationship status, and modifying if and how these automated messages are sent out is not always straightforward.

Just as important as the equipment such sites provide for displaying information is the equipment they provide for *concealing* it. 'Privacy settings' allow users to make certain kinds of information available only to certain people, facilitating what Goffman calls 'audience segregation'. We can, for example, make certain parts of our profile available to our colleagues and other parts available to our friends. Equipment for concealing information also consists of the ability to remove information. One might, for example, find it necessary to 'untag' oneself from an embarrassing photo posted by another user or to remove incriminating comments people have posted on one's wall – a process that has come to be known among Facebook users as 'wall cleaning' (see Chapter 12).

Different online social networks provide different kinds of tools for users to manage their privacy. The problem is that in some systems the privacy settings are difficult to use or 'leaky'. On Facebook, for example, one can usually gain access to the photo-album of a 'non-friend' after a mutual friend comments on a photo. Furthermore, although nearly all sites provide users with the ability to change their privacy settings, default settings have a very powerful influence on the way people manage their identities. Most people, in fact, simply accept the default settings provided by a service rather than going to the trouble of changing them. Consequently, privacy advocates have criticized sites like Facebook for setting their default privacy settings to reveal the maximum amount of information to the maximum number of people (which has obvious advantages for advertisers using Facebook as a commercial platform). There has also been concern about third party applications that make use of people's information and sometimes share it with others outside of the social network.

Rather than attempting to set different levels of privacy for different people within a particular social networking site, some people prefer to use different services for different purposes. They may, for example, use Facebook for their friends, LinkedIn for their business associates, and Twitter to contact people who have similar hobbies or interests.

Google+, the newest social networking site at the time of writing, attempts to address problems of privacy with a feature called 'circles'. When users invite new 'followers', they are able to drag their pictures into circles representing different social groups like 'colleagues' or 'family'. Later, when they share a photo or piece of information they can easily control which of their circles they want to share it with. This is not very different from the 'groups' function on Facebook, but it makes this function more visible and much easier to use. In doing so it promotes a very different kind of ideology of social organization than Facebook. Rather than promoting the 'flat' version of radical self-disclosure advocated by Zuckerberg, it promotes greater audience segregation and a more fragmented notion of identity. As Google's promotional video for the service puts it, Google+ makes online sharing 'work more like your real life relationships where you choose who gets to know what' (http://youtu.be/ocPeAdpe_A8).

Some people (see, for example, Bennett, 2011) argue that the simplest and most open privacy settings actually have the effect of helping people to better maintain their privacy. In Twitter, for example, there are only two options: complete openness (in which all 'tweets' are public and can be 'retweeted' by anyone) and completely private. Most users choose to tweet publically (since in many ways publicity is the whole point of 'tweeting'). What this means is that they do not suffer from an 'illusion of privacy' and make use of the most efficient filter available to control what they reveal: their own judgment.

Activity 10.2: Performance equipment

Consider an online social networking service that you use such as Facebook, MySpace, Orkut, RenRen, YouTube, Twitter, etc., and answer the following questions.

1.   What kind of equipment does this service make available for *displaying* information about yourself? What are the *affordances* and *constraints* of such equipment and what kinds of displays do they facilitate? How do you and other people in your social network make use of this equipment? What sorts of strategies do people use to enhance their displays in order to get other users' attention or to express certain things about themselves?
2.   What kind of equipment does the service make available for *concealing* information about yourself? What are the *affordances* and *constraints* of such equipment? How knowledgeable are you about how to use this equipment?
3.   Do you *display* and *conceal* different things to different people in your social network? What kinds of equipment does the service that you use make available for managing *audience segregation*? Do you present different identities to different audiences?
4.   To what extent do you regard your self-presentation using this service to be an 'authentic' and 'honest' reflection of your 'real-world' self? To what degree do you engage in dissembling, exaggerating, idealizing, role-playing and out-right lying? What are the social functions of such activities?

CONCLUSION

Are online social networks changing the way we think? Some people would argue that they are. They may, for example, be changing the way we think about privacy and how much we feel comfortable revealing information about ourselves to other people. They may even be changing the way we understand the notion of the self – rather than a self-contained, autonomous entity, the self may be becoming much more a matter of one's social connections. Of course, in many cultures the sense of the self as existing in a complex web of social relationships has long been the norm, as has a general lack of privacy.

Different kinds of technologies bias users to think in different ways (see Chapter 7). Two clear biases of online social networking sites have to do with the way they encourage us to think about time and the way they encourage us to think about space. The constant status updates and alerts of social networking sites encourage us to focus much more on the present than the past. We are continually introduced to new information often before we have had a chance to process old information. They also encourage us to think of all space as potentially public and to regard public actions and public discourse as naturally positive. Consequently, maintaining a public presence on an online social network is to some extent becoming part of being a 'normal' and legitimate person in some societies and social groups.

Social networking sites are also raising a host of important social issues about the rights people have to be 'secure in their persons' and the extent governments and commercial concerns can or should use information from such sites for their own purposes, even when that information is 'aggregated' rather than traceable to specific users. In order to develop the critical perspective to engage in debates about such topics, however, it is first necessary to understand the basic literacies associated with social networks: literacies associated with *managing connections* and those associated with *managing identities*.

In this chapter, we have also considered the potential for social networking sites to facilitate collective action, especially in the domain of politics. In the next chapter we will look more broadly at issues of collective action, collaboration and ways in which digital media affect how we work together.

USEFUL RESOURCES

Print

boyd, d. and Ellison, N. (2008). Social network sites: Definition, history and scholarship. *Journal of Computer-Mediated Communication 13* (1): 201–230.

boyd, d. (2008). Why youth (heart) social network sites: The role of networked publics in teenage social life. In D. Buckingham (ed.) *Youth, identity, and digital media*. Cambridge, MA: The MIT Press, 119–142.

Christakis, N. A. and Fowler, J. H. (2009). *Connected: The surprising power of our social networks*. New York: Little and Brown.

Granovetter, M. S. (1973). The strength of weak ties. *American Journal of Sociology 78* (6): 1360–1380. Available online at: http://sociology.stanford.edu/people/mgranovetter/documents/granstrengthweakties.pdf

Kirkpatrick, D. (2010). *The Facebook effect*. New York: Simon and Shuster.

Web

New York Times, Giridharadas, Anand, 'Behind Facebook's success: It takes a village'
http://www.nytimes.com/2009/03/27/world/asia/27iht-letter.html?_r=2&partner=
    rssnyt&emc=rss

The New Yorker, Gladwell, Malcom, 'Small change: Why the revolution will not be tweeted'
http://www.newyorker.com/reporting/2010/10/04/101004fa_fact_gladwell

Mashable, Social networking
http://mashable.com/follow/topics/social-networking/

Video

Clay Stirkey, Facebook killed the private life
http://www.youtube.com/watch?v=azlW1xjSTCo

Office of the Privacy Commission of Canada, Privacy in social networks
http://www.youtube.com/watch?v=X7gWEgHeXcA

Google, The Google+ project
http://youtu.be/xwnJ5BI4kLI

CHAPTER 11

Collaboration and Peer Production

As we saw in Chapters 3 and 4, reading and writing through digital media are interactive processes, with readers able to write back to authors and actively take part in text production. In addition, with mashups and remixing, creating a digital text is often a matter of piecing together the texts of others to come up with a new and original work. Although it might seem as though you are working 'alone', you are in a sense entering into 'collaboration' with the creators of the texts, images, music and sound that you are remixing. Thus, digital literacy practices increasingly involve us in interaction and/or collaboration with others.

At the same time, digital media and communication technologies also make it easier for us to enter into more formal collaborations. First, it is easier for us to establish relationships with potential collaborators: for example, we can identify people with similar interests and interact with them through the kinds of online affinity spaces described in Chapter 8. Second, thanks to the cheap availability of networked communication tools like email and chat (text, voice, video), it is easier for us to maintain collaborative relationships over a distance. Finally, we now have access to a range of dedicated writing tools, like blogs, wikis, and online office/productivity suites that make it easier to manage collaborative writing tasks.

As well as supporting existing collaborative writing processes like those found in the workplace (see Chapter 12), digital media and communication technologies have also made it possible for a new form of collaborative process to emerge. This new process is known as 'commons-based **peer production**' ('peer production' for short). In peer production, massive numbers of people, who are distributed across the globe and connected to each other by digital networks, work together voluntarily to promote projects that they are interested in. Under the right conditions, these loosely organized groups of peers can work together on projects so effectively that they are able to compete with more traditional organizations, like governments and corporations.

In the case of collaborative writing, perhaps the best-known example of this peer production process is the online encyclopaedia, Wikipedia. Although the content of Wikipedia is produced almost exclusively by volunteers, its quality nevertheless rivals professionally produced encyclopaedias like the Encyclopaedia Britannica (Giles, 2005). As we will see, the kind of peer production processes that have resulted in Wikipedia can also be found in other walks of life, including software development, archiving, academic and commercial research, entertainment and commerce.

In fact, once you become aware of the underlying principles of this new form of networked, peer-to-peer collaboration, you begin to see instances of it everywhere. As well as peer-produced content, there is peer-produced filtering and peer-produced reviewing and commentary. For example, the folksonomies and tag clouds found in social bookmarking sites (see Chapter 2) are generated using the input of large groups of internet users who tag and label the bookmarks that they share. Similarly, the list of recommendations that Amazon serves you as you browse through its online store is compiled by aggregating the selections of the many customers who bought the book you are interested in. Although you might not think of yourself as working in collaboration when you tag a bookmark or buy a book through Amazon, in reality your input, combined with the input of millions of others, provides a valuable resource for others.

In this chapter, we will consider the effect of digital media and communication technologies on collaboration. We begin by exploring the potential of digital media to facilitate collaborative writing. Then we describe peer production, the collaborative information production model that makes use of internet technologies to engage vast numbers of individuals distributed across the globe in collaborative projects.

COLLABORATION IN WRITING

In order to understand the way that digital tools can contribute to collaboration in writing, we need to understand something about the process of collaboration itself. In fact, collaboration is complex and varies from group to group. Different groups will adopt different processes and strategies depending on their particular needs and the individual style of group members. Despite this variation, we can nevertheless identify a number of common issues that collaborative writing teams must face. A first set of issues relates to the group: group formation, group organization and maintenance, and communication about group processes. A second set of issues relates to the writing task: the strategies people use to accomplish the task and how they coordinate their work (see Sharples *et al.*, 1993; Lowry, Curtis and Lowry, 2004 for more detailed accounts).

An initial issue in collaborative writing is how to form a group and define the writing task. In some cases group membership and task definition are taken as givens, as when groups of knowledge workers from the same company collaborate on routine writing tasks that emerge in the course of business. In other cases, where the writing is of a less routine nature, it may be necessary to review the goals of the collaborative writing project and identify individuals from a range of backgrounds with the necessary knowledge and skills to participate.

This process of group formation can be facilitated by participation in online affinity spaces, where individuals from different backgrounds interact with one another about a shared interest (see Chapter 8). By participating in such online spaces (for example, email lists, online forums, social networks) people expand their networks and enter into relationships with like-minded others, all of whom are potential collaborators. Such online spaces could conceivably provide useful contacts for professional collaborations as well as for more informal collaborations that arise out of non-professional interests, as is the case with fan fiction writing, for example. In addition, digital communication tools facilitate the formation of collaborative groups that are geographically distributed over large areas.

A second issue relates to organizing and maintaining the group once it has been formed and the writing task has been clearly defined. This involves negotiating a suitable process (see below), negotiating the roles of various contributors, and resolving conflict as it arises. Again, in routine workplace writing the roles of team members may be fairly stable, with given team members regularly taking on particular social roles (team leader, facilitator) or task-related roles (writer, reviewer). Conflict can arise when team members are not satisfied with each others' contributions, or when they disagree about aspects of the writing, such as the intended audience, the rhetorical purpose and so on. Such conflicts can act as both a constructive or destructive force, depending on how they are managed.

Digital media like email and chat can be used in order to address these issues of group organization and maintenance, especially in groups that are geographically distributed. However, compared to face-to-face interaction, these tools can create a sense of anonymity and increase the social distance between members of the team (what Sharples *et al.*, 1993 call **de-individuation** and Lojeski, 2007 calls **virtual distance**, see Chapter 12). This can in turn undermine the social cohesion of the group. Bearing this in mind, it is often desirable for collaborative teams to meet face-to-face during the initial stages of group formation and planning or when serious conflicts arise. In groups where this is not possible, contact with team members through more informal channels such as social networking sites might help to reduce the de-individuation effect (see Chapter 12).

A third issue relates to the strategies adopted when actually engaging in the writing task. In general, a collaborative writing project can involve both periods of close collaboration (team members meet for writing sessions, discuss and develop drafts together) as well as periods of individual work (team members divide the labour and draft on their own). Sharples *et al.* (1993) identify three different collaborative writing strategies: sequential writing, parallel writing and reciprocal writing.

In sequential writing (see Figure 11.1), one person works on the document at a time before passing control of it to the next writer. This strategy allows each writer to review and build on the existing text in a coherent way. The drawback is that each writer has to 'wait their turn' and this leads to some inefficiency.

In parallel writing (see Figure 11.2), the document is divided into different sections, which different writers work on at the same time. This allows the team to make progress on a number of sections of the writing at the same time. However, once these sections are

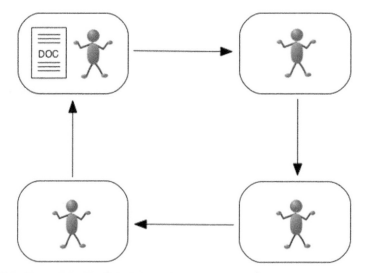

Figure 11.1   Sequential writing (adapted from Sharples *et al.*, 1993)

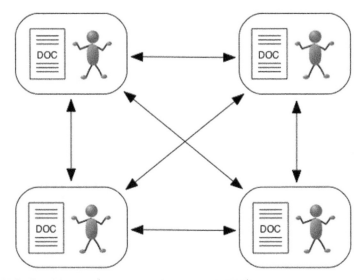

Figure 11.2   Parallel writing (adapted from Sharples *et al.*, 1993)

complete it is necessary for an editor to take control of the full draft and ensure that the sections build on each other in a logical way. Some stages of the writing task are particularly well suited to a parallel writing strategy. For example, in academic writing while one team member is editing a completed draft for formatting and style, another can compile the reference list and appendices.

In reciprocal writing (see Figure 11.3), control of the document is shared between all members of the team, who simultaneously discuss, draft and respond to each other's suggestions. This strategy is well suited to the initial brainstorming and outlining stages of a

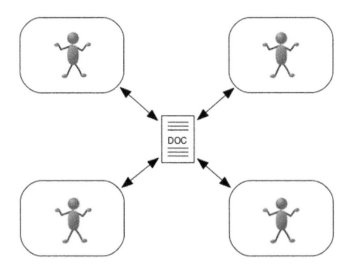

Figure 11.3   Reciprocal writing (adapted from Sharples *et al.*, 1993)

project, but can also be used to produce a full draft. For example, collaborators can meet, discuss and compose their draft with a 'scribe' making changes to the document. Alternatively, collaborators can share the document that they are working on and allow any member of the team to make changes to any section. Wiki platforms (see Case study 11) could be used to facilitate such a reciprocal writing process.

The three strategies outlined here can all be supported by technological tools to create, share, comment on and jointly edit artifacts that support different stages in the writing process (for example, mind maps, outlines, drafts). In fact, there are now a wide range of dedicated collaborative writing tools available, including brainstorming tools, word processors, online office suites and wikis. In order to support collaboration in writing, these tools must provide detailed commenting and annotation tools for peer review and feedback. After an initial draft has been created, other team members must be able to record comments and suggested changes in a way that preserves the original version of text, in case suggestions are not accepted.

One tool that provides very detailed mark-up of this kind is Microsoft Word. An example, taken from an earlier draft of this book, is provided in Figure 11.4.

In this example, Rodney has marked up a draft written by Christoph, using Microsoft Word's 'track changes' and 'comments' tool. The track changes tool provides a way for collaborators to add and delete text, while keeping track of the original version. Four changes to the text have been made here: additions to the text are displayed in purple, underlined text; deletions are recorded in the bubbles on the right. The edits are tied directly to the text and also record the editor's name as well as a timestamp. This detailed display makes the suggested edits easy for the original writer to evaluate and either accept or reject: first, the writer can tease out the contributions of different team members; second, the writer can compare the new text with the old version. If a change is not accepted, it is easy to roll back to the previous version.

Less detailed suggestions can be made using the comment tool, as shown in the figure, where Rodney asks for an example to be added (also displayed in the bubbles on the right). Once again, this comment is tied directly to the text it refers to (highlighted in purple), and this makes the comment easier to interpret. Such annotation tools are well suited to both sequential and parallel writing strategies, where the text or sections of the text are passed from one writer to another for review. Once a document has been marked up using such tools, it can be shared by email or through a file sharing service, providing collaborators with the means to discuss their written products in detail, even if they are separated by a great distance.

Online office suites like Google Documents allow writers to engage in the reciprocal writing strategy at a distance. With Google Documents, the document is stored on a server online, and any team member with the necessary permissions can edit it, so that a number of team members could work simultaneously on the entire text if desired. This method can of course become confusing when numerous authors are editing the text at the same time. In order to address this problem, the tool alerts users when other collaborators are editing or viewing the document simultaneously, and also makes chat options available so that collaborators can communicate as they edit. It also keeps track of the edits made, so that different versions of the document can be compared and older versions restored if necessary.

In such online office suites, because the document is stored on a server, there is no need to share it to the local hard drives of other team members. This kind of central storage (which is also a feature of wikis, see below) also addresses the problem of 'versioning' in collaborative writing. When documents are shared between different computers (for

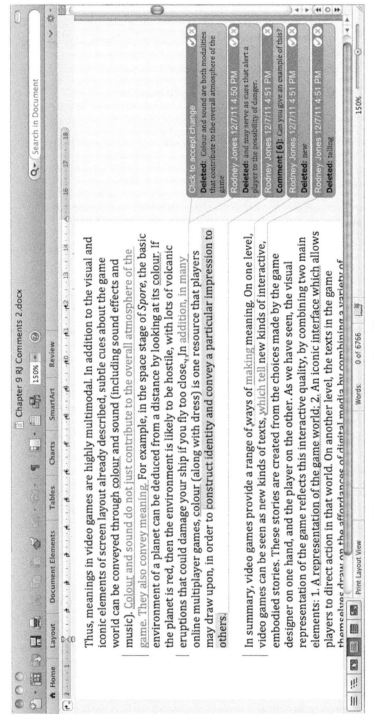

Figure 11.4 Draft with mark-up in Microsoft Word (used with permission from Microsoft)

example, by email), there is a risk that collaborators will lose track of who has the latest version, and simultaneously edit different versions of the same document on their local computers. When this happens the versions stored on different computers get out of sync and have to be reconciled.

Activity 11.1: Your collaborative writing practices

Describe and evaluate your own collaborative writing experiences, i.e. any time that you have been involved in some form of group writing or group writing project. Use the following questions to guide your discussion:

1. What was the context for the writing?

    a. Formal context, for example, school, university, training programme?
    b. Informal context, for example, Facebook, blog writing, fan fiction?

2. What motivated you to do the writing? Was your motivation: a) intrinsic, i.e. doing it for fun? b) extrinsic, i.e. doing it to meet some external pressure or reward?
3. How did you manage the collaborative writing process?

    a. Group: How did you identify group members? What roles did different people adopt and how were these roles allocated? Was there a group leader? Were there any free riders? Was there any conflict? If so, what was the conflict about, how did you talk about it and resolve it?
    b. Task: How closely did you work with your collaborators in: 1) idea formation/brainstorming? 2) drafting? 3) revising/reviewing? Did you follow a parallel, sequential, or reciprocal working strategy, or some mixture? How did you communicate suggestions and revisions to the text? How did you keep track of the most recent version of the text?
    c. Communication: What media did you use to communicate with collaborators? How did that media affect the collaborative writing? Did you notice any 'de-individuation effect'?

4. What communication tools/writing tools did you use to help you manage the collaborative writing process? How did those tools contribute to the process?

WIKINOMICS AND PEER PRODUCTION

The kind of digital media and communication tools that we have described so far make it easier to do collaborative writing in traditional contexts like the workplace. But, as we noted earlier, they also go beyond this to make possible a new kind of collaborative information production model: 'commons-based peer production' ('peer production' for short). In essence, peer production is collaboration between very large, diverse, loosely organized collections of individuals, who are distributed throughout the world and connected by a digital network. Peer production differs from traditional collaboration in the workplace in a number of ways. First, it usually involves massive numbers of collaborators from very diverse backgrounds. Second, the relationship between collaborators is one of equal peers working together and there is usually no formal 'chain-of-command' or organizational structure. Finally, the collaborators are self-selected, and motivated to contribute to the project out of a sense of enjoyment or fun.

The theory behind commons-based peer production is described in a paper written in 2002 by law professor Yochai Benkler called 'Coase's Penguin, or, Linux and the Nature of the Firm'. Benkler focuses on an early example of peer production, the development of open source software like Linux. Unlike proprietary software developed by companies like Apple and Microsoft, open source software is developed and maintained by a global community of volunteers who give their time for free. The source code underlying the software is available for anyone to use, modify and distribute, both for commercial and non-commercial purposes following the terms of the General Public License (GPL). One key term of this license is that all software products that build on open source code must also be distributed under the GPL license. In other words, future programming innovations have to be shared back to the developer community. This kind of peer production is said to be 'commons-based' because individuals do not retain the intellectual property rights to their creative work, but return the work to the 'commons' so that others can use it as well.

The open source software movement attracted a lot of attention because of its phenomenal success. As an example of this success consider the popularity of the open source server software, Apache, which competes with Microsoft products. A survey of websites conducted in February 2011 (http://news.netcraft.com) found that Apache at that time held 60 per cent of the market share (and rising), with Microsoft coming in second at 20 per cent. This invites the question: how could a group of part-time volunteers organize themselves so efficiently as to outperform one of the biggest software developers in the world?

The answer to this question probably has something to do with the unique characteristics of peer production as an economic model for the production of information (and other economic goods). According to Benkler, two kinds of economic arrangements have traditionally dominated in capitalist societies. The first is the 'market model', in which individuals sell things directly to the public, making decisions about their behaviour according to the market (for example, what people want to buy, how much money they have to spend). The second is the 'firm model', in which individuals work in a hierarchical firm and make decisions about their behaviour based on what their boss tells them to do. In a free market system, firms will emerge wherever organizing the production of goods and services is cheaper than securing those goods and services by market exchange.

Commons-based peer production, largely made possible by digital media, has arisen as an alternative to these two models. In peer production, the individual works neither alone nor for a boss who tells him or her what to do. Instead, the individual works as part of a loosely organized group of people, connected by networked computers and often distributed over a large geographical area. This system of organization is sometimes referred to as the 'crowd model'. In these groups, there is no boss to make sure that the project succeeds. Instead, things work themselves out by virtue of the sheer size of the group and everyone in the group contributing according to his or her abilities and talents.

There is an important advantage to peer production, compared to markets and firms. That advantage has to do with the way that peer production opens participation up to everyone, allowing individuals with the necessary interest and skills to self-select and take part in the project. In the firm model or market model, people do work because their boss tells them to, or because there is demand in the market and they wish to profit from it. However, the boss or the market may not always be very good at identifying the right individual for the job. By contrast, in the crowd model people do work because they are interested and consider themselves to have the necessary skills. This system is sometimes more effective because the selection of individuals is left up to the individuals themselves, and they are the ones with the best information about their own suitability.

What's more, in the kind of knowledge work that peer production involves, selecting individuals with appropriate skills for the job is very important. It's different from industrial-style factory work, where one worker is very much like another. Information production depends heavily on the quality of the human input. Not everyone can contribute to the open source software movement because not everyone has the necessary skills.

But what about the limitations of this model? One possible limitation is motivation. In the market-based system, people are motivated by the desire to earn money. In the firm-based system people are motivated by the desire to earn money and the desire for security. But peer production relies on people who are willing to forego the opportunity to make money, and work for some other motive. In peer production people are motivated chiefly by 'fun'. What we mean by 'fun' here is a complex combination of people's intrinsic desires to do things that interest them, to interact with like-minded people, to 'show-off' their talents or intelligence and to be part of something bigger than themselves. Being part of a peer production project can provide people with indirect benefits, such as the opportunity to build 'social capital', improving their reputations as they are recognized for their contributions.

Experience shows that the question of motivation is in fact a rather trivial one. It is more important to find ways to reduce the effort of participating, than it is to provide motivations to participate (of course, some threshold level of motivation is essential). The model works best if the project is sufficiently 'modular' or 'granular' to be broken down into small chunks that only take a small amount of effort to process. These chunks then need to be distributed to a very large group of people. The idea is that the many small efforts of a large number of individuals will eventually add up to a meaningful outcome. Finally, once these chunks have been isolated and processed, it must be possible to cheaply re-integrate them into a meaningful whole, some kind of final product.

As an example of a successful peer production project in research and development, consider NASA's Clickworkers project. This project provides public volunteers with the opportunity to get involved in scientific research, specifically the analysis of images from Mars. Volunteers visit a website (http://beamartian.jpl.nasa.gov/) where they can view images from Mars and either map Martian land features or count craters. The tasks require human judgment but no specific scientific training is necessary.

In this example, the task is clearly of a modular nature: it can be broken down to individual pictures which can then each be analysed by a number of 'clickworkers'. The analysis is easy and doesn't require a lot of effort. The results of the analysis can be aggregated and averaged out using some kind of algorithm in order to integrate the many contributions into a single final analysis. In all likelihood, people volunteer to analyse a few images partly for the fun of being involved in NASA research, but also because it only takes them a few minutes to do so. NASA has evaluated the research that has been conducted in this way, and found that the combined efforts of a large group of clickworkers is at least as good as the efforts of a single trained scientist working with the same images.

This kind of 'crowd-sourcing' can also work well in commercial enterprises. One example is Lego's Mindstorms. In 1998, Lego released a product with programmable pieces to turn its interlocking blocks into programmable robots and machines. Shortly after the release of the product, consumers started hacking the software and creating their own programs to do much more than what Lego engineers had designed.

Initially, Lego threatened to sue those who were violating their software license, but quickly reversed their position when they realized that they had an enormous source of creativity to co-develop their toy. Lego now has a website (http://mindstorms.lego.com) where users can share software for programming Lego toys. Furthermore, Lego offers free downloadable development software so that consumers can easily make new creations and share them with other consumers.

As this example shows, the collaborative practice of peer production has ushered in an entirely new economic model for commercial enterprises. Authors Don Tapscott and Anthony Williams call this new model 'wikinomics', described in their 2006 book of the same name. In their book they suggest that businesses must adapt to the ways of thinking of this new economic environment in order to remain competitive. Among other things, they highlight the way that peer production is affecting the roles of producers and consumers. As in the example of Lego Mindstorms, many consumers now take a more active role in design and development. In order to reflect these changing relationships, Tapscott and Williams adopt the term 'prosumer' to describe this new kind of active consumer.

Wikinomics and peer production also challenge the way that we think about authorship and ownership. Traditional wisdom and current intellectual property laws say that your creative work (including the information you produce) should belong to you alone. However, as mentioned above, commons-based peer production projects like the open source software initiative rely on contributors giving back to the community and returning their creative innovations to the commons. Adopting a traditional approach to authorship and ownership in the open software movement would be disastrous for the project because of the way that programmers innovate by building on the work of others.

None of what we have discussed here is to say that the wikinomics model is always going to outperform traditional firm and market models. Jarod Lanier, author of *You Are Not a Gadget* (2010), questions the potential of the crowd model when compared with the traditional firm and market models. He points out that, as impressive as they are, the achievements of the open source software movement are in fact limited to relatively straightforward kinds of development: for example, server software like Apache, and office software like OpenOffice. Although the crowd is effective at organizing to produce these 'software clones', true innovation, Lanier believes, relies on the vision, creativity, drive and management of individual leaders typically working in traditional hierarchical organizations. That's why, he says, the open source software collective was unable to come up with a revolutionary product like the iPhone. Instead, the individual brilliance of Steve Jobs (supported by his creative team) was needed to make this happen.

Case study 11: The wiki

The word 'wiki' comes from the Hawaiian word for 'quick' and refers to a kind of website which is designed to allow its users to quickly and easily create and edit web pages, using only a web browser. The first wiki, Wikiwikiweb was designed by American computer programmer Ward Cunningham and launched in 1995. It focuses on the topic of software development and can be visited at http://c2.com/cgi/wiki.

Since that initial wiki, wikis have been adopted in a range of different sectors, including corporate use, education and popular use. Wiki farms like Wikia, PBWiki, Wetpaint, and Wikispaces allow anyone with the time and interest to set up a wiki website and (possibly) make it available for the general public to view. In the corporate setting, wikis can be placed behind firewalls and used to support projects or as a replacement to a static intranet. In education, wikis can be used as a platform to showcase and share learning, as well as a collaborative tool to enhance group learning. And in popular contexts, wikis allow just about anyone to share insights about their passions: entertainment, travel, and cooking to name just a few. In general, wikis are particularly well suited to the creation of a knowledge base which draws on diverse contributions from a range of people: for example, plot summaries of popular TV shows, travel guides, collections of recipes.

Wikis provide a number of affordances that make them interesting collaborative tools. In particular, most wikis now provide their users (potentially anyone) with:

1. The ability to easily create, edit and hyperlink to web content;
2. A discussion page, where users can talk about the content that they create, posting comments to explain their revisions or challenge the revisions of others;
3. A 'history' function that allows users to view previous versions of the page, compare changes between different versions, and roll back to an earlier version if they want to.

These affordances can provide a number of benefits to collaborative writers. First of all, a wiki can be set up to invite contributions from anyone, even anonymous users. This provides the potential to expand the collaborative team and draw upon diverse perspectives, and such diversity is likely to have a positive effect on the project. Second, because wikis are web-based they provide an up-to-date, centralized record of the document that is under creation. This solves one problem of collaborative writing, namely keeping track of different versions of a document, which have been separately edited by different authors. Finally, wikis provide ways of discussing the document contents and reverting to earlier versions where necessary.

There are, however, some constraints associated with these features as well. For example, the fact that anyone can edit a wiki opens up the possibility of intentional disruption and vandalism of the website. Similarly, the history function can be abused, as where 'edit wars' break out with different users repeatedly rolling the wiki page back to the version that they prefer. Some wiki platforms provide the ability for a moderator to lock changes until major issues have been resolved. Authors of wikis who are using the discussion function to talk about such issues have to become very good at using text to do so, which some would argue is a relatively impoverished medium, especially compared to face-to-face interaction.

Without a doubt, the most well-known wiki at the time of writing is Wikipedia. Studying contributions to Wikipedia can provide interesting insights into the way that massive online collaboration using a wiki works. In particular, we can see that the technological affordances described above must be complemented by a system of community norms to ensure that the group works in a cohesive way.

Wikipedia presents itself as 'the free encyclopaedia that anyone can edit'. It originally started in 2001 as a supplementary project to 'Nupedia', another effort to create a free encyclopaedia. Nupedia, which relied on experts to write articles, had to be abandoned because of difficulties getting authors to agree to contribute and inefficiencies in article production and editing. The Wikipedia project, in contrast, brings together volunteers from very different backgrounds, many of whom are not recognized experts in the areas on which they write and most of whom have never met before, to collaborate to create what has become one of the largest reference websites available (http://en.wikipedia.org/wiki/Wikipedia:About).

Wikipedia is remarkable because of the nature of its mass collaborative authorship. According to Wikipedia, there are roughly 91,000 active contributors to the website, and these people are largely volunteers, not paid for their effort or expertise. Contributors are self-selected rather than vetted by experts, and yet the final product compares well with professional encyclopaedias like the *Encyclopaedia Britannica* (Giles, 2005). Furthermore, as a collaboratively written text, contributors understand that individuals cannot take credit for their work, beyond the username information that is recorded in each page's history.

With so many people working on the project, managing the group in terms of shared purpose, roles and conflict resolution becomes a major challenge. Not surprisingly, the Wikipedia community has developed a set of guidelines, policies and social norms to deal with such issues. Over time, the Wikipedia community has reduced the principles by which it operates to a core set of principles known as 'The Five Pillars'. These are:

- Wikipedia is an online encyclopaedia;
- Wikipedia has a neutral point of view;
- Wikipedia is free content;
- Wikipedians should interact in a respectful and civil manner;
- Wikipedia does not have firm rules.
  (See http://en.wikipedia.org/wiki/Wikipedia:Five_pillars)

Taken together, these Five Pillars help to provide group cohesion by: 1) stating the aim of the wiki, i.e. to construct a free, online encyclopaedia; 2) stating some expectations about how this aim will best be achieved, i.e. by writing articles with a neutral point of view, treating collaborators with respect, and not by slavishly following or enforcing community-generated rules to the letter.

Where Wikipedians disagree about the content of a Wikipedia page, it is not surprising to see them referring to one or other of these Five Pillars. The following example (Figure 11.5) comes from a Wikipedia discussion page on an article about statistical inference (http://en.wikipedia.org/wiki/Statistical_inference). The first participant raises a perceived problem of bias, a failure to meet the standard of neutral point of view (NPOV), in the comments of one editor. The second participant adds a link to the Wikipedia project page that provides detailed guidelines for achieving a NPOV. However, the original editor (the third participant in this discussion) disputes the accusation of bias, and goes on to justify the substance of what he has written in the article.

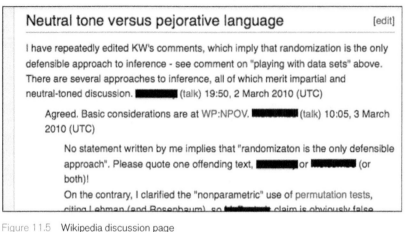

Neutral tone versus pejorative language   [edit]

I have repeatedly edited KW's comments, which imply that randomization is the only defensible approach to inference - see comment on "playing with data sets" above. There are several approaches to inference, all of which merit impartial and neutral-toned discussion. ▆▆▆▆ (talk) 19:50, 2 March 2010 (UTC)

Agreed. Basic considerations are at WP:NPOV. ▆▆▆▆▆ (talk) 10:05, 3 March 2010 (UTC)

No statement written by me implies that "randomizaton is the only defensible approach". Please quote one offending text, ▆▆▆▆ or ▆▆▆▆▆ (or both)!
On the contrary, I clarified the "nonparametric" use of permutation tests, citing Lehman (and Rosenbaum), so ▆▆▆▆▆ claim is obviously false

Figure 11.5   Wikipedia discussion page

Here, the technological affordance of the discussion page provides a venue for editors to discuss and resolve conflicts about the content of articles. However, the technological affordance alone is not sufficient to ensure that such discussions will be fruitful. Ultimately, the community must establish norms by which contributions can be evaluated, such as those relating to the NPOV in the example above. In addition, appropriate norms of interaction (i.e. netiquette) and procedures of dispute resolution also need to be established and followed. In order to collaborate effectively, a wiki community has to develop social norms which foster that collaboration.

Wikis provide a new tool for collaboration, which, as in the example of Wikipedia, is capable of facilitating a new kind of massive collaboration with associated new literacy practices. In order to make meaningful contributions, participants in such a collaborative writing project have to become good at managing relationships with a large number of partners, most of whom they have never met. Among other things, this involves: understanding group norms; understanding group writing purpose; adopting appropriate roles; communicating appropriately with the group; and resolving conflict in appropriate ways.

The collaborative literacy practices observed in wikis are not in and of themselves new. However, the potential of wikis to involve a massive, loosely organized, global community of mostly unknown volunteers is. Wikis change the quality of collaborative practices, both through the technological affordances that they introduce, as well as the social norms that grow up around established wiki communities.

THE WISDOM OF CROWDS

At the heart of peer production is the idea of 'collective intelligence', which we introduced in Chapter 2. Essentially, this is the idea that the group is often smarter than the individual. In other words, if you have a large, diverse group of people and you set them a problem to solve, then the collective solution of the whole group is often better than the best solution of any one individual. In this way the collective effort is often greater than the sum of the individual contributions that make it up.

In his 2004 book, *The Wisdom of Crowds,* author James Surowiecki illustrates the idea of collective intelligence with the example of Francis Galton, who in 1906 tested the idea (in a rather informal way) at a livestock show in the West of England. At the show, there was a competition to guess the weight of an ox, with prizes for the best guesses. It attracted 800 guesses from members of the public. Galton calculated the mean value of all the individual guesses and arrived at a collective estimate of 1,197 pounds. This collective estimate turned out to be very good indeed: the correct weight was 1,198 pounds.

The idea of collective intelligence challenges our usual instinct that the best solution to a problem can be arrived at by consulting experts. One wonders how a group of people like the one at the livestock show could be so smart. After all, the average intelligence of a crowd like that is probably just average. As it turns out, having a large number of very intelligent people in the collective is not that important to the combined intelligence of the collective. Other factors play a more important role.

Surowiecki points out four main characteristics of smart groups: 1) diversity; 2) independence; 3) decentralization; and 4) aggregation. Diversity in a group is good because then the group is able to take into account a wider range of different perspectives on the same problem. Independence is important to encourage an environment where group members arrive at their own views, which they openly state and debate. Decentralization is helpful because decentralized groups can take into account a wide range of local conditions when they make decisions. Finally, for collective decision-making to work, the group must have some means by which it can aggregate all of the contributions of different members of the group.

It follows that dumb groups are those that lack these characteristics. Instead, the following properties can be observed: 1) homogeneity; 2) centralization; 3) division; 4) imitation; 5) emotionality.

The process of networked peer production that we describe above often works to encourage the formation of these kinds of smart groups. It does this mainly by opening the process up and allowing anyone to self-select for the project. The distributed groups that result usually involve: 1) a diverse range of individuals; 2) loosely connected in a more or less decentralized network; 3) working in a more or less independent way to; 4) make a contribution which is aggregated into the collective work.

However, a note of caution is in order. The idea of collective intelligence does not imply that a collective decision will always be better than an individual one. As Lanier (2010) points out, problems that can be reduced to discrete, measurable components are better suited to collective decision-making than those that cannot. For example, the collective decision-making that determines prices in a market, with each individual simply paying an 'affordable' price for goods, tends to work fairly well. In this example, individual interests can be reduced to a single variable, namely price, which can be aggregated to arrive at a collective decision. But if the laws of a country were put on a wiki for anyone to edit, the results would be chaotic because the collective would likely fail to reach agreement. In these more complex scenarios, the individual interests of members of the collective need to be regulated by checks and balances, which more often than not place decision-making authority in the hands of individuals.

Activity 11.2: Why peer produce?

As we've suggested, one of the mysteries about peer production is what motivates people to do it in the first place. Read the different peer production stories below and consider these questions:

1. In what way is the story an example of peer production?
2. What is produced and how is it shared with peers?
3. How much time, effort and skill do you think is required?
4. How much enjoyment, social capital or money is gained?
5. What is the possible motivation of the peer producer?

Case 1: Andy is a freelance software programmer who creates web-based solutions for small businesses. He uses free, open source software and builds on existing code to create customized programs tailored to his clients' individual needs. Whenever he modifies code to build something new in this way he submits it to the open source community, where others can download and use it. In addition to his paid work for clients, Andy contributes to an open source initiative for free, and sometimes spends long hours reviewing, troubleshooting and fixing issues in the implementation of the programming language PHP.

Case 2: Jane is a secondary school English teacher, with a love of grammar, poetry and public speaking. After a long day at work, she likes to sign in to Distributed Proofreaders (http://www.pgdp.net/c/), where she volunteers her time to proofread scanned copies of public domain books that are in the process of being converted into eBooks. The website provides her with a scanned page image and the corresponding OCR text. She compares the two copies and if she finds an error she enters her comments into the web interface. Sometimes she reviews the comments of other proofreaders, checking their suggestions. She aims to do a page a day, but with all the marking that she has to do that's not always possible.

Case 3: Dan is a building contractor whose company specializes in residential buildings. In his spare time, he's heavily involved in the virtual world *Second Life* (SL). Initially, he was just curious to see what all the fuss was about. He downloaded the SL client, set up an account, created an avatar and started to explore. It was quite confusing at first, and he spent a lot of time learning how to navigate the world, and customizing his avatar (which he wanted to make look a little bit like himself, but better). After a while, he figured out that he could create his own objects in SL and share them with other residents. After designing a few accessories for his avatar, he built a classic car, the 1975 Ferrari 365 GT4 BB. He joined a classic car group in SL who have meetings to admire each other's creations, buy and sell, share experiences and help newbies.

CONCLUSION

In this chapter we have examined the way that people use digital media and communication technologies to collaborate. On one level, these technologies support collaborative writing projects in traditional contexts like the workplace by providing tools for team members to communicate with each other about their writing. On another level, the same tools have made possible a new collaborative information production model known as peer production. This model is particularly effective for knowledge work, because of the way that it opens participation up to diverse groups of individuals, allowing those with the appropriate motivation and skills to self-select for a given project. We've seen examples of how businesses, government organizations like NASA and non-governmental organizations like Wikipedia have been able to use the peer-production model and advance their interests by looking outside of the organization and drawing on the wisdom of crowds. In the next chapter we will focus on the ways that people use digital media within particular organizations and workplaces.

USEFUL RESOURCES

Print

Benkler, Y. (2002). Coase's penguin, or, Linux and the nature of the firm. *Yale Law Journal* *112* (3): 367-445.

Jenkins, H. (2006). *Convergence culture: Where old and new media collide*. New York: New York University Press.

Rheingold, H. (2002). *Smart mobs: The next social revolution*. Cambridge, MA: Perseus Publishing.

Surowiecki, J. (2004). *The wisdom of crowds: Why the many are smarter than the few and how collective wisdom shapes business, economies, societies, and nations*. New York: Doubleday.

Tapscott, D., and Williams, A. (2006). *Wikinomics: How mass collaboration changes everything*. New York: Portfolio.

Web

NASA, Be a Martian
http://beamartian.jpl.nasa.gov/

Distributed proofreaders
http://www.pgdp.net/c/

Lego Mindstorms
http://mindstorms.lego.com

Video

TED, Howard Rheingold, The new power of collaboration
http://www.ted.com/talks/lang/eng/howard_rheingold_on_collaboration.html

TED, Jimmy Wales, The birth of Wikipedia
http://www.ted.com/talks/jimmy_wales_on_the_birth_of_wikipedia.html

TED, Clay Shirky, How the cognitive surplus will change the world
http://www.ted.com/talks/clay_shirky_how_cognitive_surplus_will_change_the_world.html

CHAPTER 12

Digital Literacies at Work

In this chapter we will consider how many of the digital literacy practices we have been discussing in this book are affecting, and in some ways transforming, the world of work and helping to create what has come to be known as the **new work order** (Gee *et al.*, 1996). We will explore how workplaces have changed in the past two decades, partly due to digital technology, how people use digital tools to support teamwork, and how social media is being used to help create a sense of belonging and community in large organizations. We will also examine how digital media are affecting the ways workers market themselves and manage their relationships with colleagues, current and potential employers, clients and customers. Finally, we will consider some social and ethical aspects of the 'new work order' including such issues as privacy, job security, worker rights and the assessment and evaluation of workers.

LITERACIES FOR THE 'NEW WORK ORDER'

It is difficult to say how much the internet and digital media are responsible for the dramatic changes in the contemporary world of work, and how much changes in the world of work are responsible for the increased development and adoption of digital technologies. Much of the increase in internet use by companies has been driven by broader economic changes brought about by globalization. It is doubtful, however, that globalization would have been possible without the increased connectivity and speed of communication brought about by digital technologies.

To fully examine how workplaces and the idea of work itself has changed in the past two decades would require a separate book. What we can do is summarize the five main changes that we see as most relevant to the kinds of literacy practices that will be required in the 'new work order'. They are: 1) a shift from manufacturing work to 'knowledge work', 2) the distribution of work across large geographical distances, 3) a de-emphasis on the 'workplace' as a place where people work, 4) a flattening of hierarchies within organizations, and 5) a weakening of the relationships between employers and employees.

'Knowledge work'

Over the past several decades most 'developed' countries have experienced a dramatic shift from market-based economies characterized by mass-manufacturing of standardized products to knowledge-based economies characterized by large numbers of service jobs, manufacturing based on customization and niche markets, and global competition for jobs and markets. Traditional markets have become saturated and material products no longer command the same kind of value they could in the past. What workers of the future will be increasingly involved in is 'producing' and selling 'lifestyles', 'symbols of identity', and 'attention structures' (see Chapter 6).

Many people working in this new economy are engaged in what is known as 'knowledge work', work that is primarily focused on information processing and knowledge creation. It is not surprising that most of the new jobs in this economy are in the information-technology sector, but even in other sectors, jobs increasingly involve workers in the use of high technology, the manipulation of information, and the creation of knowledge. According to Manuel Castells, author of *The Rise of the Network Society* (1996), in the new economy wealth generation resides in the ability on the part of societies, organizations and individuals to 'create new knowledge and apply it to every realm of human activity by means of enhanced technological and organizational procedures of information processing' (Castells, 1993: 20). In organizations competing in this new economy, knowledge sharing has become more important than knowledge hoarding. In the past, 'proprietary information' was closely guarded by organizations and access to such knowledge was usually restricted to those at the top of the hierarchy. Today, however, successful organizations are those that know how to rapidly disseminate and share information both within and outside the organization in ways that make them better able to respond to greater global competition and the challenges of new markets.

The literacy practices associated with 'knowledge work' include many of those we have been discussing in this book. Workers need to be able to evaluate and find patterns and relationships in large amounts of data, to manipulate information in efficient and creative ways, to create new information and new knowledge in various forms, and to evaluate and make efficient use of 'attention structures'. These practices, however, like all literacy practices, do not just involve technical skills, but also involve the ability to successfully manage social relationships and social identities. Successful 'knowledge workers' must be adept at sharing information and knowledge, at creating and maintaining social networks through which information and knowledge can circulate, and at assuming various roles and identities within these networks.

Distributed work

Because of organizational downsizing, increased outsourcing and the globalization of manufacturing, services and markets, work today is often distributed over large geographical distances. Workers often find themselves parts of geographically distributed teams which must coordinate tasks using information technologies like email, video-conferencing, instant messaging and wikis. In a recent survey of 1,592 workers in 77 countries working in a wide variety of industries (RW³ Culture Wizard, 2010), over 80 per cent of respondents reported that they were part of a team with people based in different locations, and 63 per cent of respondents indicated that nearly half of their team members were located outside the country in which they were based.

Under such circumstances, effective communication mediated through digital technologies becomes essential to co-ordinate teams and manage tasks. This involves not just understanding how digital media work and being sensitive to the challenges involved in intercultural communication (see Chapter 8), but it also involves understanding something about the process of *mediation* itself, and how the tools that we choose (both technical tools like software packages and symbolic tools like language and types of texts) act to amplify and constrain certain kinds of relationships and certain kinds of social actions.

Taking the place out of workplace

Related to the increasingly distributed nature of work is the fact that the physical 'workplace' in the form of an office is becoming less and less important as a site of work. Many major companies, including Procter & Gamble, IBM, Accenture and AT&T, have all but eliminated traditional offices, and more than 10 per cent of workers in North America and Western Europe work from home.

Author Cynthia Froggatt (2001) refers to the increased tendency for people to work from the privacy of their own homes as 'working naked', and points out its many advantages to both organizations and individuals, including enormous savings of time previously spent commuting from home to work, enormous savings of money previously used to rent and maintain workplaces, and increased flexibility, creativity and productivity.

Like working in virtual teams, working from home requires a mastery of communication practices appropriate to different kinds of tasks and different kinds of roles. It also requires a high degree of self-management as working hours become more flexible, and the boundary between work time and leisure time, and even between the activities of work and play become fuzzier. Challenges facing those who spend all or part of their time working from home include finding an appropriate balance between work and personal life, overcoming feelings of isolation from colleagues and superiors, and compensating for a relative lack of visibility within their organizations.

From vertical hierarchies to self-managing teams

Traditionally, industrial-age organizations were organized vertically. Most decisions were made at the highest levels and then communicated to lower levels, where they were simply carried out without the need for much thought by bottom-tier employees. This wasted much of the intellectual capital within organizations, limiting productivity. In response to increased competition and more volatile markets, many organizations have sought to achieve greater productivity by organizing themselves horizontally, empowering 'self-managing teams' within lower levels of organizations to make important decisions related to their work (Manz and Sims, 1993; Mikulecky and Kirkley, 1998).

According to James Paul Gee and his colleagues (Gee, Lankshear and Hull, 1996: 29), 'old capitalism' depended on 'middle managers' to supervise workers and act as conduits of information between upper and lower levels of the organization. In the 'new work order' the roles and responsibilities of middle managers have increasingly been passed on to front-line workers themselves. Management theorists are increasingly talking less about how to control workers and more about how to 'empower' them, and organizations are increasingly looking to hire people who are 'self-directed' and exhibit 'creativity' and 'critical thinking'.

Members of the 'self-managing teams' characteristic of the 'new work order' must be able to quickly identify important problems, locate useful information, critically analyze the information, synthesize it to generate solutions to the problems identified, and then quickly communicate the solutions to others, so that everyone within the team is informed. They must also be adept at social practices of communication and identity management that are associated with effective teamwork, especially practices of knowledge sharing, networking, and appropriate self- and peer evaluation.

In such teams, the most important people will not necessarily be 'leaders', but will more likely be either 'connectors', those who link together different kinds of people in the organization and outside of the organization, or 'mavens', those who possess the most useful information and intelligence (see Chapter 10).

So what kinds of literacies will be necessary for effective work in these self-managing teams? Rob Carter, chief information officer at FedEx, argues that the best training for this may be playing massively multiplayer online games like *World of Warcraft*. The 'quests' teams engage in in MMOGs like this, he says, resemble the kind of fast paced and complicated tasks that small work teams need to engage in in today's workplace. These tasks require each member to make a unique contribution, and failure to contribute results in being socially sanctioned by one's team members (Fisher, 2009).

The rise of the nomadic worker

Another consequence of increased globalization and outsourcing is an increasingly tenuous relationship between employers and employees. In 2009 the U.S. Department of Labor estimated that by the age of 38 the average American worker will have had between 10 and 14 jobs. Their statistics also show that 1 in 4 workers is working for a different company from a year ago, and that half are working for a different company from five years ago. These statistics are similar in other places like Western Europe and Asia.

Not only are people increasingly changing jobs, but many do not even have jobs in the traditional sense as many businesses choose contract relationships over hiring new employees. This significantly complicates work relationships: many employers have very little contact with the people who do much of the work for their organizations, and many workers have very little contact with the companies they work for, because they are often hired on a part-time or temporary basis.

Because the business environment is constantly changing in unpredictable ways, workers have to be flexible and adaptable. They need to constantly 're-invent' themselves and use these 're-invented' selves to go out and find new work. People are increasingly taking what is known as a 'portfolio' approach to their careers – an approach based on almost constant self-promotion and 'self-reinvention' as workers cope with less secure employment situations and quickly changing job markets.

This is another area where literacy practices associated with online social networking become important for workers. Workers who are successful at moving easily from one job to another or at gaining lucrative contract work are those who are able to effectively make use of the 'strong weak ties' in their social networks, and those with the impression management skills to create 'profiles' which bring together evidence of past achievements and experience in effective and creative ways that command the attention of potential employers.

It should be clear by now that many of the literacy practices necessary for success in the 'new work order' are very different from those people used to get ahead in traditional market-based organizations. Unfortunately, many schools, universities and training programs do not do enough to integrate these new literacies into their curricula.

The problem often has to do with fundamental notions of what literacy is. Most business communication courses take a very narrow view of literacy, focusing on 'skills' associated with operating certain technologies or producing certain kinds of texts rather than helping people understand how these tools and texts are tied up with the ways that we make meaning, conduct social relationships, create social identities and think. Even higher order abilities like 'creativity' and 'critical thinking' are often presented as discrete, decontextualized 'skills'. According to the practice oriented view of literacy we have been advocating in this book, 'skills training' is only a very small part of what is needed to help prepare people for work. People also need the ability to analyze how work-related interactions and transactions occur at a nexus of technological tools, social relationships and personal skills, and how different elements of this nexus amplify or constrain certain meanings, certain relationships and certain identities.

Activity 12.1: Preparing for the world of work

Based on the discussion above, consider the degree to which the things you have learned and the literacy practices you have engaged in as part of your formal schooling have prepared you for the workplace practices described above. Also consider how your non-school-based literacy practices, including participating in blogs, social networking sites, photo/video sharing sites, online forums or discussion groups, instant messaging, online shopping and auction sites, and online gaming, might have prepared you for these workplace practices.

Sorting through and evaluating large amounts of data	Sharing information and knowledge	Using text-based digital communication
Identifying and solving problems	Anticipating future problems and new opportunities	Working in virtual teams
Self-management	Taking on different roles and identities	Flexibly adapting to changing circumstances
Self-marketing and profile building	Social networking	Re-inventing yourself

---

THE PROMISES AND PITFALLS OF THE 'WIKI-WORKPLACE'

The work-related practices we described above are supported by a large and ever-growing array of technological tools, from more traditional tools like telephones, to more sophisticated technologies like teleconferencing and voice over internet protocol. It is these technologies that make possible and support practices like virtual teamwork, telecommuting, and 'anytime anywhere' work.

The digital tools currently used in workplaces include communication tools like email, instant messaging software, and virtual meeting and teleconferencing software; information sharing tools like file sharing software, blogs and podcasts, forums and bulletin boards, and virtual team spaces; push technologies like RSS feeds and aggregators; and collaborative work tools like groupware and wikis. It is this last type of tool, especially wikis, which have inspired the most enthusiasm among managers and business journalists. Writing in *Businessweek*, for example, Don Tapscott (2007) argues that such tools help to facilitate the global, 'self-organized' teams that are part of the 'new work order' and make use of many of the digital literacy practices younger employees bring to the workplace. Wikis, he claims, 'will arrive in the workplace, whether companies are ready or not'.

As we explained in Chapter 11, wikis are online environments that facilitate the collaborative creation of documents. They provide both connectivity and flexibility, allowing people to contribute to projects when, where and in the way that they want to. They also have the advantage of automatically recording the entire flow of the work on a project as it progresses, allowing people to look back at the history of a document and see how it has been altered and enabling them to efficiently build knowledge and negotiate ideas.

Many organizations have reported great success in using wikis and other collaborative tools to coordinate the work of virtual teams and to encourage greater participation of workers at all levels of the organization. One example is Xerox Corporation, where a wiki was used in order to help the company define its technology strategy. Typically, high-level strategy documents are created by people in the upper levels of organizations. By setting up a wiki, Xerox allowed workers in its research and development teams to collaboratively define the company's strategy and create the relevant strategy documents (Tapscott and Williams, 2006).

For every success story in using online collaborative tools, however, there are numerous tales of difficulties and frustrations. In fact, most workplaces have yet to adopt such solutions, opting instead for more traditional communication tools like telephones and email to manage the work of virtual teams. In a survey of the use of communication technologies in the workplace, D'Urso and Pierce (2009) found that the ten most frequently used were (in this order): Email, internet, landline telephones, voicemail, fax devices, cell phones, intranets, audio teleconferencing, Listserv or group email, and instant messaging. Wikis came in at number 22, with only 2.2 per cent of respondents using them, and for most of those users (92 per cent), use was mandatory, suggesting that people were using wikis not because they wanted to but because they had to. Other digital collaborative tools fared equally badly, with only 2.8 per cent of respondents reporting use of group decision and support systems, and only 1.6 per cent reporting use of corporate blogs.

The apparent lack of enthusiasm by many organizations to adopt the digital collaborative tools we discussed in the last chapter, despite their clear affordances, may be part of a more general ambivalence about virtual teamwork itself. In the international survey of distributed work mentioned above (RW[3] Culture Wizard, 2010), respondents were also asked about their experiences with virtual teams. A majority found it more difficult in virtual teams than in face-to-face teams to manage conflict, make decisions, and express their opinions. They also stated that delivering quality output and generating innovative ideas were both more challenging in a virtual environment. Finally, 81 per cent of respondents reported difficulty in establishing rapport and trust with virtual team members and 90 per cent reported insufficient time to build relationships when working in virtual teams.

Some of the difficulties associated with using online-collaborative tools in virtual team-work may stem from the same narrow view of digital literacies we mentioned above, a view which focuses almost exclusively on the 'skills' needed by workers to operate technologies without considering the social practices and social relationships that form the *context* for effective and efficient work. As a result, the introduction of tools to facilitate virtual teamwork sometimes actually makes it more difficult for people to work together. Digital communication tools, for example, might discourage people from using the telephone or face-to-face communication in situations where these older media might be more appropriate. Online collaborative tools might also contribute to workers receiving more data than they need, resulting in time wasted determining what data is relevant to their jobs and what data is not (see Chapter 2).

Other difficulties with proprietary collaborative tools include the fact that sometimes they are not particularly user-friendly and get in the way of the smooth execution of tasks or the smooth flow of communication. Often, because of security reasons, they create 'walled gardens' that make it more difficult for members of teams to share and collaborate outside of the organization or beyond the firewall. Many younger people in organizations complain that the collaborative tools they use at work are not as good as commercial tools like Facebook and Twitter. This is nowhere more evident than in universities where both students and professors complain that expensive proprietary 'learning management systems' like Blackboard lack the flexibility, functionality and elegance of the online tools they are accustomed to using in their everyday lives (Selwyn, 2007).

The greatest barrier to using collaborative work tools in virtual teams, however, remains the fact that they often do not sufficiently address issues of rapport and trust among users. Along with the survey cited above, lower levels of trust and rapport in virtual teams as compared to face-to-face teams have been reported in numerous other studies (see, for example, Merriman *et al.*, 2007). In Chapter 11 we called this increased sense of anonymity and distance 'de-individuation'. Consultant Karen Sobel Lojeski (2007) calls it 'virtual distance', and claims that it is the inevitable result of *mediation*. Her argument is that the lack of rapport and trust that members of virtual teams experience is less a matter of the physical distance separating them and more a matter of the technological tools that they use to communicate and how they manage these tools. Indeed, even workers in the same workplace can experience virtual distance if most of their communication is done via email and instant messaging.

Dealing with virtual distance requires that team members understand the effects of mediation and take steps to address those effects. Appropriate tools cannot be designed simply with the aim of facilitating workplace tasks. They also have to be designed to facilitate the creation and maintenance of social relationships among collaborators. Sometimes the tools that are the best at doing this are not necessarily those which facilitate 'work' in the traditional sense, but those which facilitate 'socializing'.

DIGITAL MEDIA AND THE CREATION OF CONTEXT

Above we discussed some of the advantages and disadvantages of using collaborative tools in the management of tasks by virtual teams. The problems many organizations confront in this regard, we said, come from taking a 'skills-based' view of technology and teamwork and not paying enough attention to the social context (social relationships and personal experiences) that support successful teamwork. An exception to this is the increasing use of social media in workplaces.

The difference between the use of social media tools and the use of collaborative digital workspaces is that while the later emphasize tasks and texts, the former emphasize context. Most wikis, for example, facilitate the collaborative authoring or editing of documents but create few chances for users to get to know and get to trust one another. Social media tools, on the other hand, allow collaborators to share information more freely, whether it is relevant to the task at hand or not. In fact, in many organizations social media is not explicitly used to accomplish any specific workplace tasks at all, but rather to facilitate the formation of relationships and the sharing of information that make it easier to get future tasks done in both virtual and face-to-face groups. Other organizations are attempting to merge the two functions, building tools like wikis, online whiteboards and other kinds of collaborative work tools into social networking sites, and commercial software suites for collaborative work like IBM's Lotus Connections and Microsoft's SharePoint are increasingly including social networking functions.

In their study of the role of Twitter in informal communication at work, Dejin Zhao and Mary Beth Rosson (2009) conclude that social media has the potential to act as a kind of 'digital water cooler'. They see Twitter as a virtual space where people gather and informally chat about things that are related to their own interests that might include work and might not. In the study they noticed a number of different, but interconnected ways that people use Twitter in the workplace: 1) to provide frequent, brief updates about personal life activities; 2) as a source of real-time information; and 3) as a 'people-based RSS feed'. Although Twitter, with its minimalist interface and 140-character limit on message length, lacks many of the affordances of other online workspaces, it has an advantage over many other tools in that it facilitates not just the exchange of information but also the building of relationships.

Many organizations, such as IBM, Microsoft and Deloitte (see below), have recognized the importance of fostering a conducive social context for collaborative work and instituted their own internal social networking sites in order to help their employees get to know one another and share information more easily. The main advantage of using social media for workplace and organizational communication is that it helps to address precisely the 'trust' and 'rapport' related difficulties people have with working in virtual teams we discussed above. Social media tools emphasize relationships more than tasks. They allow people to share what they want when they want to and to choose whom they want to be in their circle of communication, giving them more of a sense of control over their communication and their work. Social media tools also help to facilitate a sense of common purpose among members of teams and organizations and to facilitate the creation of a supportive corporate culture.

In their study of the ways employees of IBM use that company's internal social networking site, called Beehive, Joan DiMicco and her colleagues (DiMicco et al., 2008) at the IBM research center in Cambridge, Massachusetts found that people primarily use such tools not so much to collaborate on tasks as to get to know other people in the organization better, strengthen the weak ties in their networks (see Chapter 10), and reach out to other employees they do not know. One participant in their study said, 'Beehive helped me ... maintain loose social ties with people I don't have a close, frequent connection with' (715). Another said:

> Browsing lists of my contacts ... helped me get better knowledge of who I should know within IBM, by seeing who appears in multiple contact lists. I also learned about informal communities that exist within IBM – the cat lovers, the photographers, and maybe even the people who play strange musical instruments.
>
> (715)

The collection of strong ties, weak ties, and 'strong weak ties' that become visible in online social networks actually mirrors and helps to support the organizational structures that are becoming increasingly dominant in contemporary workplaces. These self-managing teams with porous boundaries often need to form and disperse very quickly and often depend as much on effective communication with people outside the team but peripherally connected to it as they do on communication among people inside the team.

Case Study 12: Deloitte

One of the first large companies to promote the widespread use of social media among its employees was the international accountancy firm Deloitte. Two notable examples of their efforts are the firm's internal online social networking site 'D Street' and the YouTube-based 'film festival' it sponsors called 'What's Your Deloitte?'. Both of these projects serve as illustrations both of how thoroughly digital literacy practices have permeated contemporary workplaces and how, in some cases, it is the 'social' aspects of these tools that have proven to be most valuable to companies.

D Street, Deloitte's internal social networking site, was launched in 2007. Part of what motivated D Street creator Patricia Romeo to initiate the project was her observation that many employees were already using social networking sites like Facebook and LinkedIn at the office. Another motivation was recruitment: Romeo wanted to find a way to make the firm appeal to the younger generation of workers accustomed to using social media to interact with people.

D Street has capabilities similar to Facebook, providing Deloitte employees with profiles pre-populated with basic information including name, job title and contact information. The employees can personalize their profiles by sharing photos, videos, resumes, community affiliations and information about their hobbies and interests. Accessing a colleague's profile on D Street has many of the same qualities as visiting them in their office where you might see a picture of their kids or souvenirs of their favorite sports team on the wall.

DiMicco and her colleagues (2008) found that employees use personal profiles on workplace social networking sites to engage in a process of 'people sensemaking', which they describe as 'the process a person goes through to get a general understanding or gist of who someone is' (1). This process facilitates the establishment of common ground, which, in turn makes future work-related collaboration more successful.

Other important features of the system are that it allows employees to introduce colleagues to one another, to join 'affinity groups', and to create their own blogs. Users also have the ability to link with external social networking sites like Facebook and

Twitter, allowing people to pursue their relationships beyond the 'walled garden' of the company.

After launching the site, the firm found not only that employees reported feeling more connected to one another, but that cross-division collaboration increased. The site also helped with the management of the flexible work arrangements, which were becoming more and more common in the firm. Avinash Jhangiani, a senior consultant at the firm, talked about how D Street had helped him expand his internal contacts at the company and to get involved in a volunteer project which allowed him 'to share (his) passion with nonprofit organizations and . . . enhance (his) personal brand within the organization' (Brandel, 2008).

Another successful social media initiative of Deloitte is 'What's Your Deloitte?', also launched in 2007, a contest in which its employees are invited to create short videos answering the question, 'What's your Deloitte?' Organizers of the project received over 400 submissions from employees during the first round of the competition and posted the fourteen winning videos on a Deloitte Film Fest YouTube page.

This project gives employees a chance to communicate about their personal experiences using a social media tool that is familiar to them from their daily lives, and, at the same time, to make a contribution to creating the public face of the company. The winning films are mostly playful, poking fun at the firm, like 'The Green Dot' (http://youtu.be/idOuHBuhXtY), in which an employee portrays himself as a 'client services superhero', and 'Food for Thought' (http://youtu.be/ainJ2VKJ_wU), in which employees spoof the culture of food at the workplace. These unfiltered and sometimes irreverent portrayals of what it's like to work at Deloitte have ended up serving as useful recruitment tools aimed at younger workers for whom they have much more credibility than traditional firm-produced recruitment materials. Like D Street, 'What's Your Deloitte?' is an example of the company encouraging employees to use digital tools in ways that, while not directly related to performing particular work-related tasks, end up contributing significantly to overall productivity by helping to create a *context* for effective communication across the organization (see above).

Both of these examples exemplify many aspects of the 'new work order' mentioned above. They encourage the strengthening of social relationships across administrative and geographical boundaries, facilitating the formation and management of self-regulating teams. Furthermore, by reducing 'virtual distance', they make the self-regulation of these teams easier, since people who trust one another are more likely to feel comfortable communicating openly and sharing their opinions.

They also help to encourage creativity and innovation, first by cultivating an environment of trust and 'fun', and second, by giving people more opportunities to pursue personal passions and hook up with others who share those passions. D Street even uses the vocabulary of digital literacies when it refers to the online spaces where people can share these passions as 'affinity groups' (see Chapter 8).

SOCIAL MEDIA AND CAREER ADVANCEMENT

Social media tools are not just a good way for enterprises to foster cooperation in their organizations and recruit new staff. They are also useful for individuals in managing their careers and finding new employment opportunities. In a world of increasingly temporary relationships with employers, social media help individuals stay connected to important relationships that can help them both to do today's job better and to find out about future opportunities. Many of these relationships constitute what Mark Granovetter, whose work we discussed in Chapter 10, called 'strong weak ties'. It is, in fact, telling that Granovetter's observations about the strength of weak ties is based on research that had to do with people looking for jobs.

More and more young professionals are using social networking sites like Facebook and LinkedIn to form and maintain work related connections. LinkedIn, in fact, markets itself as a tool for job seeking, providing ways for people to upload their resumes and connect with potential employers. The personal profiles that people create on LinkedIn contain a wealth of work related details, which enables users to filter and search for contacts based on skills, knowledge, personal connections, or affinities that might be useful for specific purposes. It also helps people to build their 'personal brand' through the information they include in their profiles and endorsements of their work from other members.

Of course, many people already have a presence in social networking sites before they enter the workforce, a presence which they built up during their high school and university studies. Many of the connections they have made with professors, classmates, classmate's friends, internship hosts and acquaintances from extra-curricular and voluntary activities end up being extremely useful to them when they enter the world of work.

On the other hand, the public identity one wishes to portray often changes once one makes the transition form school to the workplace. As a result, some people find it necessary to manage the image projected on their social networking sites (see Chapter 10), especially since these sites are often the first places potential employers go in search of additional information about possible recruits. Image management sometimes involves choosing new profile pictures and changing profile information and can even involve going back through one's previous public interactions and removing incriminating pictures and comments from friends, a process that has come to be known as 'wall cleaning' (see Chapter 10). In the activity that follows you will be asked to analyze the social networking strategies of three different people who have made the transition from school to work. You will also be asked to consider how you might use social networking to advance your own career.

Activity 12.2: Wall cleaning, networking and resume building

A. CASE STUDIES

Read the three case studies below (from DiMicco and Millen, 2007) and discuss the different ways the three people have integrated their social media use into their careers and workplace practices.

Case 1: Ben is in his early 20s and joined the company as a full-time software engineer in January 2006. He is an active Facebook user, beginning in 2005, checking every day, multiple times a day. He primarily uses the site for maintaining friendships with close, but geographically distant, friends. He has over 200 friends on the site, 35 of which are colleagues. When he joined his company, he did not change anything about his profile or the pictures of himself. His current profile links to many photos of him drinking alcohol (including directly out of a beer keg) and attending numerous college parties. He feels that Facebook is 'for fun' and relates only to 'personal life' and hopes that if his manager ever did see this page he would understand that it has 'nothing to do with his professional life'.

Case 2: Ethan is in his early 20s and joined his company as an entry-level consultant six months ago. He joined Facebook in college to keep up with his current friends and used it primarily for getting to know new friends better. He now uses the site to keep in touch with these friends, but his usage has gone from an hour a week to 10 minutes a week. He has over 200 Facebook friends and most of the colleagues he met at company orientation are listed as friends. Before starting his job, he purposefully 'cleansed' all information about himself on the internet: from Facebook, his blog, and his personal website. In particular, he removed all photos of himself involving 'drinking alcohol'. Because of that he is not concerned about strangers, managers, or mentors seeing his information online.

Case 3: Anne joined Facebook at the urging of her coworkers. Since joining, she has posted dozens of photos of herself and has received dozens of wall posts from her coworkers. Most of her Facebook friends are coworkers whom she started with at the same time. These are people she goes to lunch with and socializes with after work. She works closely with some, but others could be considered part of her extended work network. She believes that she has become better friends with these coworkers because of Facebook and because of the site spends much more time talking to them face-to-face than she would otherwise.

B. PERSONAL REFLECTION

Discuss how you might integrate your personal social networking practices into your career and workplace practices. In particular, talk about:

1. If and how you might change your privacy settings or separate people into groups on your social networking site;
2. If and how you might alter the content you or your friends have posted on your social networking site (or establish a new profile, perhaps on a different site) to create a 'professional identity' that you might use to 'market yourself';
3. If and how the people in your social network might be useful in helping you find a job or advance your career in the future.

CRITICAL PERSPECTIVES ON THE 'NEW WORK ORDER'

The changes in the nature of work we have been describing in this chapter and the literacy practices associated them are not universally regarded as positive. For many people the 'new work order' and the 'digitalized workplace' associated with it raise serious questions about such things as the rights of workers and personal privacy.

With the loosening of ties between workers and employees, for example, there has come a lessening of job security for many workers. Despite efforts by employers to give their staff a feeling of 'belonging', rapid economic changes have led to increased downsizing and outsourcing. As a result, employers sometimes end up sending mixed signals to those who work for them, giving the impression that they want employees who are both 'eager to stay, and ready to leave' (Gee, Lankshear and Hull, 1996). Contract workers and freelancers, while enjoying flexibility and freedom, are not able to enjoy the benefits and pension plans that, at least in the past, usually accompanied full time employment. Those who work from their homes often end up working more rather than less. Without the rigid temporal boundaries of the 9 to 5, Monday to Friday 'working week', the 'working week' has come to be defined as 'however long it takes to get the job done'.

Those who still work in offices, on the other hand, are often finding themselves and their workplace activities under almost constant surveillance by employers using the very same digital tools that are meant to empower workers and make their jobs easier. In his book *The Naked Employee: How Technology Is Compromising Workplace Privacy* (2003), Fredrick Lane warns that employers are increasingly regarding it as their right to monitor any employee communication that takes place over corporate networks and even to install spyware on employees' computers. He also notes how the internet has enabled employers and potential employers to gather information about people's private lives to an extent never before possible. Even workplace social networking tools which have the seemingly benign mission of helping workers to get to know one another better also give employers access to information about their employees' private lives that might not have been otherwise available to them.

Furthermore, a more transient workforce and the nearly universal use of digital technology for personnel management has resulted in a heavier reliance on quantitative measurements to assess the 'quality' and 'value' of work. 'Portable' certification of skills and achievements like test scores have become more and more important for employment purposes, and once people are employed, their performance is often measured based on what Colin Lankshear (1997) calls a 'techno-rationalist' view of the world in which 'quality' is broken down into distinct, measurable components, sometimes referred to with terms like 'key performance indicators'.

Finally, flattened hierarchies and 'self-management' does not necessarily mean that people are given the freedom to really self-regulate or to challenge their employers. Often the social norms and peer surveillance of 'self-managing' teams can be just as oppressive as the watchful eye of a foreman, and, for all the rhetoric about the need for 'critical thinking' in the workplace, there are limits to how 'critically' employees are permitted to think. As long as their critical thinking is directed towards innovation and improvement within the parameters of the organization's goals, it's well received. But when it extends to holding these goals themselves or the larger social, political, economic or environmental consequences of the organization's actions up to scrutiny, that's often a different story.

While for some workers, especially those who are highly educated and possess professional qualifications, the 'new work order' has brought exciting new opportunities for innovation, creative collaboration, and personal growth, the work of many 'knowledge workers' in the new economy is just as tedious and disempowering as the jobs of factory workers in the industrial economy. Jobs in fields like quality control and customer service, which often involve workers following computer-generated protocols, leave little room for creativity or fulfillment. Many of these jobs pay low wages and carry with them few or no benefits and little job security.

In his book *A Hacker Manifesto* (2004), McKenzie Wark argues that there will be three main classes of people in the new economy. The first consists of those who own the networks along which information travels and so constitute a new 'ruling class'. The second consists of those who are involved in the creation of new knowledge, including programmers, artists, writers, scientist and musicians (whom he calls 'hackers'). The third consists of workers who manage data but are not really engaged in the creation of new knowledge, low-level coders, proofreaders and copy editors, call centre operators and clerical workers. Despite the rhetoric of the 'new work order', this last group of knowledge workers will be as alienated from the fruits of their labors as workers at any time in the past. To be a 'hacker' and get a job that involves true knowledge creation, an understanding of digital literacies is not enough on its own. Such jobs require people who have not only mastered the 'new literacies' we have discussed in this book, but who have also mastered 'old literacies' like writing well, engaging in deep analysis and sustained and reasoned argument, and mastering high order theoretical knowledge in their particular fields.

CONCLUSION

In this chapter we have talked about the role of digital literacies in the workplace. First we considered how the world of work is changing, and how digital technologies are, to some extent, facilitating or even driving these changes. Then we discussed some of the advantages and disadvantages to using digital technologies for workplace collaboration. Finally we discussed how organizations are using social media to foster more cohesive and creative workforces and how individuals are using them for career advancement and professional development.

In some ways it is particularly appropriate to end this final chapter by considering practices of workplace social networking. First, they vividly illustrate how, in the 'new work order', corporations must come to terms with (and, in some cases, incorporate) many of the ostensibly 'non-work related' digital literacies we have been examining in this book. Second, they illustrate an important fact that that we have been emphasizing throughout this book – the fact that digital literacies are not just about mastering particular 'skills' (like being able to use track changes in Microsoft Word or to collaboratively author documents on a wiki), but also about being able to form and cultivate the 'right' kinds of social relationships and to present oneself as the 'right' kind of person using the tools available in different situations.

USEFUL RESOURCES

Print

DiMicco, J. M., and Millen, D. R. (2007). Identity management: Multiple presentations of self in Facebook, *Proceedings of the ACM Conference on Organizational Computing and Groupware Technologies* (GROUP 2007). New York: ACM Press, 383–386.

D'Urso, S. C., and Pierce, K. M. (2009). Connected to the organization: A survey of communication technologies in the modern organizational landscape. *Communication Research Reports 26* (1): 75–81.

Gee, J. P., Hull, G., and Lankshear, C. (1996). *The new work order: Behind the language of the new capitalism.* Boulder: Westview Press.

Froggatt, C. G., (2001). *Work naked: Eight essential principles for peak performance in the virtual workplace.* San Francisco: Jossey-Bass.

Wark, M. (2004). *A hacker manifesto.* Cambridge, MA: Harvard University Press.

Web

Time, The future of work
http://www.time.com/time/specials/packages/article/0,28804,1898024_1898023_1898169,00.html

Wikinomics, The Wiki workplace
https://www.socialtext.net/wikinomics/the_wiki_workplace

Don Schawbel, How to leverage social media for career success
http://mashable.com/2009/04/07/social-media-career-success/

Video

Deloitte, What's Your Deloitte? (Examples)
   Food for thought: http://www.youtube.com/watch?v=ainJ2VKJ_wU
   The green dot: http://www.youtube.com/watch?v=idOuHBuhXtY
   Dude, where's my proposal: http://www.youtube.com/watch?v=eH1Bu7G5Hrs
   Is this heaven: No it's deloitte: http://www.youtube.com/watch?v=k4Wn_h5ce7c

CNN, The future of the workplace
http://youtu.be/PwqycgOPEh8

Afterword
Mediated Me 2.0

IT'S ALL ABOUT YOU

The media critic Marshall McLuhan, whose work we discussed at the very beginning of this book, said: 'We shape our tools and thereafter our tools shape us' (1964). What McLuhan was trying to capture in this statement was the power of media to affect the kinds of meanings we can make, the kinds of relationships we can have with others, the kinds of people we can be, and the kinds of thoughts that we can think.

What we have tried to emphasize in this book, however, is that this process is not as simple and sequential as McLuhan makes out, that even as our tools shape us, *we never stop shaping our tools*, creatively adapting them to different situations, mixing them with other tools, 'modding' them, and otherwise 'hacking' them to fit our particular needs and goals. While a big part of mastering digital literacies is understanding the affordances and constraints of the technological tools available to us, another big part is understanding ourselves, our particular circumstances, our needs, our limitations, and our capacity for creativity.

Literacies are not things we develop just for the sake of developing them. We develop them to do certain things, become certain kinds of people, and create certain kinds of societies. And so the most basic underlying questions governing your development of digital literacies are: 'What do you want to do with them?' 'Who do you want to be?' and 'What kind of society do you want to live in?'

How you engage with digital literacies has a direct impact on the kind of friend, lover, colleague and citizen you become. Every time you use digital tools, you create yourself and the society that you inhabit in small and subtle ways through what you click, what you share, and the different connections that you make. We develop technological tools and the social practices that they become part of collectively. All of us play a role in and have a stake in this development. This is especially true given the participatory affordances of digital media. We all have the responsibility for shaping our digital futures.

Digital media open up a staggering range of possibilities for us. They make available new ways to create information and knowledge, to express ourselves, to reach out to others and form relationships, and to explore our potential as humans. They also bring along with them a range of questions, some of which we have mentioned in this book: questions about privacy, questions about property and ownership, questions about freedom of speech and our capacity for political action, questions about what to pay attention to and about the extent to which our view of the world is distorted by the tools that mediate our experience and by our own agendas, questions about how to learn and how to educate our children, questions about truth and deception, friendship and love. We have not, of course, managed to answer any of these questions definitively, but hopefully we've given you some tools to go about answering them for yourselves.

More important, however, are the questions that we have not raised, those that are specific to your own situation, your own needs, or the particular social or cultural circumstances in which you live, or questions that will arise from new technologies developed after this book is published. These are questions that you will have to formulate yourself. The Spanish painter Pablo Picaso famously said, 'Computers are useless. They can only give you answers'. Perhaps the most important digital literacy you can master is learning how to ask the right questions.

Glossary

Adaptation: Making a tool fit the goals of the user or the circumstances of its use, often referring to the act of finding new ways to use tools which were not necessarily intended by the designers of those tools.

Affinity space: (see **online affinity space**).

Affordance: A feature of a cultural tool which makes it easier for us to accomplish certain kinds of actions.

Agent-based algorithm: An algorithm that works through the interaction of a set of procedures and some 'agent' who can apply the procedures in an 'intelligent' way.

Algorithm: A step-by-step process or set of operations to be followed to solve a particular problem.

Alternate reality game: An online game, which usually takes place over a designated time period, in which players compete to solve simulated real-world problems and share their solutions through collaborative platforms like wikis, blogs, photo- and video-sharing sites.

Appropriation: The act of introducing a particular tool into a particular social context, sometimes referring to situations in which tools are introduced into contexts in which they do not normally appear.

Asynchronous communication: Communication in which there is a delay between the time messages are produced and the time they are received.

Attention economy: The theory that the basis of the new economy is neither material goods nor information, but rather 'attention'.

Attention structure: The patterns of orientation to time and space which individuals use in order to attend to elements of an interaction.

Attentional tracks: The 'tracks' in our minds which we use to pay attention to different activities and interactions.

Avatar: The representation or agent of a player in a video game.

Bias: (see **media bias**).

Blog: An easy-to-use website that displays content or posts in chronological order similar to a journal or diary and provides a form for readers to comment.

Blogging: The practice of writing a blog.

Blogroll: On a blog, a list of links to other blogs which the blogger regularly reads.

Bonding: Strengthening relationships with other people.

Bridging: Creating relationships between different groups of people or 'clusters' in a network.

Closed system: A software system that can only run on certain devices and can only be re-programmed by the manufacturer or its licensed agents.

Cluster: A group of people joined together by proximity or common goals or interests.

Code mixing: Mixing different languages together in speech or writing.

Collective intelligence: Shared or group intelligence that emerges naturally from many people working independently to solve a common problem.

Commenting: The practice of leaving comments in a blog or online forum.

Community: (see **online community**).

Contextualization cues: Signals which create the context in which messages should be interpreted.

Constraint: A feature of a cultural tool that makes it more difficult to accomplish certain kinds of actions.

Continuous partial attention: A stressful state where people continuously, but only partially, pay attention to information from digital communications (like messages in email and social networking sites) motivated by a fear of 'missing out'.

Connectors: People in a social network who connect different groups of people together.

Cookie: A small piece of code or program that is installed on a user's computer, usually in the web browser, which can record data about the user and communicate that data to the server.

Cultural tool: A material or abstract artifact which we use to accomplish social actions.

Cultures-of-use: The conventions, norms and values for using a particular tool that grow up among particular groups of users.

Data: 'Facts' in a 'raw' or unorganized form, such as sensory perceptions, numbers, symbols or words, that represent ideas, objects or states of being.

Data signals: The data used by search engines to determine what to search for and how to rank search results.

Database of intentions: A term used by author John Battelle to describe the aggregation of search terms and clicking behavior collected by Google which he believes can reveal something about the collective consciousness of human cultures.

De-individuation: A sense of social distance between members of a virtual team caused by the anonymity of digitally-mediated communication.

Demand image: An image that portrays its subject looking directly out of the image at the viewer, 'demanding' some sort of action or response (see **offer image**).

Digital story: A short film which combines digital images, video and audio in order to create a personally meaningful narrative.

Digital storytelling: The practice of creating a digital story.

Directory: A website which lists 'useful' links, usually classified in a hierarchical taxonomy.

Discourse systems: Systems of discourse used by particular groups which include ideologies, face systems, forms of discourse and practices of socialization.

Discourses in place: In discourse analysis, the texts and tools that are available for an interaction in a particular situation.

Embodied stories: The kind of stories encountered in video games, which are 'embodied' because they depend on the actions taken by the player.

Emoticon: A symbol denoting a facial expression, gesture or bodily posture used in text-based digital communication.

Emoting: Signaling actions in text-based communication by describing them between asterisks (*).

Face systems: Rules for how we conduct relationships based on power and social distance.

Fan machinima: (see **machinima**).

Fan modification: (see **modding**).

Filters: Any device or procedure which engages in filtering.

Filtering: The process of selecting and prioritizing data and information.

Flaming: Verbally abusing somebody over the internet.

Folksonomy: (see **social tagging**).

Forms of discourse: The forms (for example, styles, genres) that discourse takes in different contexts.

Frame: (as verb) Provide a context for, as when a caption provides the context for an image or vice versa.

Given information: In the grammar of visual design, information presented on the left of an image, which the speaker assumes to be known or agreed because it is common shared knowledge or because it has already been introduced in the discourse.

Hacking: Appropriating, adapting, modifying and remixing digital media in creative ways to make it better fit one's purposes or the demands of a particular situation.

Hashtag: In Twitter, a tag which adds descriptive information to a post, preceded by '#'.

Hierarchical taxonomy: A structure for the organization and classification of data in which some pieces of data are considered superordinate ('parents') and some subordinate ('children').

Hierarchical structure: A structure for the organization of a hypertext in which parts of the text are linked to other parts of the text based on a hierarchical relationship, with superordinate ('parent') and subordinate ('child') items.

Historical body: In discourse analysis, the person or participant to an interaction, with all of his or her memories and experiences.

Hyperlink: An electronic text element, like an image, phrase or word, which when selected redirects the reader to another electronic text on the network.

Hyperlinking: The practice of using hyperlinks to associate one electronic text to another on a network like the internet.

Hyperpersonal communication: A term coined by Joseph Walther to describe the sense of intimacy that sometimes accompanies text-based digital communication.

Hypertext: Electronic text which is hyperlinked to other electronic text on a network like the internet.

Hypertext link: (see **hyperlink**)

Hypertextual structure: A structure for the organization of a hypertext in which parts of the text are linked to other parts of the text or other texts on the network based on relationships of association.

Ideology: A system of ideas, practices and social relationships that govern what is considered right or wrong, good or bad, and normal or abnormal.

Ideal (textual structure): In the grammar of visual design, information presented at the top of an image, which represents the aspired to promise, hope, or ideologically foregrounded information.

Ideational function of language: The function of language by which we represent the world and construct propositions about it.

Illusory attention: According to Michael Goldhaber, the attention which a 'star' gives a 'fan' to create the illusion of individual attention.

Impression management: The process of controlling the information one reveals about oneself in order to project a particular social identity.

Information: That which is created when different pieces of data are connected in meaningful ways and/or are connected to particular people or particular tasks.

Information overload: The state of being overwhelmed by a feeling of having 'too much information' leading to stress and the inability to make decisions or set priorities efficiently and effectively.

Instant messaging: A communication service that allows users to chat semi-synchronously over the internet.

Interaction order: In discourse analysis, the social relationships between participants of an interaction.

Interactivity: The ability for readers and writers to interact about texts on the internet.

Intercultural communication: Communication between people who participate in different discourse systems.

Interpersonal function of language: The function of language which helps to create relationships between writers and readers or speakers and hearers.

Knowledge: That which results from the interpretation of information, its integration with experience, and its application to solving specific problems.

Linear structure: A structure for the organization of a hypertext in which parts of the text are linked to other parts of the text in a sequence for readers to follow.

Lock-in: The state in which it becomes difficult for a user to abandon a certain technology or change to an alternate technology because the personal or social costs of doing so are too high.

Lurking: Being present in an online environment such as a chatroom or message board but not participating in any interactions.

Linking: (see **hyperlinking**).

Machinima: Digital video made using a video game's real-time 3-D animation engine.

Mashing: Creating a **mashup**.

Mashup: A combination of two or more cultural products (such as texts, songs, or software applications).

Mavens: People in social networks who are in the possession of material, intellectual or emotional commodities which other people need or desire.

Media: (see **medium**).

Media bias: The way different media distort our view of reality and how we can interact with it.

Media ideology: A set of beliefs which users of a particular tool use to explain how the tool 'should' be used.

Media richness: The range of modes (text, speech, images, etc.) that a medium can incorporate into its signal.

Mediation: The process of communicating between one thing or person and another using media.

Medium: A material or abstract artifact used to communicate between things or people.

Mediational means: A medium used as a means for social action.

Meme: An idea which spreads like a virus.

Memeing: Spreading or promoting an idea.

Mental algorithm: A set of mental procedures agents follow when undertaking tasks such as searching for relevant data.

Metadata: Data which describes a piece of data by linking it to a concept or pointing to another piece of data.

Mixed code: (see **code mixing**).

Mixing: Combining tools, often in a way in which the constraints of one tool are cancelled out by the affordances of another (see **remixing**, **mashup**).

Mod: A modified video game.

Mode: (see **semiotic mode**)

Modifying: Physically altering a tool to make it more suitable to our purposes (see **modding**).

Modding: The practice of modifying a video game either by adding content (like a new level or new items) or by creating an entirely new game from elements of an old game.

MOO: Short for MUD Object Oriented, a text-based virtual world which uses an object oriented database and where users can interact with each other.

MUD: Short for Multi User Dungeon or Multi User Domain, a text-based virtual world where people can interact with each other.

Multimedia: The use of multiple media or content forms, such as video, audio, images and text, in a document.

Multimodal: (see **multimodality**).

Multimodality: The use of multiple semiotic modes, such as visual, aural, spoken and written modes, in a text.

Multitasking: Distributing attention to perform multiple tasks simultaneously.

Networked associations: A way of organizing data based on its often multiple relationships with other pieces of data in a complex network.

New information: In the grammar of visual design, information presented on the right of an image, which the speaker assumes is yet to be agreed upon because it is not common shared knowledge or because it has not already been introduced in the discourse.

New work order: The term given by scholars to the new practices of management associated with the new economy.

Offer image: An image that 'offers' its subject (person or animal) for contemplation, by portraying the subject obliquely, not looking directly out of the image (see **demand image**).

Online affinity space: a virtual place where people interact to promote a particular shared interest or common goal.

Online culture: The ideology, face-systems, norms of communication, and practices of socialization (discourse systems) associated with particular online communities, social networks or affinity spaces.

Online community: A group of people who meet in a virtual space to pursue a common purpose or goal.

Opacity: The state in which the way a tool works becomes difficult for a user to understand and learn how to alter.

Opaque: (see **opacity**)

Open source: Referring to software systems for which the 'source code' is publicly available, allowing anyone to reprogram them.

Open system: A software system that can be run on different devices and can be reprogrammed by users.

Organization system: A system for the storage and retrieval of data which makes it easier for us to find relevant data and turn it into useful information.

PageRank algorithm: The algorithm used by the Google search engine to rate the relevance of items returned in a search based on their hypertextual relationships with other items on the web.

Participation: The practice of creating online content for others to consume, or contributing to such content creation by interacting in online platforms like blogs, wikis, social networking sites, etc.

Peer production: An economic model for collaborative information production, in which massive numbers of volunteers loosely connected by a network work together to promote projects that they are interested in.

Perpetual contact: Being in continuous or constant contact with others via digital media.

Perma-link: The permanent, unique url for a post in a blog or an online forum entry.

Persistence: The fact that text and images in digital media can be preserved in memory, either on servers or on devices, for later retrieval.

Personal filter: (see **personalized algorithm**).

Personalized algorithm: An algorithm that filters and ranks data based on your personal choices or an analysis of your past behaviour.

Polyfocality: The distribution of attention across multiple focal points.

Pragmatics: A branch of linguistics concerned with how people 'do things with words'.

Presupposition: The presentation of a proposition as 'given' or 'assumed'.

Proposition: A statement about the world and how it works.

Read-only web: The early phase of the World Wide Web, characterized by high technical barriers to publication, with users primarily reading the content of professional content producers.

Read-write web: The more recent phase of the World Wide Web, characterized by low technical barriers to publication, with users not only reading but also writing content.

Real (textual structure): In the grammar of visual design, information presented at the bottom of an image, which represents concrete reality and factual information.

Remix: A digital text that builds on the prior digital texts of others by technically editing and modifying them in order to produce a new creative work.

Remix culture: A culture or society that values re-mixing, allowing and encouraging the production of creative works that build on existing creative works of others.

Remixing: The practice of producing a remix (see **remix**).

RSS feed: ('Really Simple Syndication') A web feed format used to push updated web content to subscribers.

Semiotic mode: A meaning-making system such as speech, writing, gesture, image or moving image.

SMS: 'Short messaging service', the text messaging protocol used by mobile telephones.

Social algorithm: An agent-based algorithm that allows groups of people to filter and rank data for one another.

Social filter: (see **social algorithm**).

Socialization: The process of learning to participate in a discourse system.

Social language: A variety of language which marks one as a 'certain kind of person' or a member of a particular social group.

Social networking site: A website that allows users to construct a profile, make connections with other users and share data with people they are connected to.

Social tagging: The process by which users of a system independently add metadata to shared content, resulting in a 'folksonomy'.

Storyboard: A visual script for a film which consists of a series of images that depict visual shots accompanied by scripted text and notes about soundtrack.

Strong ties: Connections in a social network between close friends or people who often have interactions with each other.

Strong weak ties: Connections in a social network which are originally weak (see **weak ties**) but eventually end up becoming important or useful, often because they serve the function of connecting disparate groups.

Synchronous communication: Communication that takes place in 'real time' with little or no delay between when messages are produced and when they are received.

Syntax: The way words are arranged in a phrase, clause or sentence.

Tag: (see **metadata**).

Tag cloud: A visual representation of the metadata users have attached to a particular piece of content, usually using font size to represent the frequency with which different tags were used.

Tagging: The act of attaching metadata to content.

Technological algorithm: An algorithm that is automatically run by a machine or software application.

Technological determinism: An approach that sees technology as having the power to control our thoughts and/or actions.

Technological dystopianism: A belief that technology will bring about negative consequences for humans.

Technological utopianism: A belief that technology will bring about only or primarily positive consequences for humans.

Technologization of practice: The gradual association of particular social practices or conventions of use with certain technologies to the extent that it becomes difficult to use these technologies in ways that do not conform to these conventions.

Transaction costs: The amount of effort, time or other resources expended in making a transaction such as sending a message.

Transparent: (see **transparency**).

Transparency: The state by which tools become so easy or 'natural' to use or people become so adept at using them that they become less aware of their mediating properties.

Video blog: A website, similar to a blog, with regular posts that users can comment on, but posts take the form of video clips which are also uploaded to video sharing sites like YouTube.

Video blogging: The practice of creating and maintaining a video blog.

Virtual distance: A loss of intimacy and trust as a result of mediation.

Vlogger: Someone who maintains a video blog.

Vlogging: (see **video blogging**).

Weak ties: Connections in a social network between distant acquaintances or people that have infrequent contact with each other.

Web 1.0: (see **read-only web**).

Web 2.0: (see **read-write web**).

Weblog: (see **blog**).

Web portal: (see **directory**).

Wiki: A website that is designed to allow users to quickly and easily create and edit web pages, view revision histories and discuss content.

References

Ames, M. G., Go, J., Kaye, J. J., and Spasojevic, M. (2010). Making love in a network closet: The benefits and work of family videochat. *Proceedings of the CSCW 2010.* New York: ACM Press, 145–54.

Appelbaum, S. H., Marchionni, A., and Fernandez, A. (2008). The multi-tasking paradox: Perceptions, problems and strategies. *Management Decision, 46* (9): 1313–25.

Baehr, C. M. (2007). *Web development: A visual spatial approach.* Upper Saddle River, NJ: Prentice Hall.

Bakhtin, M. M. (1986). *Speech genres and other late essays.* Austin: University of Texas Press.

Baron, N. (2004). See you online: Gender issues in college student use of instant messaging. *Journal of Language and Social Psychology 23*: 397–423.

Baron, N. (2010). *Always on: Language in an online and mobile world.* New York: Oxford University Press.

Barthes, R. (1977). The death of the author. In *Image, music, text: Essays selected and translated by Stephen Heath.* London: Fotana, 142–8.

Barton, D. (1994). *Literacy: An introduction to the ecology of written language.* Oxford: Blackwell.

Battelle, J. (2005). *The search: How Google and its rivals rewrote the rules of business and transformed our culture.* Boston: Nicolas Brealey Publishing.

Bays, H. (1999). The gift economy in internet relay chat: Giving immaterial and material gifts. In J. Armitage and J. Roberts (eds) *Exploring cybersociety: Social, political, economic and cultural issues.* Newcastle: University of Newcastle School of Social, Political and Economic Sciences.

Beavis, C. (2004). Good game: Text and community in multiplayer computer games. In I. Snyder and C. Beavis (eds) *Doing literacy online: Teaching, learning, and playing in an electronic world.* Creskill, NJ: Hampton Press, 187–206.

Benkler, Y. (2002). Coase's penguin, or, Linux and the nature of the firm. *Yale Law Journal, 112* (3): 367–445.

Bennett, S. (2011, June 18). Defending your privacy: Is Twitter more secure than Facebook? *All Twitter.* Retrieved from http://www.mediabistro.com/alltwitter/infographic-social-media-security_b10357 on August 10, 2011.

Berg, S., Taylor, A. S., and Harper, R. (2005). Gift of the gab. In R. Harper, L. Palen and A. S. Taylor (eds) *The inside text: Social, cultural and design perspectives on SMS.* Amsterdam: Springer, 271–85.

Berlinski, D. (2000). *The advent of the algorithm: The idea that rules the world.* Boston: Houghton Mifflin Harcourt.

Black, R. W. (2005). Access and affiliation: The literacy and composition practices of English-language learners in an online fanfiction community. *Journal of Adolescent and Adult Literacy 49* (2): 118–28.

Black, R. W. (2006). Language, culture, and identity in online fanfiction. *E-Learning and Digital Media 3* (2): 170–84.

Black, R. W. (2007). Digital design: English language learners and reader reviews in online fiction. In M. Knobel and C. Lankshear (eds.) *A new literacies sampler.* New York: Peter Lang, 115–36.

Blood, R. (2002). *The weblog handbook: Practical advice on creating and maintaining your blog.* Cambridge, MA: Perseus Publishing.

Bolter, J. D., and Grusin, R. (1999). *Remediation: Understanding new media.* Cambridge, MA: MIT Press.

boyd, d. (2008). Why youth (heart) social network sites: The role of networked publics in teenage social life. In D. Buckingham (ed) *Youth, identity, and digital media.* Cambridge, MA: The MIT Press, 119–42.

boyd, d. m., and Ellison, N. B. (2008). Social network sites: Definition, history, and scholarship. *Journal of Computer-Mediated Communication 13* (1): 210–30.

Brandel, M. (2008, August 11). The new employee connection: Social networking behind the firewall. *Computerworld.* Retreived from http://www.computerworld.com/s/article/322857/The_new_employee_connection_Social_networking_behind_the_firewall?taxonomyId=16andpageNumber=1 on July 6, 2011.

Buckingham, D., and Burn, A. (2007). Game literacy in theory and practice. *Journal of Educational Multimedia and Hypermedia 16* (3): 323–49.

Burbules, N. C. (1998). Rhetorics of the Web: Hyperreading and critical literacy. In I. Snyder (ed) *Page to screen: Taking literacy into the electronic era.* London: Routledge, 102–22.

Carr, N. (2011). *The shallows: What the internet is doing to our brains.* New York: W.W. Norton and Co.

Castells, M. (1993).The informational economy and the new international division of labor. In M. Carnoy, M. Castells, S. Cohen, and F.M. Cardoso (eds) *The new global economy in the information age: Reflections on our changing world. University Park*, Penn: Pennsylvania State University Press, 15–43.

Castells, M. (1996). *The rise of the network society.* Cambridge, MA: Wiley-Blackwell.

Clark, A. (2003). *Natural born cyborgs.* Oxford: Oxford University Press.

Crystal, D. (2001). *The language of the internet.* Oxford: Oxford University Press.

Crystal, D. (2008). *Txting: The gr8 db8.* New York: Oxford University Press.

Crystal, D. (2011). *Internet linguistics: a student's guide.* London: Routledge.

Danet, B. (1998). Text as mask: Gender, play and performance on the internet. In S. Jones (ed) *CyberSociety 2.0. Revisiting computer-mediated communication and community.* London: Sage, 129–58.

Danet, B., and Herring, S. (eds) (2007). *The multilingual internet: Language culture and communication online.* New York: Oxford University Press.

Davidow, W. H. (2011). *Overconnected: The promise and threat of the internet.* Harrison, NY: Delphinium Books.

Dawkins, R. (2006). *The selfish gene*, 30th anniversary edition. Oxford: Oxford University Press.

DeCastell, S., and Jenson, J. (2004). Paying attention to attention: New economies for learning. *Educational Theory 54* (4): 381–97.

Dillon, A., Richardson, J., and McKnight, C. (1989). The human factors of journal usage and the design of electronic text. *Interacting with Computers 1* (2): 183–9.

DiMicco, J. M., and Millen, D. R. (2007). Identity management: Multiple presentations of self in Facebook. *Proceedings of of the ACM Conference on Organizational Computing and Goupware Technologies (GROUP)*. New York: ACM Press, 383–6.

DiMicco, J. M., Millen, D. R., Geyer, W., Dugan, C., Brownholtz, B., and Muller, M. (2008). Motivations for social networking at work. *Proceedings of CSCW 2008*. New York: ACM Press, 711–20.

Doctorow, C. (2001). Metacrap: Putting the torch to seven straw-men of the meta-utopia. Retrieved from http://www.well.com/~doctorow/metacrap.htm on April 4, 2011.

D'Urso, S. C., and Pierce, K. M. (2009). Connected to the organization: A survey of communication technologies in the modern organizational landscape. *Communication Research Reports 26* (1): 75–81.

Fink, E. (2011). The virtual construction of legality: 'Griefing' and normative order in Second Life. *Journal of Law, Information, and Science 21*(1).

Fisher, A. (2009, May 14). When Gen X runs the show. *Time Specials*. Retrieved from http://www.time.com/time/specials/packages/article/0,28804,1898024_1898023_1898086,00.htm l on August 18, 2011.

Foo, C. Y., and Koivisto, E. (2004). Defining grief play in MMORPGs: Player and developer perceptions. *Proceedings of the 2004 ACM SIGCHI International Conference on Advances in Computer Entertainment Technology* (Vol. 74). New York: ACM, 245–50.

Foucault, M. (1977). *Discipline and punish: The birth of the prison*, trans. A Sheridan. London: Penguin.

Froggatt, C. C. (2001) *Work naked: Eight essential principles for peak performance in the virtual workplace*. San Francisco: Jossey-Bass.

Gee, J. P. (2003). *What video games have to teach us about learning and literacy*. New York: Palgrave Macmillan.

Gee, J. P. (2004). *Situated language and learning: A critique of traditional schooling*. New York: Routledge.

Gee, J. P. (2007). *Good video games + good learning: Collected essays on video games, learning, and literacy*. New York: Peter Lang.

Gee, J. P. (2008). *Social linguistics and literacies: Ideology in discourse*, 3rd edition. London: Routledge.

Gee, J. P. (2010). *An introduction to discourse analysis*, 3rd edition. London: Routledge.

Gee, J. P., and Hayes, E. R. (2011). *Language and learning in the digital age*. New York: Routledge.

Gee, J. P., Lankshear, C., and Hull, G. (1996). *The new work order: Behind the language of the new capitalism*. Boulder, CO: Westview.

Gershon, I. (2010). *The breakup 2.0: Disconnecting over new media*. Ithaca, NY: Cornell University Press.

Giles, J. (2005). Internet encyclopaedias go head to head. *Nature 438*: 900–1.

Gladwell, M. (2000). *The tipping point: How little things can make a big difference*. New York: Little Brown.

Gladwell, M. (2010, October 4). Small change: Why the revolution will not be tweeted.

The New Yorker. Retrieved from http://www.newyorker.com/reporting/2010/10/04/101004fa_fact_gladwell on July 30, 2011.

Goffman, E. (1959). *The presentation of self in everyday life*. New York: Doubleday.

Goffman, E. (1974). *Frame analysis: An essay on the organization of experience*. New York: Harper and Row.

Goldhaber, M. H. (1997). The attention economy and the net. *First Monday 2* (4–7). Retrieved from http://firstmonday.org/htbin/cgiwrap/bin/ojs/index.php/fm/article/viewArticle/519/440 on May 6, 2011.

Granovetter, M. S. (1973). The strength of weak ties. *The American Journal of Sociology 78* (6): 1360–80.

Hafner, C. A., and Miller, L. (2011). Fostering learner autonomy in English for science: A collaborative digital video project in a technological learning environment. *Language Learning and Technology 15* (3): 68–86.

Halliday, M. A. K. (1994). *An introduction to functional grammar*, 2nd edition. London: Edward Arnold.

Highland, M. (2006). *As real as your life (director's cut)*. Retrieved from http://www.youtube.com/watch?v=fxVsWY9wsHk on March 4, 2011.

Huffaker, D. A., and Calvert, S. (2005). Gender, identity, and language use in teenage blogs. *Journal of Computer-Mediated Communication 10* (2). Retrieved from http://jcmc.indiana.edu/vol10/issue2/huffaker.html on June 4, 2011.

Innis, H. (1951/1964). *The bias of communication*. Toronto: University of Toronto Press.

Jenkins, Henry (2006). *Convergence culture: Where old and new media collide*. New York: New York University Press.

Jewitt, C. (2005). Multimodality, 'reading', and 'writing' for the 21st century. *Discourse: Studies in the Cultural Politics of Education 26* (3): 315–31.

Jewitt, C. (2010). Digital multimodal experiences of the museum visitor. Paper presented at the Fifth International Conference on Multimodality, University of Technology, December 1–3, Sydney.

Johansson, M., and Verhagen, H. (2010). And justice for all – the 10 commandments of online games, and then some . . . *Experiencing games: Games, play, and players: Proceedings of DiGRA Nordic 2010*. Retrieved from http://www.digra.org/dl/.

Johnson, S. (2006). *Everything bad is good for you*. New York: Riverhead Books.

Joinson, A. N. (2008). Looking at, looking up or keeping up with people? Motives and use of Facebook. *Proceedings of the Twenty-sixth Annual SIGCHI Conference on Human Factors in Computing Systems*. New York: ACM, 1027–36.

Jones, R. H. (2002). Mediated action and sexual risk: Discourses of sexuality and AIDS in the People's Republic of China. Unpublished PhD dissertation. Macquarie University, Sydney.

Jones, R. H. (2005a). Attention structures and computer-mediated communication among Hong Kong secondary school students. Paper presented at the Annual Meeting of the American Educational Research Association (AERA), April 11–15, Montreal, Canada.

Jones, R. H. (2005b). Rhythm and timing in computer-mediated communication. Paper presented at the 9th International Pragmatics Conference, July 10–15, Riva del Garda, Italy.

Jones, R. H. (2005c). Sites of engagement as sites of attention: Time, space and culture in electronic discourse. In S. Norris and R. H. Jones (eds) *Discourse in action: Introducing mediated discourse analysis*. London: Routledge, 141–54.

Jones, R. H. (2008). Technology, democracy and participation in space. In V. Koller and R. Wodak (eds) *Handbook of applied linguistics Vol. 4: Language and communication in the public sphere.* New York: Mouton de Gruyter, 429–46.

Jones, R. H. (2009). Inter-activity: How new media can help us understand old media. In C. Rowe and E. L. Wyss (eds) *Language and new media: Linguistic, cultural, and technological evolutions.* Cresskill, NJ: Hampton Press, 11–29.

Jones, R. H. (2010). Cyberspace and physical space: Attention structures in computer mediated communication. In A. Jaworski and C. Thurlow (eds) *Semiotic landscapes: Text, image, space.* London: Continuum, 151–67

Jones, R. H. (2011). Discourses of deficit and deficits of discourse: Computers, disability and mediated action. In C. N. Candlin and J. Crichton (eds) *Discourses of deficit.* Palgrave Macmillan, 275–92.

Jones, R. H. (2012a). *Discourse analysis: A resource book for students.* London: Routledge.

Jones, R. H. (2012b). Constructing and consuming 'displays' in online environments. In S. Norris (ed.) *Multimodality and practice: Investigating theory-in-practice-through-method.* New York: Routledge, 83–97.

Kirkpatrick, D. (2011). *The Facebook effect: The inside story of the company that is connecting the world.* New York: Simon and Schuster.

Kleinman, Z. (2010, August 16). How the internet is changing language. *BBC News Technology.* Retrieved from http://www.bbc.co.uk/news/technology-10971949 on July 17, 2011.

Koechlin, E., Basso, G., Pietrini, P., Panzer, S., and Grafman, J. (1999). The role of the anterior prefrontal cortex in human cognition. *Nature 399* (6732): 148–50.

Kress, G. R. (2003). *Literacy in the new media age.* London: Routledge.

Kress, G. R., and van Leeuwen, T. (2006). *Reading images: The grammar of visual design,* 2nd edition. London: Routledge.

Lam, W. S. E. (2000). L2 literacy and the design of the self: A case study of a teenager writing on the internet. *TESOL Quarterly 34* (3): 457–82.

Landow, G. P. (2006). *Hypertext 3.0: Critical theory and new media in an era of globalization.* Baltimore: John Hopkins University Press.

Lane, F. S. (2003). *The naked employee: How technology is compromising workplace privacy.* New York: AMACOM.

Lanham, R. A. (1994). The economics of attention. *Proceedings of 124th Annual Meeting, Association of Research Libraries.* Retrieved from http://www.arl.org/resources/pubs/mmproceedings/124mmlanham~print.shtml on February 26, 2011.

Lanham, R. A. (2006). *The economics of attention: Style and substance in the age of information.* Chicago: University of Chicago Press.

Lanier, J. (2010). *You are not a gadget: A manifesto.* New York: Alfred A. Knopf.

Lankshear, C. (1997). Language and the new capitalism. *International Journal of Inclusive Education 1* (4): 309–21.

Lankshear, C., and Knobel, M. (2002). Do we have your attention? New literacies, digital technologies, and the education of adolescents. In D. Alvermann (ed) *Adolescents and literacies in a digital world.* New York: Peter Lang, 19–39.

Lankshear, C., and Knobel, M. (2006). *New literacies: Everyday practices and classroom learning,* 2nd edition. Milton Keyes: Open University Press.

Lave, J., and Wenger, E. (1991). *Situated learning: Legitimate peripheral participation.* Cambridge: Cambridge University Press.

Lee, C. (2007). Affordances and text-making practices in online instant messaging. *Written Communication 24*: 223–49.

Lemke, Jay L. (1998a). Metamedia literacy: Transforming meanings and media. In D. Reinking, M. McKenna, L. D. Laboo, and R. D. Kieffer (eds) *Handbook of literacy and technology: Transformations in a post-typographic World.* Mahwah, NJ: Lawrence Erlbaum Associates. Retrieved from http://www-personal.umich.edu/~jaylemke/reinking.htm on Aug 6, 2011.

Lemke, J. L. (1998b). Multiplying meaning: Visual and verbal semiotics in scientific text. In J. R. Martin and R. Veel (eds) *Reading science: Critical and functional perspectives on discourses of science.* London: Routledge, 87–113.

Lessig, L. (2004). *Free culture: How big media uses technology and the law to lock down culture and control creativity.* New York: Penguin Press.

Lessig, L. (2008). *Remix: Making art and commerce thrive in the hybrid economy.* New York: Penguin Press.

Lévy, P. (1997). *Collective intelligence.* New York: Basic Books.

Ling, R. (2004). *The mobile connection: The cell phone's impact on society.* San Francisco: Morgan Kaufmann.

Lojeski, K. S. (2007). When distance matters: An overview of virtual distance. Virtual Distance International. Retrieved from http://virtualdistance.com/Documents/When%20Distance%20Matters%20-%20An%20Overview%20of%20Virtual%20Distance.pdf on August 21, 2011.

Lowry, P. B., Curtis, A., and Lowry, M. R. (2004). Building a taxonomy and nomenclature of collaborative writing to improve interdisciplinary research and practice. *Journal of Business Communication 41* (1): 66–99.

MacLeod, R. (2000). *Attention marketing in the network economy.* Paper presented at The Impact of Networking: Marketing Relationships in the New Economy, 17–20 September, Vienna.

Manovich, L. (2007). What comes after remix? Retrieved from http://manovich.net/DOCS/remix_2007_2.doc on July 9, 2011.

Manz, C. C., and Sims, H. P. (1993). *Business without bosses: How self-managing teams are building high performing companies.* New York: Wiley.

Massey, A. J., Elliott, G. L., and Johnson, N. K. (2005, November). Variations in aspects of writing in 16+ English examinations between 1980 and 2004: Vocabulary, spelling, punctuation, sentence structure, non-standard English. Research Matters: A Cambridge Assessment Publication, Special Issue. Retrieved from http://www.cambridgeassessment.org.uk/ca/digitalAssets/113937_Variations_in_Aspects_of_Writing.pdf on June 14, 2011.

McGonigal, J. (2011). *Reality is broken: Why games make us better and how they can change the world.* New York: Penguin Press.

McLuhan, M. (1964). *Understanding media: The extensions of man,* 1st edition, New York: McGraw Hill; reissued MIT Press, 1994, with introduction by Lewis H. Lapham; reissued by Gingko Press, 2003.

The Mentor (1986). The conscience of a hacker. Retrieved from http://records.viu.ca/~soules/media112/hacker.htm on August 10, 2011.

Merriman, K. K., Schmidt, S. M., and Dunlap-Hinkler, D. (2007). Profiling virtual employees: The impact of managing virtually. *Journal of Leadership and Organizational Studies 14*: 6–15.

Mikulecky, L., and Kirkley, J.R. (1998). Changing workplaces, changing classes: The new role of technology in workplace literacy. In D. Reinking, M. McKenna, L. D. Labbo, and R. Kieffer (eds) *Handbook of literacy and technology: Transformations in a post-typographic world*. Mahwah, NJ: Erlbaum, 303–20.

Miller, D. and Slater, D. (2000). *The internet: An ethnographic approach*. Oxford, U.K.: Berg.

Morozov, E. (2011). *The net delusion: The dark side of internet freedom*. New York: Public Affairs.

Nelson, T. H. (1992). *Literary machines: The report on, and of, Project Xanadu concerning word processing, electronic publishing, hypertext, thinkertoys, tomorrow's intellectual revolution, and certain other topics including knowledge, education and freedom*. Sausalito, CA: Mindful Press.

Newitz, A. (2006, September 1). Your Second life is ready. *Popsci*. Retrieved from http://www.popsci.com/scitech/article/2006-09/your-second-life-ready July 3, 2011.

Nielsen, J. (2006, April 17). F-shaped pattern from reading web content. *Alertbox*. Retrieved from http://www.useit.com/alertbox/reading_pattern.html on August 10, 2011.

Norris, S., and Jones, R. (eds) (2005). *Discourse in action: Introducing mediated discourse analysis*. London: Routledge.

Ong, W. J. (1996). *Orality and literacy: The technologizing of the word*. London: Routledge.

Pariser, E. (2011). *The filter bubble: What the internet is hiding from you*. New York: Penguin Press.

Pinker, S. (2010, June 10). Mind over mass media. *New York Times*. Retrieved from http://www.nytimes.com/2010/06/11/opinion/11Pinker.html on August 10, 2011.

Plester, B., Wood, C., and Bell, V. (2008). Txt Msg n school literacy: Does mobile phone use adversely affect children's literacy attainment? *Literacy 42* (3): 137–44.

Plester, B., Wood, C., and Joshi, P. (2009). Exploring the relationship between children's knowledge of text message abbreviations and school literacy outcomes. *British Journal of Developmental Psychology 27* (1): 145–61.

Prensky, M. (2001). *Digital game-based learning*. New York: McGraw-Hill.

Prensky, M. (2003). Digital game-based learning. *Computers in Entertainment 1* (1): 21–21.

Putnam, R. D. (1995). Bowling alone: America's declining social capital. *Journal of Democracy 6* (1): 65–78.

Raine, L. (2010). Networked creators: How users of social media have changed the ecology of information. Pew Internet and American Life Project. Retrieved from http://www.slideshare.net/PewInternet/networked-creators on May 19, 2011.

Rheingold, H. (2002). *Smart mobs: The next social revolution*. Cambridge, MA: Perseus Publishing.

Rothenberg, E. (2010, October 27). Do you 'like' your privacy invaded? *Huffington Post*. Retrieved from http://www.huffingtonpost.com/erik-rothenberg/do-you-like-your-privacy_b_775086.html on August 6, 2011.

Rowlands, I., Nicholas, D., Williams, P., Huntington, P., Fieldhouse, M., and Gunter, B. (2008). The Google generation: The information behaviour of the researcher of the future. *Aslib Proceedings 60* (4). Retrieved from http://www.emeraldinsight.com/10.1108/00012530810887953 on August 10, 2011.

Rushkoff, D. (2010). *Program or be programmed: Ten commands for a digital age*. OR Books.

RW3 Culture Wizard (2010). *The challenges of working in virtual teams*. New York: RW3 LLC.

Schrage, M. (2001). The relationship revolution. *Merrill Lynch Forum*. Retrieved from http://www.ml.com/woml/forum/index.htm on April 5, 2011.

Scollon, R. (2001). *Mediated discourse: The nexus of practice*. London: Routledge.

Scollon, R., Bhatia, V. K., Li., D. C. S., and Yung, V. (1999). Blurred genres and fuzzy identities in Hong Kong public discourse: Foundational ethnographic issues. *Applied Linguistics* *20* (1): 22–43.

Scollon, R., and Scollon, S. B. K. (1981). *Narrative, literacy and face in interethnic communication*. Norwood, NJ: Ablex.

Scollon, R., and Scollon, S. W. (2004). *Nexus analysis: Discourse and the emerging Internet*. London: Routledge.

Scollon, R., Scollon, S. W., and Jones, R. H. (2012). *Intercultural communication: A discourse approach*, 3rd edition. London: Wiley-Blackwell.

Selwyn, N. (2007). 'Screw blackboard . . . do it on Facebook!': An investigation of students' educational use of Facebook. Paper presented at the Poke 1.0 – Facebook Social Research Symposium, November 15, University of London.

Sharples, M., Goodlet, J. S., Beck, E. E., Wood, C. C., Easterbrook, S. M., and Plowman, L. (1993). Research issues in the study of computer supported collaborative writing. In M. Sharples (ed) *Computer supported collaborative writing*. London: Springer, 9–28.

Simon, H. (1971). Designing organizations for an information-rich world. In M. Greenberger (ed) *Computers, communications and the public interest*. Baltimore: The John Hopkins University Press, 37–72.

Snee, T. (2011, August 4). Texas tweeter writes top application tweet. *University of Iowa Tippie College of Business, News and Events*. Retrieved from http://tippie.uiowa.edu/news/story.cfm?id=2642 on August 10, 2011.

Snyder, I. (1996). *Hypertext: The electronic labyrinth*. Carlton South, Vic: Melbourne University Press.

Snyder, I. (ed) (1998). *Page to screen: Taking literacy into the electronic era*. London: Routledge.

Steinkuehler, C. A. (2006). Massively multiplayer online video gaming as participation in a discourse. *Mind, Culture and Activity, 13* (1): 38–52.

Stone, A. R. (1995). *The war of desire and technology at the close of the mechanical age*. London: MIT Press.

Stone, L. (n.d.). Continuous partial attention. Retrieved from http://lindastone.net/qa/continuous-partial-attention/ on March 16, 2011.

Street, B. (1984). *Literacy in theory and practice*. Cambridge: Cambridge University Press.

Sunstein, C. (2002). *Republic.com*. Princeton, NJ: Princeton University Press.

Surowiecki, J. (2004). *The wisdom of crowds: Why the many are smarter than the few and how collective wisdom shapes business, economies, societies, and nations*. New York: Doubleday.

Tapscott, D. (2007, March 26). The wiki workplace. *Businessweek*. Retrieved from http://www.businessweek.com/innovate/content/mar2007/id20070326_237620.htm on August 4, 2011.

Tapscott, D., and Williams, A. D. (2006). *Wikinomics: How mass collaboration changes everything*. New York: Portfolio.

Thorne, S. L. (2003). Artifacts and cultures-of-use in intercultural communication. *Language Learning and Technology* 7 (2): 38–67.

Thorne, S. L. (2008). Transcultural communication in open internet environments and massively multiplayer online games. In S. Magnan (ed), *Mediating discourse online*. Amsterdam: John Benjamins, 305–27.

Thurlow, C. (2006). From statistical panic to moral panic: The metadiscursive construction and popular exaggeration of new media language in the print media. *Journal of Computer-Mediated Communication 11*: 667–701

Thurlow, C. (2011). Determined creativity: Language play in new media discourse. In R. Jones (ed) *Discourse and Creativity*. London: Pearson, 169–90.

Turkle, S. (1995). *Life on the screen: Identity in the age of the internet*. New York: Simon and Schuster.

Unsworth, L. (2004). Comparing school science explanations in books and computer-based formats: The role of images, image/text relations and hyperlinks. *International Journal of Instructional Media 31* (3): 283–301.

Unsworth, L. (2008). Multiliteracies and metalanguage: describing image/text relations as a resource for negotiating multimodal texts. In J. Coiro, M. Knobel, C. Lankshear, and D. J. Leu (eds) *Handbook of research on new literacies*. New York: Lawrence Erlbaum, 377–405.

Vaidhyanathan S. (2011). *The Googlization of everything (And why we should worry)*. Berkeley: University of California Press.

Valenzuela, S., Park, N. and Kee, K. F. (2009). Is there social capital in a social network site?: Facebook use and college students' life satisfaction, trust and participation. *Journal of Computer-Mediated Communication 14* (4): 875–901.

van Leeuwen, T. (2012). Design, production and creativity. In R. Jones (ed.) *Discourse and creativity*. Harlow, UK: Pearson Education, 133–42.

Virtual online worlds: Living a Second Life. (2006, September 28). *The Economist*. Retrieved from http://www.economist.com/node/7963538 on July 2, 2011.

Waddington, P. (1998). *Dying for information? A report on the effects of information overload in the UK and worldwide*. London: Reuters. Retrieved from http://www.cni.org/regconfs/1997/ukoln-content/repor~13.html on April 1, 2011.

Walther, J. (1996). Computer-mediated communication: Impersonal, interpersonal, and hyperpersonal interaction. *Communication Research 23*: 3–43.

Wark, M. (2004). *A hacker manifesto*. Cambridge, MA: Harvard University Press.

Warschauer, M. and Grimes, D. (2007). Audience, authorship and artifact: The emergent semiotics of Web 2.0. *Annual Review of Applied Linguistics 27*: 1–23.

Wertsch, J. V. (1993). *Voices of the mind: Sociocultural approach to mediated action*. Cambridge, MA: Harvard University Press.

Wesch, M. (2007). *Web 2.0 . . . The machine is us/ing us*. Retrieved from http://youtu.be/6gmP4nkOEOE on April 9, 2011.

Wesch, M. (2008). *An anthropological introduction to YouTube*. Retrieved from http://youtu.be/TPAO-IZ4_hU on April 11, 2011.

Williams, D., Yee, N., and Caplan, S. E. (2008). Who plays, how much, and why? Debunking the stereotypical gamer profile. *Journal of Computer-Mediated Communication 13* (4): 993–1018.

Witmer, D. F. and Katzman, S. L. (1997). On-line smiles: Does gender make a difference in the use of graphic accents? *Journal of Computer-Mediated Communication 2*: 4. Retrieved from http://jcmc.indiana.edu/vol2/issue4/witmer1.html on August 14, 2011.

Wolf, M. (2007). *Proust and the squid: The story and science of the reading brain*. New York: Harper Collins.

Wylie, D. (2010, October 1). EA removes Taliban option from "Medal of Honour." *National Post*. Retrieved from http://arts.nationalpost.com/2010/10/01/ampersand-arcade-ea-removes-taliban-option-from-medal-of-honor/ on May 5, 2011.

Zhao, D., and Rosson, M. B. (2009). How and why people Twitter: The role that micro-blogging plays in informal communication at work. *Proceedings of GROUP 2009*. New York: ACM Press, 243–52.

Index